King Death

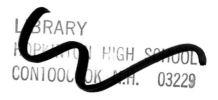

King Death

The Black Death and its aftermath
in late-medieval England

Colin Platt

University of Toronto Press
Toronto Buffalo

First published in 1996 by UCL Press
The name of University College London (UCL) is a registered trade mark used by UCL Press
with the consent of the owner.

Published in North America by
University of Toronto Press Incorporated

Canadian Cataloguing in Publication Data
Platt, Colin
       King Death: the Black Death and its aftermath in
late-medieval England

Includes bibliographical references and index.
ISBN 0-8020-0930-1 (bound) ISBN 0-8020-7900-8 (pbk.)

1. Black death – social aspects – England. 2. Black
death – England – History. 3. England – Social conditions
– 1066–1485. I. Title.

RC179.G7P5 1996   942'.03'7   C95-933375-4

ISBNs:
0-8020-0930-1 (cloth)
0-8020-7900-8 (paperback)

Typeset in Bembo.
Printed and bound by
Biddles Ltd., Guildford and King's Lynn, England.

Contents

Preface

"The ceaseless labour of your life," Montaigne once said, "is to build the house of death." And if there is one historical period to which his maxim most applies, it is to the centuries which followed the Great Pestilence. The Black Death came to Europe in 1347; it stayed until about 1700. Some of its later visitations, including the Great Plague of London of 1665–6, were among the most devastating. However, it was in the first 150 years – the approximate span of this book – that Christian men and women learnt to live with plague. Another thing they learnt was how to die of it.

Those who bought manuals on the Art of Dying (*Ars Moriendi*) in the Late Middle Ages, or who left the message "Learn to Die" (*Disce Mori*) on their monuments, were not thinking primarily of plague. From well before the pestilence, Purgatory's recognition as an official doctrine of the Church had added hugely to the industry of death. Nevertheless, the pains of Purgatory – much worse, it was taught, than anything known on Earth – would begin to seem more terrible when Death arrived both suddenly and too soon. In that ancient didactic legend, *The Three Living and the Three Dead*, three young princes are out hunting when they meet their own cadavers at a crossroads. "As ye are now, so once were we," the Dead warn, "As we are now, so shall ye be." Abrupt and brutal, contemptuous of rank and wealth, Death was the guest of every late-medieval household "in pestilence time", when plague threw wide the door to let him in.

The young (with little to lose) and the old (with nothing to gain) are not so frightened of death. Less courageous are the many in the middle. Driven by fears of hideous torment beyond the grave, propertied men and women in late-medieval England invested hugely, whether as individuals or in gilds, in the provision of after-death soul-care. It is this alone that accounts for the recession-proof rebuilding of almost every major church which is the most visible material legacy of the fifteenth century. But there is another important legacy we still enjoy which is more directly associated with the pestilence. What the Black Death began was a severe labour shortage which persisted little changed for a century and more, and which was not entirely over even then. Labour shortages may occur for different reasons at any time. But for such a crisis to last as long is quite exceptional. The results were as extraordinary as the condition. In barely 50 years, as labour learnt its strength and flexed its muscles, most of the ties of feudal bondage fell away. That "flood of British freedom" which poets still celebrate and politicians habitually invoke at blue-rinse conferences has not been flowing (as Wordsworth once supposed) since "dark antiquity", but originated in the aftermath of the Black Death.

Using the term "post-plague" as a period flag throughout this book has been one way of underlining the Black Death's importance. But bubonic plague, as we shall see, was not the only potent instrument of change in late-medieval England. A second was alterations in inheritance practices; a third was the developing role of gentry JPs in the localities; a fourth was family shrinkage, and a fifth the related freedom to marry late. My own research interest has always been in socially inspired change in the arts. And I return briefly to that subject in the most highly illustrated chapter of my book. But for a fruitful diversion into other specialities which has taught me personally so much, I dedicate this book gratefully to Theo, my son, who was the first to insist that I had been living long enough with my "black[-monk] abbots", and that it was time I wrote instead on the Black Death.

Farley Chamberlayne 1996

The ancient counties of England before reorganization under the Local Government Act (1972). The new county boundaries, shortly to be revised again, came into being on 1 April 1974. *University of Southampton Cartographic Unit.*

CHAPTER ONE

Mortalities

What does it matter how many people died in the Black Death? I shall argue in this book that it matters a great deal. But there is truth also in the view that "so much of the population was surplus by the fourteenth century that the early famines [of 1315–17] and the mid-century pestilences [of 1348–9] were more purgative than toxic".[1] And the remarkable resilience of English institutions, both during and after the Black Death, would certainly support such a conclusion.[2] By 1361, when the plague returned to England on the first of many visits, that resilience was already under challenge. "The beginning of the plague was in 1350 minus one", records the well-known contemporary inscription on the church tower at Ashwell (Hertfordshire). Then in larger letters below, cut soon after the second outbreak – the *pestis puerorum* or *mortalité des enfants* of 1361 – had carried off the new-born children of the survivors, the carver's despair is palpable: "wretched, fierce, violent [pestilence] . . . [only] the dregs of the populace live to tell the tale."[3] And that was just the beginning of over three centuries of deadly visitations, until bubonic plague inexplicably disappeared.[4]

Among the most vivid accounts of the Black Death's origins and symptoms are those of its earliest survivors. Giovanni Boccaccio, author of *The Decameron*, wrote one of the best of them. Boccaccio witnessed the plague in Florence in the spring and summer of 1348:

> Some say [he begins] that it descended upon the human race through the influence of the heavenly bodies, others that it was a punishment signifying God's righteous anger at our iniquitous way of life. But whatever its cause, it had originated some years earlier in

1

the East, where it had claimed countless lives before it unhappily spread westward, growing in strength as it swept relentlessly on from one place to the next ... Its earliest symptom, in men and women alike, was the appearance of certain swellings [buboes] in the groin or the armpit, some of which were egg-shaped whilst others were roughly the size of the common apple. Sometimes the swellings were large, sometimes not so large, and they were referred to by the populace as *gavoccioli*. From the two areas already mentioned, this deadly *gavocciolo* would begin to spread, and within a short time it would appear at random all over the body. Later on, the symptoms of the disease changed, and many people began to find dark blotches and bruises on their arms, thighs, and other parts of the body, sometimes large and few in number, at other times tiny and closely spaced. These, to anyone unfortunate enough to contract them, were just as infallible a sign that he would die as the

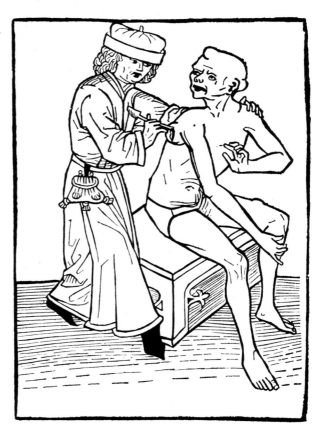

1. "Its earliest sympton . . . was the appearance of certain swellings in the groin or the armpit, some of which were egg-shaped while others were roughly the size of the common apple." In this woodcut, from a late-fifteenth-century Nuremberg treatise on bubonic plague, a doctor is shown lancing one of the buboes Boccaccio describes. *The Wellcome Centre Medical Photographic Library.*

gavocciolo had been earlier, and as indeed it still was . . . Few of those who caught it ever recovered, and in most cases death occurred within three days from the appearance of the symptoms we have described, some people dying more rapidly than others, the majority without any fever or other complications.[5]

2. A manuscript talisman against the plague (*contra pestilentia*) from a fifteenth-century English leech book. *The Wellcome Centre Medical Photographic Library.*

From March until July, wrote a fellow Florentine, Marchionne di Coppo Stefani, "all the citizens did little else except to carry dead bodies to be buried . . . At every church they dug deep pits down to the water level; and thus those who were poor who died during the night were bundled up quickly and thrown into the pit. In the morning when a large number of bodies were found in the pit, they took some earth and shovelled it down on top of them; and later others were placed on top of them and then another layer of earth, just as one makes *lasagne* with layers of pasta and cheese."[6]

"It is reliably thought," reported Boccaccio, "that over a hundred thousand human lives were extinguished within the walls of the city of Florence."[7] It was an over-estimate, of course: among the first of many. But what worried Boccaccio and his contemporaries, in any event, was as much the

3. Plague victims are buried at Tournai (Flanders) in the autumn of 1349: a miniature illustrating the contemporary *Chronicle* of Abbot Gilles li Muisis – "After the feast of St John [29 August] the mortality began in the parish of St Piat in Merdenchon Street, and later it began in other parishes, so that every day the dead were carrried into churches: now 5, now 10, now 15. And in the church of St Brice, sometimes 20 or 30. And in all the parishes the priests, the parish clerks and the grave diggers earned their fees by tolling the passing bells by day and night, in the morning and in the evening; and thus everyone in the city, men and women alike, began to be afraid; and no one knew what to do." (Rosemary Horrox (trans. and ed.), *The Black Death* (Manchester, Manchester University Press, 1994), pp. 51–2). *The Wellcome Centre Medical Photographic Library.*

manner of those deaths as their sum. "Bodies were here, there and every-where," writes Boccaccio, so that every customary ceremony was set aside. "There were no tears or candles or mourners to honour the dead; in fact, no more respect was accorded to dead people than would nowadays be shown towards dead goats."[8] Fifty-two thousand are said to have died in Siena that same summer, and another 28,000 in its suburbs. And while figures like these are obvious fictions, there is no mistaking the personal anguish they recall:

> Father abandoned child; wife, husband; one brother, another . . .
> And none could be found to bury the dead for money or friendship
> . . . And in many places in Siena great pits were dug and piled deep
> with the multitude of dead . . . And I, Agnolo di Tura, called the
> Fat, buried my five children with my own hands.[9]

It was not much later, in the autumn of 1348, that the Black Death visited England. "It began first in India," wrote Henry Knighton, its most reliable English chronicler, "then in Tarsus, then it reached the Saracens and finally the Christians and Jews . . . Then the most lamentable plague penetrated the coast through Southampton and came to Bristol, and virtually the whole town was wiped out. It was as if sudden death had marked them down beforehand, for few lay sick for more than two or three days, or even for half a day. Cruel death took just two days to burst out all over the town. At [Knighton's own] Leicester, in the little parish of St Leonard, more than 380 died; in the parish of Holy Cross more than 400; in the parish of St Margaret 700; and a great multitude in every parish."[10]

These are Mickey Mouse numbers again. But Knighton, while writing some 40 years later, was a conscientious and discriminating historian.[11] And the picture he paints of England's post-plague desolation carries more con-viction than his statistics:

> After the aforesaid pestilence many buildings of all sizes in every city
> fell into total ruin for want of inhabitants. Likewise, many villages
> and hamlets were deserted, with no house remaining in them,
> because everyone who had lived there was dead, and indeed many
> of these villages were never inhabited again. In the following winter
> there was such a lack of workers in all areas of activity that it was
> thought that there had hardly ever been such a shortage before; for
> a man's farm animals and other livestock wandered about without a

4. A Black Death cemetery under excavation at East Smithfield, just south of the Tower of London. To the south again was the site of the Cistercian abbey of St Mary Graces, founded in 1350 by Edward III in part fulfilment of an earlier vow but also as a memorial to his late confessor, Archbishop Thomas Bradwardine, who died of the plague within weeks of his elevation to Canterbury. While many of these London plague victims were given coffin burials, there were at least two mass graves at East Smithfield – and probably many more – in which the dead (carefully laid) were stacked up to five bodies deep (Duncan Hawkins, "The Black Death and the new London cemeteries of 1348", *Antiquity* **64**, 1990, pp. 637–42). *Museum of London Archaeology Service.*

shepherd and all his possessions were left unguarded. And as a result all essentials were so expensive that something which had previously cost 1*d* was now worth 4*d* or 5*d*.[12]

Knighton, a canon of Leicester Abbey, died in 1396. And it was in that same year that Thomas Burton, of Meaux Abbey (East Yorkshire), completed the first draft of his *Chronica Monasterii de Melsa*. Burton, more even than Knighton, had the instincts of a professional historian. "No one," he promises, "who finds anything in what follows which he did not know before, should think that I invented it; he must rest assured that I have only included what I have found written in other works or in a variety of documents, or have heard from reliable witnesses, or have myself seen."[13] Accordingly, Burton's figures are more accurate than most, and the total he gives of 42 monks and seven lay brethren at Meaux in 1349 is likely to be a true record. Only ten of Meaux's monks and not a single lay brother survived the Black Death that summer. In 1396, almost 50 years later, when Burton could count them for himself, there were still no lay brethren and just 26 monks in his community.[14]

Among monks and nuns plague mortalities were not the only cause of declining recruitment. Another was changing fashions in religion. Nevertheless, it is a fact that very few religious houses in late-medieval Britain ever fully recovered their pre-plague numbers, and this was as true of such huge and well-endowed communities as Christ Church (Canterbury) as of only moderately wealthy abbeys like Burton's Meaux. Christ Church was the premier cathedral priory of medieval England. And one of the consequences of the community's great wealth and of its unbroken post-Dissolution life as secular cathedral was the preservation of unusually complete archives. At sleepy provincial Meaux, a Cistercian abbey with no great tradition of record-keeping, Burton had had to rescue "many ancient documents and long forgotten parchments . . . some [of] which had been exposed to the rain, and others put aside for the fire".[15] But the estate and other records of a great Benedictine landowner like Christ Church Priory were always acknowledged to be among the more precious of its assets. There is no doubting the report at Christ Church of only four mortalities in the Black Death. But then the *pestis secunda* of 1361 carried off another 25 of the priory's community, while cutting a further swath through its tenantry.[16]

Concerning those Canterbury tenants, it has been argued persuasively from the surviving estate records that the two earliest plagues were indeed "more purgative than toxic". But there was still no sign in the 1390s of population recovery. And after a last Indian summer of satisfactory returns on their manors, even the monks of Christ Church felt the pinch of real recession.[17] Two important fifteenth-century documentary sources, complementary from 1395 to 1505, establish the circumstances which inhibited recovery. One of those sources, the Canterbury profession lists, recorded individual admissions to the fraternity. The other, the priory's obituary lists, resumed in 1395 after a full generation's silence following the plague of 1361, giving time, cause and circumstances of each death.[18]

These records together, for eleven decades at Canterbury, furnish a unique source of mortality data. And what they show with shocking clarity at this well-founded house is the continual stalking presence of sudden death. At Christ Church, through this time, almost a third of the monks' deaths resulted from frequently recurring epidemic diseases, of which bubonic plague, tuberculosis and the sweating sickness were the great killers. Tuberculosis, in particular, carried off the younger monks, reducing life expectation at birth, already chronically low in late-medieval England, to less than 23 years. No fewer than 17 times during these decades the annual crude death rate at Canterbury soared to above 40 per thousand. By any recognized standard of today, these are appalling statistics. Yet they derive neither from the Third World nor from the truly disadvantaged urban poor, but from a late-medieval community of wholly exceptional privilege: well watered, well fed and well housed.[19]

Privileges of this kind must explain in some degree the early immunity of the Christ Church monks from the Black Death. Yet other great religious houses, as advantaged in every way, were worse hit. Westminster Abbey, one of the wealthiest, lost fully half of its fellowship in the early summer of 1349, including the abbot and 26 of his monks. And although Westminster, in the longer term, was one of the very few English religious communities to be restored to full strength, it had been so immediately impoverished by the death of tenants as to be forced into a one-off sale of plate.[20] The losses of other houses were catastrophic. Forty-six monks died at Benedictine St Albans, along with the abbot, the prior and subprior. At Cistercian Newenham, out of a pre-plague community of 20 monks and three lay brethren only the abbot and two monks remained alive. Just two canons survived at Augustinian Bodmin, while at some of the poorer and remoter houses nobody was left alive to mourn the dead.[21]

There is no evident pattern in reported mortalities like these. But neither is there any reason to disbelieve them. Other sources confirm that, while the plague struck irregularly, its return was so frequent and its overall impact was so great as to cost the population, whether in the short term or the long, between a third and a half of its pre-plague strength. A recent study of the Essex tithing data, for example, has concluded unambiguously that "at the beginning of the sixteenth century local population stood at well under one-half the level it had achieved two centuries earlier, and that England experienced renewed demographic growth only from the second quarter of the sixteenth century".[22] Crucially, this huge loss of lives was no slow descent, but a sudden headlong plunge to a low floor. Of the four Essex communities for which such calculations can be made, Market Roding was the least damaged in 1349 with mortalities of just 25.6 per cent; Great Waltham's population fell by 44.4 per cent; Chatham Hall by 44.6 per cent; High Easter by as much as 53.8 per cent. While it is true that a fair proportion of these Black Death victims were replaced almost immediately by immigration and new births, the overall picture at all four Essex townships was of continued "decline into the early fifteenth century and prolonged stagnation for the remainder of the 1400s".[23]

These Essex calculations suggest overall mortality in the Black Death of around 45 per cent, which compares well with known mortalities in other regions. But such averages frequently conceal much graver losses. Thus of 28 Durham townships where the overall loss, at "slightly over 50 per cent", was near this suggested norm, only two communities experienced death rates of less than 30 per cent; eight had death rates of between 50 and 59 per cent, and at another eight – over a quarter of the whole – more than 60 per cent of Durham Priory's tenants died, rising to peaks of 72 and 78 per cent at Nether Heworth and Jarrow respectively.[24] Similar variations occurred on the Bishop of Worcester's Middle England estates, where the reduction of tenants in the Black Death was as much as 76 per cent at Bibury and 80 per cent at Aston; where three manors experienced losses of 60 per cent or over; where another three manors lost 50, 54 and 55 per cent; and where the overall average was reduced to 42 per cent by a mere handful of mortalities as low as 19–21 per cent at the bottom end of the scale. In reality, only a third of the bishop's estates had below average losses, whereas over a half of his remaining manors lost 50 per cent of their tenants – or many more.[25]

In agricultural communities dependent on a young labour force, *who* died might be as important as *how many*. Halesowen was another large West Midlands manor, the property of Premonstratensian canons of that name. And there, on "a cautious estimate", the 1349 death rate among adult males of 20 and over was between 40 and 46 per cent. No directly comparable figures exist for women. But some 42 per cent of Halesowen's women – only slightly less than the men – are thought to have died in the Black Death, which also carried off large numbers of their children. The younger the child and the older the man, the more likely he was to fall victim. Thus plague-fatality rates rose in the parish from just over 20 per cent of the young adult population to somewhat over 60 per cent of the elderly. Almost all the survivors of the Black Death in Halesowen were still in their twenties and thirties.[26]

Dreadful though these figures are, they at least help explain the strikingly rapid social and economic recovery from the Black Death observable at so many contemporary manors. In the case of Halesowen, fully 82 per cent of plague-vacated holdings were taken up by new tenants within the year. Most of those tenants were young and locally born, the biggest single group (42 per cent) being the sons and daughters of the dead. For these young people the plague presented an unlooked-for opportunity to rise at once into the privileged tenant class. In a society previously characterized (not just at Halesowen) by over-abundant labour, by soil exhaustion and by declining productivity, the time had come for Malthusian checks.[27]

As at Halesowen, so also at Walsham-le-Willows. The Black Death came to this Suffolk parish in mid-March 1349. When it left in mid-May just two months later, what remained was a community drastically pruned at each end but still very strong in the middle. At least 64 per cent of Walsham's children died of the plague, with over 50 per cent of the forties-plus, and some 90 per cent of the elderly. But of the parish's working males only 14 per cent in their twenties died, and just 20 per cent in their thirties.[28] Looked at this way, the total mortality at Walsham-le-Willows in 1349 – calculated as "in the range of 45 per cent to 55 per cent" – need hardly have touched the economy. Before the Black Death, with a population exceeding 1,250 and quite possibly even as high as 1,500, Walsham was seriously overcrowded. It would never regain that higher figure, and in 1851 (its next and final peak) still numbered only 1,297. Assuming that some 500 healthy adults survived the Black Death, to inherit the family land and to reap what their dead relatives had sown, Walsham's chances of recovery were very fair. All the more significant, therefore, is the irrefutable evidence of long-term shrinkage. In the second outbreak of plague in 1361 Walsham lost very few. Yet by the 1390s entry fines on new tenancies had fallen to less than a third of their pre-plague level, and the land market at Walsham, increasingly busy in the five decades before the Black Death, was only half as active as before.[29]

Frenetic activity in the peasant land market has come to be recognized as one of several indicators of chronic over-population and of a "mounting rural crisis" before the Black Death. And nowhere was this more obvious than in north-eastern Norfolk, "the most densely settled district within the most densely populated county in the country".[30] Hakeford Hall, in Coltishall, north of Norwich, was a small but representative manor of the region, for which the court rolls have (exceptionally) survived. They record unremitting activity in the land market before the Black Death, featuring panic buying in years of plenty and multiple forced sales in times of dearth. If any rural society were ripe for a Malthusian crisis, that should have been Norfolk's crowded Coltishall. But the balance (almost a symmetry) of land sales and re-purchases within the peasant community helped to ward off catastrophe. The crisis, when it came, was not self-made, being "a result not of economic but of biological factors".[31]

In 1349 and over the next 20 years, which probably included return visits of the plague both in 1361 and 1369, Coltishall lost an estimated 80 per cent of its pre-Black Death population. And whether from disease or other causes – migration and a reduction in marital fertility have both also been suggested – Coltishall's numbers continued to drift downwards.[32] The local land market, in these circumstances, was transformed. A new kind of purchaser entered that market. And while the number of transactions fell steadily through the years, Coltishall's nascent yeoman farmers, engrossing their neighbours' lands, bought more heavily all the time and pushed up the size of each purchase. Half-acre plots had been the normal currency of pre-plague exchanges in the township. By the end of the fourteenth century that average had trebled to 1.4 acres. And it was to rise again during the next two generations to a mean of 6.8 acres – almost five times what it had been in 1400.[33]

Evidently, the pace of change at Coltishall was slow at the beginning, only speeding up from the end of the century. And few contemporary landowners can have moved as quickly as the Abbot of Eynsham at stricken Woodeaton (Oxfordshire), where "at the time of the mortality or pestilence, which occurred in 1349, scarcely two tenants remained in the manor, and they expressed their intention of leaving unless Brother Nicholas de Upton, then abbot and lord of the manor, made a new agreement with them and other incoming tenants" on more favourable terms: which is what he immediately allowed.[34] Others dragged their feet, hoping for better times. But Abbot Nicholas's instinctive reaction was in point of fact the right one, for

11

5. *Death and Mourning*, from the early-fifteenth-century *Pricke of Conscience* window at All Saints, North Street, York. Of the 15 panels in this window illustrating the signs of the end of the world, this is the last but one. Death waits as three mourners – one with his hands in the air in a gesture of grief – lament the passing of a man and his wife. The inscription reads: "Ye xiiij day all that lives than / sall dy bathe childe man & woman" (E. A. Gee, "The painted glass of All Saints' Church, North Street, York", *Archaeologia* **102**, 1969, p. 161). *RCHME Crown copyright.*

6. Detail of *St Christopher carrying the Christ Child*, from the east window of All Saints, York. In the full-length figure, St Christopher has his feet in the water as he carries the Child across a river; below him are the kneeling donor figures of Nicholas and Margaret Blackburn, with the inscription: "*Orate pro animabus* . . . Pray for the souls of Nicholas Blackburn senior once mayor of the city of York and Margaret his wife." Although St Christopher's protection was most frequently invoked by travellers, it was also believed to be effective against sudden death, including death by plague (Gee, "The painted glass of All Saints' Church", pp. 155–6). *RCHME Crown copyright.*

he was smart enough to recognize, as a witness of those events, that nothing would ever be the same. Another contemporary of the Black Death, the great Arab historian Ibn Khaldun, saw this clearly. "Civilization both in the East and the West," he wrote, "was visited by a destructive plague which devastated nations and caused populations to vanish. It swallowed up many of the good things of civilization and wiped them out . . . The entire inhabited world changed."[35] And so indeed it did; which is not to say that there had been no earlier intimations of what was coming.

In particular, population growth – in many regions, although not in all – had already shown signs of abating.[36] In England's more heavily populated counties, of which Essex was one, a case has been made for "sustained demographic decline", beginning with mortalities as high as 15 per cent in the Great Famine of 1315–17.[37] And with a deteriorating climate, with spoiled harvests and with crop yields already low and still falling, the situation might easily develop – as it can again today – where "labour is so plentiful that its marginal productivity is negligible, or nil, or even negative".[38] Such societies are notoriously catastrophe-prone. And early-fourteenth-century England had more than its share of human and natural disasters. However, there is little to establish that the social and economic pressures – the so-called "endogenous factors" – which chiefly brought these failures about had launched an irreversible demographic decline before the pestilence. Coltishall was only one of many English townships where no ascertainable pre-plague levelling-off in population took place. "Yet," writes its historian,

> even though the relentless increase in numbers may have driven the population [of Coltishall] perilously close to the brink of the Malthusian precipice, no major subsistence crisis ever materialized . . . [whereas] plague accomplished within twelve months what the recurrent famine had signally failed to achieve during the preceding seventy years.[39]

"It was," concludes Barbara Harvey, who began this debate, "the advent of plague, an exogenous factor, that transformed the economic life of Western Europe in the later Middle Ages, and the changes which actually occurred after that event could not have been predicted in the first half of the century."[40]

None could have predicted those changes in the 1350s either, even after the dead had moved in. And many, including the newly installed tenants of the canons of Halesowen, had cause rather to celebrate their good fortune. However, what Halesowen's young survivors then experienced in their turn was the repeated brutal culling of their children. It was Halesowen's babes and infants of the 1350s and 1360s who mostly died in the plagues of 1361, 1369 and 1375. And the long-term consequence of those deaths was an increasingly ageing population in the parish, "overwhelmed at the end of the fourteenth century by the middle-aged and elderly and doomed to a long period of stagnation and decline".[41] Such populations have obvious difficulty in reproducing themselves. In late-medieval Essex, birth and death rates, neither altering appreciably for a century or more from 1400, reached perfect balance. Yet that new demographic equilibrium was at only half the level formerly achieved by the same communities before the pestilence.[42]

More than a century of zero growth in late-medieval England brought all kinds of unforeseeable consequences. No part of contemporary society was free of them. Nevertheless, there was still room in the first decades following the Black Death for reasonable expectations of recovery. Thus, vacant plots found ready takers at Meopham and Havering, Durrington and Cuxham, Kibworth Harcourt and Chalfont St Peter. But sooner or later, each one of those economies would show the strain. Steeply rising wages, for example, pushed up fixed costs at Meopham in the 1380s.[43] By 1369 at Havering two return visits of the plague had resulted in vacant plots and unpaid rents.[44] At Durrington falling receipts became a problem as early as the 1350s; nor did wages return again to pre-plague levels.[45] Customary renders ceased at Cuxham well before the end of the fourteenth century, and rents went into a decline.[46] At Chalfont St Peter from the 1360s tenants were scarce, cottages collapsed and holdings increasingly fell vacant.[47] In the second plague of 1361 Kibworth Harcourt, already devastated by the Black Death, lost another ten landholders; there were exceptional mortalities at Kibworth again in 1375–6, 1378–9, 1389–93, 1396–8 and 1412; the manor's annual death rate, averaging 5 per cent in the 1390s, was consistently higher than it had been in pre-plague times.[48]

These manors, and others like them on the champion lands, were the crown jewels of the contemporary farming system. At the far end of the scale were the tiny assarting hamlets of chilly Bilsdale, in north-east York-shire, already battered by foul weather before the Black Death and aban-doned by their peasant cultivators not long afterwards.[49] Light-soiled Breckland, spread over several counties of East Anglia, was another region on the agricultural margin. But Breckland's terminal decline was delayed for some decades by the greater flexibility of its landowners. Not all of them moved with equal speed. Nevertheless, short-term leases at special rates were already familiar in Breckland in the 1350s; the local land market had largely recovered by the end of that decade; and total rental incomes were often back to pre-plague levels by the 1370s. Breckland's peasant farmers, never as wretchedly poor as the Bilsdale assarters, stayed with their land. Cereal growers switched to barley. Sheep-farming prospered with the growing textile industry. And heathland rabbiting, on a major commercial scale, became a new and highly profitable speciality.[50]

That initial prosperity, continuing into the 1380s and sometimes longer, sharply contrasted with what followed. The clearest indicator of change, in Breckland as elsewhere, was a gradual collapse of the land market. Rents fell; arrears accumulated; Breckland land values were down by a third. Even sheep-rearing no longer offered a solution. Weakened by over-supply, fleece prices collapsed in the 1390s. They would recover again somewhat during the next three decades, only to touch bottom in the severe and prolonged slump of the mid-1450s when, on at least one Breckland manor, the clip remained unsold "for want of merchants".[51]

A common nightmare image of late-medieval England was of sheep which ate up the men. In Breckland, it was more likely to be rabbits. Either way, a steady haemorrhage of labour, whether through migration or early deaths, caused rural settlement to fall back. Some of the smaller villages were lost in these circumstances; many more shrank dramatically in size. And while fifteenth-century Breckland escaped the worst of the desertions, its population again slumped by a third.[52] When the losses levelled out, as they did from the mid-century, some obvious winners then emerged. Breckland's pastoral communities had survived comparatively well, and almost all its desertions were on the arable. Furthermore, the majority of those desertions were in the Norfolk Breckland, and only one of Breckland's Suffolk hamlets was abandoned.[53] Yet the overall picture, even in cloth-rich Suffolk, was disturbing. With few exceptions, fifteenth-century village wealth stayed well below pre-plague levels. In 1428 the 74 Suffolk communities judged too small to pay tax "were only part of a great continuum of decline".[54]

Suffolk is a county of contrasts. Of those 74 hamlets exempt in 1428, fully 80 per cent were still qualifying for tax relief in 1449 and several had been lost altogether. Yet, while this was happening, an almost equal number of Suffolk's villages prospered in the cloth trade, or saw the rise of rich communities of wealthy graziers. In the first half of the century cloth exports through Ipswich multiplied several times over, before falling back again in the 1450s.[55] But throughout the fifteenth century, as the dizzying fluctuations of the cloth trade show, Suffolk was experiencing both "contraction *and* growth, declining wealth *and* new opportunity".[56] It is this apparent paradox, not limited to East Anglia nor to that century alone, which has suggested an alternative view of post-plague England as an economy in excellent health.[57] But "the chief economic problem of the fourteenth century", as Dr Bridbury himself admits, "remains a population problem even when we have shifted it from mid-century [the Black Death] to the 'seventies'".[58] Call no society happy that loses as many children as ever enter adult life, where death rates rise and life expectations fall, and where the living are beleaguered by the dead.

Of such a society, the experience of religious houses need not be typical. Epidemics spread more rapidly in closed communities, and may – in total contrast to more normal societies beyond the walls – seek out the young and the strong.[59] Nevertheless, there remains much of value in the exceptionally complete archives which the monks have left behind, whether at Christ Church (Canterbury) or at Westminster. "To a remarkable extent," writes Barbara Harvey of fifteenth-century Westminster, "the Abbey's experience of mortality resembled that of Christ Church, Canterbury."[60] And one of her more important conclusions from the Westminster data is that the community's death rate, far from easing from the 1450s, had reached another crisis before the end of the century, so that throughout "the long period 1410–1509, the trend was normally above 30 per thousand per annum, and in the period 1460–1509 it was above 40 per thousand per annum in no fewer than twenty years".[61] Life expectations fell in proportion. Whereas a Westminster monk aged 20 in 1400 could hope to live another 30 years, his equivalent a century later would probably die in his forties, if not before.[62]

The monastic community at Westminster, suppressed in January 1540, survived just long enough to see the up-turn. True, there were above-average mortalities at Westminster in 1523–4 and again in 1527–8. But the trend from the 1510s was in the contrary direction: towards a healthier life and later death.[63] Much the same was happening in Westminster's secular community, outside the abbey walls. But one important difference was at least the hint of a recovery in St Margaret's parish, beginning as early as the 1470s. Some of that increase may be attributable to greater fertility, but it is more likely to have resulted from immigration. In any event, recovery was checked (as at the abbey) by exceptionally high annual death rates of as many

7. *Skeletons dancing on an open grave*: a woodcut illustrating moralizing verses in a Nuremberg printed book of 1493. *The Wellcome Centre Medical Photographic Library.*

as 50–60 per thousand between 1490 and 1510. And when the upturn began again in the 1510s Westminster's monks also experienced its effects.[64] Significantly, nothing else had changed, whether in the abbey or in its surrounding parish, to increase or reduce community numbers; and only one conclusion can result. In Westminster at least, among all the other variables (including fertility) which might otherwise have affected this suburban population from the Great Pestilence until the early sixteenth century, "it is surely hard to deny pride of place to mortality".[65]

CHAPTER TWO

Shrunken towns

In the long-running debate about the severity of urban decline in late-medieval England one conclusion stands out. "For better or worse," Dr Rigby has written of the east coast port of Grimsby, "it is population size which remains our main indicator of changes in urban fortunes."[1] Over-crowded Grimsby, purged by the Black Death, probably lost at least 30 per cent of its pre-plague population in the spring and summer of 1349. But greater significance attaches to a second and more reliable figure: the well-established loss of over 40 per cent between 1377 (the first poll tax) and 1524 (the lay subsidy). Far from Grimsby recovering through the fifteenth century — which one well-known historian has nevertheless described as "a period of spaciousness and promise" for English towns — the port's population continued to slip away, reduced by as much as four times the national average.[2]

The condition of Boston, another Lincolnshire port, was even worse. It had been one of provincial England's most successful new towns. From 1086, when unrecorded in Domesday, Boston had climbed by 1200 to a position of great importance in the east coast trade. It grew especially rapidly before 1300, and then continued to prosper throughout the fourteenth century, supported by the growing export trade in cloth. When that trade fell off, as it did in the next century, Boston's ability to attract new settlers collapsed also. Of Boston as of Grimsby, Dr Rigby sees population decline as "the key indication of the town's decay in the later Middle Ages". And Boston's loss again far exceeded the national average. Taking the 1377 poll tax as the first fixed point, Boston's population would fall by 50 per cent before the diocesan household survey of 1563 gave the next reliable local count. In contrast, the estimated national totals for those two dates are much the same.[3]

Population generally had begun to rise again before 1563. And the fact that Boston's community was still so far below its earlier poll-tax figure is further proof of continuing decline. By itself, Boston's loss in the Black Death of 1349 could probably have been restored relatively quickly. But the plague had returned repeatedly in later years, and heavy mortalities had continued. In the event, the only way communities like Boston and Grimsby – or bustling Westminster, for that matter – could maintain their numbers was through continuous inward migration. And if a town should ever lose its ability to attract new blood, its collapse could be shockingly rapid. One urban community which, despite heavy mortalities, never lost its allure was late-medieval London. Nevertheless, even that great city's otherwise fortunate mercantile elite was unable to reproduce itself through two centuries. "It is unmistakably clear," wrote Sylvia Thrupp, "that at no part of the period did the average number of heirs that a merchant left behind him in the direct male line reach two." Rather, she continues, "with a sinister uniformity the figures hover closer to the figure one", while a high proportion of London's richer merchants either abandoned the city for a country retreat or left no surviving sons to replace them.[4]

It was immigration, then, which for many decades topped up otherwise diminishing urban communities. And that was undoubtedly the experience of post-Black Death Colchester, where the huge population losses of 1349 and 1361 were very quickly made up, to be followed by half a century of growth.[5] However, compensating immigration lasted only as long as prosperity. From the 1410s Colchester's economy began to fail, and migrant workers showed less willingness to settle there. Colchester's population only barely held up through the epidemics of 1412–13, 1420–21, 1426–7, 1433–4 and 1439. And when, after a short intermission, extraordinary mortalities returned again in 1463–4, there was no way of reversing a population shrinkage for which neither new births nor new faces could fully compensate. Throughout the fifteenth century and well into the sixteenth, the number of newly enrolled burgesses at Colchester fell steadily, intensifying the downward pressure on a population already weakened by high mortalities and fewer births.[6]

For Colchester's only recently enlarged economy those pressures need not have been fatal. And far from losing out altogether during its long fifteenth-century decline to smaller cloth-making communities like rival

8. In the fifteenth century, when the overseas trade of Boston was in near-terminal decline, the power and wealth of its parish fraternities – in particular the rich and fashionable Corpus Christi Gild – had never been greater. Boston's huge Stump, to which extra stages continued to be added through much of the century, accordingly tells us more about contemporary priorities in religion than about the wealth of the community which built it. *A. F. Kersting.*

Lavenham, Colchester was still markedly richer in the 1520s than it had been in 1334. Comparison of the two subsidy payments shows Colchester's contribution in 1524 more than keeping pace with its neighbours. But what had evidently happened in the course of those years was a growing concentration of personal wealth in fewer hands. For the more fortunate of its burgesses, Colchester's rebuilt townhouses were markedly more comfortable than they had ever been before; they had more plentiful private chambers and more abundant furnishings; many had been given a second storey.[7] Likewise in once-prosperous Boston, where the economy had fallen into irreversible decline, "sore decay" and "fair dwellings" co-existed in the 1530s, when John Leland passed his verdict on the borough. Here too wealth had polarized, so that a community which – exceptionally – paid far less tax in 1524 than it had before the pestilence, was nevertheless the home of many rich.[8]

Contradictions of this kind even within single communities, as well as the very different showings of individual towns in the taxation returns of 1334 and 1524, have caused some historians of late-medieval urban England to reject any one model.[9] But it was already plain by 1350 that successful new towns had ceased to be established in England well before that date, and that few communities except London were still growing. Some of the older boroughs were particularly at risk. Probably the best-known of the failures was late-medieval Winchester, which had already peaked soon after 1100. From that time on Winchester had continued to lose status to London, its earlier rival. But although Winchester descended steadily in the rank order of English towns – thirteenth-century Boston was among several post-Domesday newcomers to overtake it – its population fell more slowly than its wealth. Even before the Black Death, some decline in overall numbers and a contraction of settlement may have resulted in the closure of parish churches. But that redundancy of five parish churches before 1349 was as nothing to what followed the pestilence. In the next half-century another 19 of Winchester's churches closed, reducing the total by a third. Then seven more parish churches were lost during the fifteenth century, to be followed by another 14 closures before 1600, of which 11 pre-dated 1550.[10]

With no fewer than 57 recorded churches in twelfth-century Winchester, there was obvious over-provision. And some of the later closures, especially the last, were the result of rationalizations. But so exact is the correspondence between known church closures and the best estimate of plague losses – both 30 per cent – in late-fourteenth-century Winchester, that the one must relate to the other. Nor did this contraction stop short at 1400. For the rest of the fifteenth century and well into the next Winchester experienced worsening recession. During those years a combination of lay piety and clerical inertia kept many of the less viable churches open. But another third of Winchester's population had been lost by 1550, and the area of settlement was still shrinking.[11] This second contraction was more serious than the first, for there was nothing to compensate for the decline. In the late fourteenth century, like so many English towns, Winchester had been protected from the worst consequences of plague mortalities by a contemporary boom in the cloth trade. It had enjoyed some success in attracting migrant workers, among them fullers from Flanders. But from the early 1400s, first Winchester's weavers and then its fullers ran into difficulty. A clothing industry which remained in the sixteenth century "by far the most important commercial activity in the city" was nevertheless "but a shadow of what it had formerly been [in 1400]".[12]

Industrial shrinkage was clearly viewed by contemporaries as the chief cause of Winchester's difficulties. Its effects had become obvious by the mid-fifteenth century, when a new petition was addressed to the King. Winchester's petition of 1452, like other versions that preceded it, paints a picture of tumbledown decay. And some of its claims, including the estimate of 997 houses in ruins – in reality, more houses than the city possessed – are obvious hyperbole. But other details in the petition are more accurate. The citizens knew their lost parish churches, and got those numbers right. They listed correctly those Winchester streets – excluding only three – where the devastation was already near-complete. And, as they rightly saw in 1452, the first collapses had begun as far back as the 1360s. Like earlier petitioners surrounded by the evidence of a cloth industry in ever-deepening recession, they blamed Winchester's empty plots on that collapse. But in point of fact it was bubonic plague – its consequences still obvious in lost or vacant tenements – that had done the greater mischief. Dr Keene's conclusions, while properly cautious on other matters, on this point at least are unambiguous. "There can be little doubt," he writes of Winchester in 1452, "that by far the greater part of the loss of houses and churches obvious in the mid-fifteenth century had come about during the third quarter of the fourteenth century as the immediate result of the principal outbreaks of plague in 1349 and 1361/2."[13]

Dr Keene's *Survey of medieval Winchester* (1985) was a pioneering study, soundly based on the reconstruction of tenement histories. There has been no other urban survey half as thorough. And what Keene noted was the increasingly dismal predicament of a formerly prosperous ancient borough, in all likelihood shared by many others. Certainly, one common experience was falling rents, again attributable to high mortalities and low demand.

Winchester's rents had fallen sharply in the immediate aftermath of the first plagues of 1349 and 1361, but had recovered almost as quickly in the 1360s. They stayed firm through the rest of the fourteenth century; but then, as in other towns, began to fall. That fall did not apply to all types of housing. Significantly, rent losses were greatest among those larger properties built during Winchester's prosperity. They were particularly acute in the old cloth-making parishes, but were hardly felt at all in the cheaper and meaner housing next to the city's gates, where small tradesmen still created a demand.[14]

Industrial and commercial failures, such as those of fifteenth-century Winchester, undoubtedly contributed to falling rents throughout the urban community. But they can seldom explain the full severity of rent losses, especially among the younger and more vigorous of the boroughs. Rents in suburban Westminster, for example, would recover strongly again before the end of the fifteenth century. But they did so only after a severe contraction,

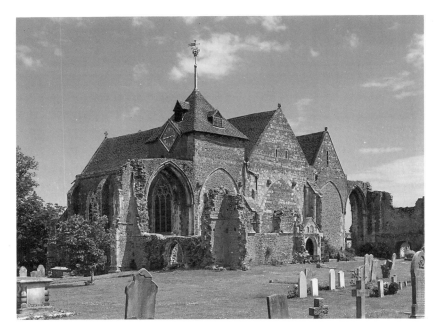

9. Deteriorating weather and coastal inundations caused the port of Old Winchelsea to be abandoned and a new hill-top town to be laid out in 1283. But the prosperity of New Winchelsea, threatened first by the war with France and then by the plague, lasted little more than a generation. Many building plots in the town were never taken up. The new parish church, which was begun on a grand scale in the early years of the plantation when this big aisled chancel was built, was probably never taken further than the east wall of the crossing, seen here in ruins from the north-west. *A. F. Kersting.*

beginning in about 1400. When, in the 1470s, new growth resumed, it was Westminster's smaller and cheaper tenements that attracted the returning migrants, unable to afford big-city rents.[15] Another borough often said to have escaped the worst recession was late-medieval Newcastle. And it is true that Newcastle's population was growing fast again by 1515. But that growth similarly followed a demographic collapse as acute as any in the less fortunate boroughs which never managed an equivalent recovery. Through the fifteenth century rents in Newcastle had fallen steadily. And while some of that falling demand was owed (as at Winchester) to recession in the cloth trade, the clear association of unpaid rents with epidemic years shows plainly where the blame must belong.[16]

Empty plots and ruined tenements blighted most fifteenth-century townscapes. For many comfortably-off individuals these were the only obvious reminders of decline. But that decline, in any event, had been a long time coming, and was never felt with equal force by every sector. One of the last English communities to fall a victim to recession was mid-fifteenth-century Oxford; Canterbury had succumbed not long before. But good rents were still obtainable on premium properties in both boroughs, and it was the poorer private landlords (excluded from prime locations by the dead hand of the Church) who suffered first. Sharing only the commanding presence of big corporate landowners, the two towns had very different economies. Yet both exhibited the same "resilience and even buoyancy" in the post-Black Death decades, sustained by immigration and by other extraordinary factors, including (in Oxford's case) the huge inward investment of college-founding bishops. Then rents began to fall, but in such different trading circumstances – yet with such identical effect – that only unremittingly high mortalities could explain them.[17]

Oxford and Canterbury, like Westminster and Newcastle, climbed back to health again in the sixteenth century. Wells, in contrast – a much smaller borough – had fallen mortally ill. This was not necessarily the diagnosis of contemporaries. "For ordinary [Wells] people," writes their latest historian, "urban decline would have been a meaningless, incomprehensible notion, at most a reference to the growing number of vacant or ruined properties."[18] But the decay of Wells in the post-plague years proved irreversible. From Bishop Robert's time in the mid-twelfth century, Wells had seen continual expansion. However, that had ceased by the 1320s if not before, and there were streets on the borough's periphery – New Street, Tucker Street and Beggar Street among them – which although laid down before 1300 were never more than partially settled. In the fifteenth century empty plots were common even in prime trading locations like the High Street. The 1340s development of Moniers Lane had shrunk to just two tenements by the 1470s, and would subsequently disappear altogether.[19]

Falling rents chart that decline. Borough rental accounts survive at Wells for the years 1427–8 and 1550–51. And they show that the Community (governing body), as in other English towns, had made substantial property purchases following the Black Death, to provide against future expenses. In 1427–8 almost a quarter of Wells's entire housing stock was in the Community's hands. Yet of those 120–30 tenements another quarter again had been let at reduced rents, and the Community's receipts in 1428 were already down by almost 15 per cent. Nor did the reductions stop there. Rents went on falling in the fifteenth-century borough. Moreover, Wells's continuing crisis may have been worse than it looked, for many of the larger losses were sustained on High Street sites which had the best commercial frontages in town. By 1551, while the Community owned more properties than it had ever held before, its rents brought in less than in the 1420s.[20]

What had kept receipts steady in the earlier period had been inward migration from the locality. However, it had become very obvious before 1450 that the Somerset villagers who had once replenished Wells could no longer be relied upon to come there. Burgess admissions, which had begun to decline in the 1410s, reached a low point in the mid-fifteenth century. They then experienced a brief recovery in the later 1460s and 1470s, but started falling again in the 1480s, when potential migrants chose either to stay at home or to settle in competing market centres like neighbouring Glastonbury. There is nothing to suggest that admissions policy in Wells changed over these years. Entry prices remained the same, and there is no evidence of that manipulation of burgess admissions for political ends which is believed to have occurred at other boroughs. While it is true that Wells burgess-ships went increasingly in the fifteenth century to locally born sons, the rising proportion of admissions by patrimony was less a result of protectionist policies than of a growing failure of outsiders to seek entry. Individual foreigners still settled in post-plague Wells: an Irishman, several Hollanders and a Danziger. But the booming cloth industry, which had raised so many of Somerset's larger villages to new prominence by 1500, did little to improve the fortunes of this minor cathedral city, only 20 miles from commercially dominant Bristol and – under that great oak – reduced like its small-town neighbours to client status.[21]

Plainly, Bristol's success was one important cause of the comparative failure of Wells; and it is a useful reminder of the many contributing circumstances that, when added to plague, brought about small-town contraction. Certainly Wells was not alone in suffering the shopping blight, most damaging to the profitable luxury trades, imposed by a larger regional centre. And those provincial capitals in their turn – York and Norwich, Lincoln and Exeter, Chester, Gloucester and Bristol – were themselves experiencing some customer desertion, as the rich shopped increasingly in London. Poorer customers were necessarily more loyal. Even so, informal rural exchanges took a larger share of trade, as more bargains were struck in the fields or at an inn, and as urban craftsmen settled in the villages. Where many small-town populations were already dominated by husbandmen, it required only a minor relocation of specialized trades and services to remove the substantive difference between those lesser towns and the larger agricultural villages of their region, much reducing their credibility as market centres.[22]

Always more liable to fail were the village markets which had multiplied especially in the thirteenth century but of which as many as 50 per cent had ceased to trade by 1500.[23] In contrast, the typical English market town, while commonly experiencing some reduction of its customer base, never entirely lost its role in the locality. In particular, towns of moderate population ("a thousand or so") and of reasonable market spread survived well enough on the exchanges of local peasantry to be counted among the "success stories" of the recession.[24] Accordingly, it is hardly surprising that for many historians today "it goes against the grain to talk about [late-medieval] urban decay".[25] But post-plague urban shrinkage, whatever its main cause, did indeed claim genuine victims. Boston was one of those; Winchester was another; Wells was a third. And in all three towns exceptional mortalities undoubtedly played a part in their decline. Less clear was the Black Death's role at late-medieval Great Yarmouth in bringing down that once wealthy herring port.

Great Yarmouth's collapse is well documented. Once ranked among the top four urban taxpayers of 1334, Yarmouth fell further, proportionately, in the later Middle Ages than any English town except Winchester or Shrewsbury. It was to recover some prosperity after 1500. But in 1349, when the Black Death arrived, the bad times had already begun. What ruined Yarmouth's trade was war at sea. London and Bayonne, formerly its principal markets, ceased to be large-scale customers for Yarmouth herring; privateering raised the cost of seaborne trades in wine and salt; taxation and

10. Another failed urban plantation was the Bishop of Winchester's Newtown (Francheville), on the Isle of Wight, founded in 1256. While initially so successful that Edward I believed it worth his while to acquire Newtown from the then bishop (John of Pontoise) in 1284, the town was regularly raided by French pirates in the following century, and never recovered its prosperity. The two main streets – High Street (left) and Gold Street (right) – were both originally much longer, but have now mostly reverted to grass tracks. Newtown's market was just the other side of the parish church (centre). *Ministry of Defence Crown copyright.*

defence charges rose sharply.[26] Reacting only slowly to increasing threats to its monopolies, Yarmouth lost ground to its competitors. And it was the low-cost village fisheries, along the same coast, which temporarily gained advantage from its troubles. But by 1400 even the part-time rustic fishermen of Leiston and Walberswick, Benacre, Aldeburgh and Sizewell were finding

Chapell fyelde alias
Brome fyelde. 50—3—32

Towne fyelde
15—3—29

Watts With the.
Barn yearde 2—0—21

Barne Crofte
2—2—32

William bedithes Barne Crofte
4—3—0

M ciffes gave berfing

backsydes

in Wallingers londe

Backsydes

fryers meade

fryers
fre schoole hows

Borsteed

the Chelmer or auncient Bner

11. A pioneering early map by John Walker the Elder of Chelmsford in 1591. Walker's "trew platt" shows the borough still focusing on its big funnel-shaped market-place, closed by the parish church on the north. Some colonisation of the market has already taken place, but Chelmsford's burgesses have otherwise competed for the best commercial frontages, whether on the market or along its principal approach roads. *Reproduced by courtesy of the Essex Record Office.*

it hard to sell their catches. With demand already low and still falling, the entire East Anglian fishing industry was in jeopardy.[27]

It is that overall decline, which no combination of local circumstances can entirely explain away, that hands the debate back to the demographers. Yarmouth may have been the victim of extraordinary forces – among them a growing popular preference for freshwater fish [28] – which none could have predicted or accommodated. But it was just one of at least 80 English urban authorities seeking the powers, between 1536 and 1544, to "re-edify" their towns. And only a handful of those petitions were special pleading. The Re-edification Act of 1540, for example, lists 36 towns, including Great Yarmouth, where "there have been in times past divers and many beautiful houses of habitation . . . [which] now are fallen down, decayed, and at this day remain unre-edified, and do lie as desolate and vacant grounds".[29] Other towns named that year were York, Lincoln, Canterbury, Coventry, Bath, Chichester, Salisbury, Winchester, Bristol, Scarborough, Hereford, Colchester, Rochester, Portsmouth, Poole, Lyme, Faversham, Worcester, Stafford, Buckingham, Pontefract, Grantham, Exeter, Ipswich, Southampton, Oxford, Great Wycombe, Guildford, Stratford, Kingston upon Hull, Newcastle upon Tyne, Beverley, Bedford, Leicester and Berwick.

Such a catalogue, made in 1540 after general recovery had begun, must always remain highly suspect. It includes successful provincial capitals like Exeter and Bristol among the vast majority of other towns known to have been in genuine trouble. Many towns, moreover, never featured on any list, having no parliamentary representative to make their case for them.[30] But one fact survives every criticism. Whether or not the post-plague towns were better places to live, they "were certainly emptier than they had been before the Black Death".[31] If plague had come just once, English towns might have survived it leaner and fitter than before, relieved of their "unwanted surplus of impoverished people".[32] Alternatively, if the pestilence had gone away after only half a century or so, when new recruitment of rural labour was still possible, then there might again have been some advantage in its culls. However, that automatic topping-up of urban populations which pre-1400 England took for granted could no longer be relied upon from that date. To borrow Tolstoy's well-known aphorism: "All happy [towns] resemble one another, but each unhappy [town] is unhappy in its own way."[33] And today, understandably, there are at least as many explanations of late-medieval England's urban crisis as there are towns generally agreed to have been its victims. One concerns the "flight from office" of which there is some evidence at Coventry but little at York;[34] another postulates a failure of local entrepreneurship such as may have contributed to Hull's fifteenth-century recession;[35] a third stems from the shortage of coin, which so crippled English trade in the later Middle Ages as to limit even the richest merchant "barons" of the capital.[36] But alongside these special causes – and each town had another – at least one major obstacle to recovery was shared by all. In every case, what had finally stanched the flow of re-invigorating immigration was population stasis in the countryside as well.

CHAPTER THREE

Villages in stasis

The plague bacillus can go anywhere. But it will travel faster and further in the aggravated conditions known as septicaemic or pneumonic plague, when direct person-to-person infection can take place. In those extreme but rare variants of bubonic plague, both probably present in the Black Death of 1348–9, plague bacilli may concentrate in the bloodstream in such huge quantities that they can be carried by the human flea (*Pulex irritans*), or transmitted by coughed-up droplets and blood-bearing sputum. Such conditions, however, have remained exceptional. And it has always been more common for plague to be carried by the rat flea (*Xenopsylla cheopis*), and to be limited in range by the black rat's usual run of not more than 200 metres. Other rodents subsequently spread the plague bacilli much further, especially in close-knit communities such as towns. But, except in grand pandemics like the Black Death itself, bubonic plague has stayed throughout its history primarily urban-based, seldom reaching out with full force into the surrounding countryside, and killing many more in the towns than in their hinterlands.[1]

That being so, plague alone is unlikely to have been the cause of the failure of rural populations in fifteenth-century England to make up for the heavy mortalities in the towns. And there are other reasons also, not lost on contemporaries, for seeing the late-medieval countryside as comparatively healthy. Rural living standards had never been better. Whereas the normal fare of English peasantry before the Black Death had consisted of barley bread and oatmeal pottage, with very little meat and some thin ale, diet improved radically after 1349, as more land became available, and as labour thinned out and wages rose. There was wheat bread on the husbandman's table in late-medieval rural England; beef and mutton replaced bacon; fresh fish was preferred by many villagers over Yarmouth's salted herring; and harvest workers, now greatly in demand, were plied with strong ale to keep them happy.[2]

Rural housing had also taken a turn for the better. Substantial stone-built village long-houses pre-dated the Black Death, as did major improvements in timber framing. But comfortable multi-room farmhouses – the Kentish Wealden house and the Pennine aisled hall, or their variants (below, pp. 164–7) – were unknown in England before the Late Middle Ages. And equally significant for the better health of rural people was the separation of the farmer's family from his livestock. When, for example, the Earl of Stafford's agents rebuilt John Bromefeld's farmhouse at Tillington in 1437–8, they provided him not with the mixed-purpose long-house of traditional plan but with a separate dwelling-house and a barn to go with it. Old materials were re-used from another farm in the locality, and the total cost to Humphrey Stafford's estate was quite small. But the old-style shared accommodation – with animals at one end and family at the other – was no longer believed appropriate for a tenant of Bromefeld's standing, who must have his own parlour and his hall.[3]

Relatively immune from plague, insulated by land surpluses against harvest failure, better fed and better housed than ever before, England's peasant families nevertheless failed to multiply. And where fifteenth-century rural populations came to rest – at barely half their pre-plague totals – was on a near-perfect balance of births and deaths. That balance left little over for migration to the towns, which consequently entered their worst period of contraction. Yet although rural stagnation is well established at this date, its causes are still very obscure. One possible clue, Lawrence Poos suggests, may be found in the Walden parish records. Walden, in northern Essex, is a large mixed parish (both rural and urban) where an account was kept during the mid-fifteenth century of the fees paid at "churchings" after childbirth. The record is defective in several ways, and covers no more than five decades. However, it has enabled Poos to calculate a crude annual birth rate in mid-century Essex of just 30 per thousand, which matches exactly the much better-documented birth rates of the late seventeenth century, when England's population again entered a decline.[4] It matches contemporary death rates also, and Walden's essentially stationary population in the Late Middle Ages was never simply the product of fewer births. But that equality of birth-rate figures in late-medieval and post-Civil War England is still significant. If Walden is at all typical, then the low fertility which was arguably a main cause of the pre-1700 population collapse may equally have characterized the Late Middle Ages.

In reality, Walden was representative only of the most crowded parts of England. Essex (thickly settled with cross-infecting little towns) was one of those counties always more liable to plague than the comparatively empty regions of the north. Until the early 1700s plague remained the big killer in East Anglia and the southern Midlands, in the Home Counties and throughout the south-east, whereas famine was still the main cause of exceptional mortalities in Cumbria and northern Lancashire, Northumbria, the North Riding and the Pennine valleys.[5] There were other persisting differences between the regions, including a more traditional marriage system in the north. However, one common aspiration – crucial to reproduction – was slowly spreading. The English, it is now thought, were early pioneers of the nuclear family, which they may have favoured in some areas – especially in the south – as early as the mid-thirteenth century.[6] Later marriages and fewer children both resulted from that preference, so that when plague mortalities were also high, there was little short-term prospect of recovery.

Certainly, it was the practice of late marriage which kept families small in early-modern England. And the parish register studies that have shown this to have been the case have also now established beyond reasonable doubt that secular variations in nuptiality and fertility were of as much importance in population control as such exogenous factors as plague or famine.[7] England's parish registers begin only in the 1540s. Yet there is every reason to suppose that the marriage patterns they record are much older than the registers, while post-dating the Black Death in many areas. In pre-plague England overcrowding had been endemic, and rural communities had responded – as they still do today in some Third World countries – by reproducing more prolifically than ever. "People are not poor because they have large families," it was once said of northern India. "Quite the contrary, they have large families because they are poor."[8] And that dependence on child labour and then on adult offspring for old-age care is the unavoidable accompaniment of deprivation. England, in contrast, saw lower rents and higher wages banishing excessive poverty in the post-plague decades, and the extended family gradually lost its rationale. In ever-growing numbers and from a comparatively early date, the English (with other northern Europeans) found themselves swapping a "situation where people cannot afford not to have children, [for] one where they cannot afford to have many of them".[9]

That situation already existed before the Black Death in some of England's more densely populated counties. And market-intensive Essex, with its diversified economy, was probably among the first to pioneer the nuclear family. Elsewhere the traditional extended family – the oldest of human associations – was more usually reinforced by pre-plague crowding. Such was the case, for example, on the West Midlands manor of Halesowen, where plague mortalities in 1349 exceeded 40 per cent (above, p. 10). In Halesowen subdivision of patrimonial holdings for multi-occupation became common in the late thirteenth century, as the manor's population climbed unceasingly. Consequently, when Hugo Alwerd inherited his father's yardland at Ridgeacre in the mid-1290s, there was nothing unusual in the way he shared it out – with Agnes (his re-married mother), who continued to live there, with his sister (Lucy), and with his three brothers (William, Thomas and Philip) – thus dividing the family's single holding between six households.[10]

In less-favoured locations such crowding could only end in catastrophe. And for substantial parts of pre-plague England growth had already halted before the Black Death, with communities either levelling-out or in retreat.[11] However, Halesowen's villein families were luckier than most. Their long and bitter struggle with the abbot, their lord, was already largely over before 1300.[12] The manor was well placed on major trading and droving roads; its economy was varied, with several sorts of agriculture and some rural industry; rents had stabilized, labour services were light, and fines in the manor court were low. If some of the earlier troubles returned after the Black Death as the abbot did his utmost to raise receipts, the generally favourable local circumstances which had supported a large population at Halesowen before the plague continued to attract inward settlement. For almost five decades vacant family holdings were immediately taken up by distant relatives. But then, as in the towns, immigration slowed down, to cease almost completely by 1400. Without regular infusions of new blood, the manor's old tenant families died out quickly. Halesowen's "functionally extended familial system", writes Dr Razi with rare precision, "broke down in the fourth decade of the fifteenth century".[13]

In point of fact, Halesowen's traditional family system took nearer 70 years to unravel. And that period of transition might have lasted even longer had it not been for the contemporary exodus of serfs. Unable to extract worthwhile concessions from their abbot, Halesowen's more enterprising villeins departed for nearby manors where – no questions asked – they could readily sell their labour and live as freemen.[14] It is probable that the abbot

himself poached bondmen from other manors in the locality. And this artificially induced labour mobility in late-medieval rural England weakened
still further the old extended families, broken already by return visits of the
plague and as hard to put together again as Humpty Dumpty. In late-fourteenth-century Halesowen it had remained usual for sons to succeed their
fathers on family holdings. But such intra-family successions fell away
sharply after 1400, causing a tenement take-up rate of almost 70 per cent in
the 1390s to reduce to half in the 1410s, and then to drop again after 1430,
when it settled at just 40 per cent for the rest of the century.[15]

For a community which had been stable for so many years, these are truly
extraordinary statistics. And they establish a dissolution of the family–land
bond in fifteenth-century Halesowen as complete as any that had already
taken place in the more progressive rural parishes of the south or east.[16] That
dissolution is only partly explained by the post-feudal exodus of bondmen;
for there were other factors also – not confined to the Late Middle Ages –
that contributed still more to the breaking of ancient ties and to the separation of peasant families from their land. Many of those conditions would re-
emerge in the chronic labour shortages of the late seventeenth century. And
a prominent feature of both periods was the full employment of young
women – usually (but not exclusively) in domestic service – which necessarily delayed marriage and sometimes prevented it altogether. Less easy to
quantify, but of huge long-term consequence, was the slowly growing preference among the English of all classes for individual households over shared
ones. "As the young Bees do seek unto themselves another hive," wrote
William Whateley, vicar of Banbury, in 1624, "so let the young couple
another house . . . [for] the mixing of governors in a household, or subor-
dinating or uniting of two Masters, or two Dames under one roof, doth fall
out most times, to be a matter of much unquietness to all parties."[17] Yet, far
from being new doctrine in Puritan England, this wisdom had been current
for two centuries.

Over that long time, a household formation system which required late
marriage had won wide acceptance in rural England. Large families were
still found there – as in the 23 children (12 daughters and 11 sons) of the
twice-married Ralph de Nevill, Earl of Westmorland (d. 1425). But such
great and costly broods were never common in late-medieval England, even
among the wealthy. And for a typical working family, where the mother had
been in service for several years before her marriage, the probability of many
children was always low. Whereas south European women of this period had

usually found a partner before twenty-one, the average age at marriage of a northern bride rose in the fifteenth century to twenty-three or over. Only at that comparatively advanced age would the coveted separate household come within reach of many couples, and the marriage chest be filled to overflowing.[18]

It was thus the coincidence of separate household systems with abundant jobs for women that created a crisis of replacement in fifteenth-century rural England. Late marriage, resulting from such employment, was no absolute bar to many children. But while successive annual births remain perfectly possible for mature women of all ages until menopause, they are rare even in those societies where marriage is early and in which children are most highly prized. In pre-industrial Europe, the typical interval between births was nearer two (or even three) years than one. That gap might be less if a child died in infancy, as many did. But mothers – and fathers too – might also die young in the epidemic-prone communities of the Late Middle Ages. And any limitation, however caused, of average child-bearing years was certain to have a disproportionate effect on a population's ability to replace itself.[19]

Domestic service, delayed marriage and low fertility are all better recorded in late-seventeenth-century England.[20] Nevertheless, the parallels between the periods are close enough. A recent study, for example, of fifteenth-century matrimonial cause papers from the consistory of York has arguably shown a cycle of female employment differing hardly at all from the national pattern of two centuries later. In late-medieval Yorkshire, country girls usually entered domestic or farm service in their early to mid-teens. They then stayed in those (or related) jobs for ten or more years, before leaving in their mid-twenties to marry and bear children.[21] Exactly that cycle would be repeated again by working women of the late seventeenth century. And another century on, it took an average serving couple at least ten years to save enough between them to set up house.[22] Such engrained habits of thrift are likely to have had a long history. In the poll tax returns of 1377, 1379 and 1380–81, some 20–30 per cent of English urban populations were classed as servants, the majority of whom were single women. Attracted to the towns by good wages and low living costs, they would have remained there, characteristically, for as long as it took them to save for a home of their own.[23]

More women than men were in service in the towns; men outnumbered women as farm servants. However, no matter where they worked, most shared the same ambition, which was to accumulate sufficient savings for independence. At two periods in particular – during the Late Middle Ages and in the century from 1650 – that dream approached reality, for high wages and low prices had persuaded employers of the clear cost advantages of live-in servants. Wealthy townspeople had always enjoyed such help. But it now suited farmers also – many of whom were switching to less labour-intensive pastoral regimes – to maintain permanent establishments of relatively inexpensive live-in servants rather than hire seasonal labour at daily wage-rates.[24]

England's labouring children left home early for a variety of reasons, among them the desire to avoid domestic conflict and the need of their parents to save money.[25] And when, after a long absence, they returned with capital of their own, they were old enough to decide what to do with it. Special arrangements to attract first-time tenants – from reduced entry fines to small cash incentives and waived services – were common in the Late Middle Ages. They offered markedly better deals than those enjoyed by

12. Hard physical labour is here being illustrated in the miniature of a peasant digging which accompanies Hunger's moralizing speech in William Langland's *Piers Plowman*. The manuscript is dated 1427. *The Bodleian Library, Oxford: MS Douce 104, fol. 39r.*

established tenants, and contributed once again to a breakdown of the family–land bond in fifteenth-century England more complete than at any time until the present. On Durham Priory's estates, where such favourable terms were routinely conceded to new tenants, transfers within the family fell from fully two-thirds of the peasant land market just before the Black Death to only 10–15 per cent in the 1380s. They then remained at that low level for much of the fifteenth century, until experiencing some revival round about 1500, as the abler peasant consolidators on the priory's estates built up farms of sufficient consequence for their sons.[26]

It might be thought that those consolidators, tenants of multiple hold-ings, would be the natural founders of yeoman-farmer dynasties of their own; and some were. Yet recent research has put more emphasis on transi-ence. "The outstanding feature of fifteenth-century Coleshill," wrote Rosamond Faith of one Berkshire parish, "was the rise of a peasant aristo-cracy which came to nothing."[27] And while that was evidently not the experience of all late-medieval consolidators, including those of Durham, it was still comparatively rare for successful peasant families of the first post-plague generations to survive much beyond 1400.[28] The richer the tenant, the more likely he was to leave his name on the land. And there is good evidence everywhere of a return to family farming in Tudor England.[29] However, what chiefly characterized rural society in the immediate after-math of plague was high mobility and growing polarization. The old-style virgate and half-virgate family holdings which remained the common local land units in early-fifteenth-century Leighton Buzzard had been broken up, with few exceptions, before 1500. And what took their place from 1450 in this large Bedfordshire parish was a socially polarizing mix of labourers' smallholdings with the increasingly substantial property accumulations of *fin-de-siècle* rentiers like William Taillour.[30]

It was in this period again that Edmund Grey's manor of Blunham, also in Bedfordshire, saw some of its most significant changes. There are two surviv-ing fifteenth-century Grey rentals of Blunham: for 1457 and 1498. And what they show between them is a very similar fragmentation of former family holdings, associated with a rapid turnover of new tenants. Of eight half-virgate holdings known to have had just one tenant each in 1457, 44 separate parcels had been made by 1498, shared among 21 holders. And of the 50 dif-ferent Blunham families the two rentals name, just 19 occur in them both.[31] A fair proportion of those name-changes probably resulted from the mar-riage of female heirs; and it is unlikely that Blunham's migrants travelled far.

But what is certain is that post-1450 Blunham was less a functioning manorial community of the traditional kind than a loose association of individuals.

Throughout the fifteenth century it was continuing labour shortages on Spalding Priory's estates that drove successive priors to extraordinary lengths in the ceaseless pursuit of their bondmen. And Spalding's fugitive villeins fled further than most, over half of them migrating 20 miles or more, and many seeking refuge in the anonymity of towns – at Wisbech, King's Lynn or even London.[32] Spalding's priors, even so, enjoyed more success in locating their departed serfs than in bringing them back to their villages. And in a rural society where systematic landowner bullying was rare, it was always more usual for the domesticated former villeins of late-medieval England to re-settle within easy walking distance of their relatives. This was only occasionally to the benefit of population-hungry towns, just six of which were named among the 21 recorded destinations of Hampton Lovett villeins who departed their Worcestershire manor in the late fifteenth century. In point of fact, most of those migrants never left their native county, settling within a radius of between five and 13 miles of Hampton Lovett.[33]

By 1500, one new reason for ignoring the towns was that many jobs there had disappeared with the recession. And what commonly happened was that country women of this period, who had formerly made up as much as half of the post-plague urban workforce, now found themselves excluded from the more remunerative crafts and trades, and driven to marry earlier in consequence.[34] Partly as a result, birth rates began to rise again in many rural areas. Yet village women of this class had enjoyed particular freedom in the later Middle Ages, able to follow work wherever it led them and to opt to marry late or not at all.[35] Late marriage is largely a personal choice. Over the population as a whole, it leaves much less mark on the historical record than the more obtrusive interventions of plague or famine. Yet with every community growing older in fifteenth-century England, with the disease-ridden towns still shrinking, and with rural births and deaths in perfect balance, alterations in average age of marriage might well have been decisive in causing the population to rise or fall. In other words, it is not impossible – as some have already argued – that nuptiality, rather than mortality or any other imposed condition, was the single late-medieval demographic variable of greatest consequence.[36]

The decision whether or not to marry late was clearly open to many country people in fifteenth-century England. Increasingly also, young couples could choose where to live. Their choices resulted in the abandonment of many settlements, and have left their mark today in the earthwork remains of deserted villages and hamlets still plainly visible on modern landscapes. Population loss was the underlying cause of all desertions. However, every deserted village – like every shrunken town – had its own peculiar reasons for abandonment. Of these, one of the more frequent was the shift to mixed farming – pastoral as well as arable – which often followed a slackening of manorial discipline and the collapse of old-style communal systems in the open field. And closely related to that relaxation of landowner pressure was the new mobility of one-time bondmen, making voluntary migration in almost every case the "key" factor in a settlement's desertion.[37] More important by far than heavy plague mortalities or adverse climatic change in marginal areas – each of which claimed some victims among the smaller English villages – was the abiding desire of the ex-villein for self-betterment.

For many that self-betterment might best be achieved by engrossing the vacant holdings of former tenants. But whereas the consolidators in larger villages kept communities alive, they just as often contributed to the eventual destruction of lesser settlements already disadvantaged. On a cold and rain-swept Cotswold hillside, even the most enterprising peasant engrosser was unable to make a living in fifteenth-century Roel, from which Robert Hethe (the embittered former tenant of three once-separate holdings) departed in 1453 "with threatening and odious words".[38] The climate was not Robert's only, nor even his worst, enemy at Roel. If his village is compared with neighbouring Hawling, with which it had many parallels before the pestilence, one important difference stands out. Hawling was a mixed community: chiefly of customary tenants, but also of day-labourers (cottagers) and some freeholders. Roel, in contrast, had only the first: all bondmen of the Abbot of Wynchcombe. Why those tenants should have abandoned Roel while others (not the same) still came to Hawling was not because Roel was less fertile or its bondmen more oppressed, but because their options in the two communities were quite different.[39]

Two Oxfordshire desertions of the Late Middle Ages, at Thomley and Tubney, show what was happening in many areas. Of the two villages, Thomley was the weaker: a late-cleared forest assart and cradle-sick child, with no single dominant landowner, no market, no church and no mill. Yet even little Thomley had filled up with settlers in the overcrowded thirteenth century when, lacking firm lordship, it had developed a precociously active peasant land market well before 1300, inimical to family–land bonds in the community. A similarly active land market developed only much later in the more conservatively managed Tubney, nevertheless becoming sufficiently vigorous in the second half of the fourteenth century to cause many long-established Tubney families to disappear from view, less than a third of the surnames in a 1394 assessment matching those of pre-plague subsidy listings. By 1400 Thomley was practically empty. And although Tubney struggled on for another century or so, the enclosure of former holdings had begun there already before 1445, starting probably with the plots which former bond-men had abandoned and which had remained un-tenanted and un-tilled on their departure.[40]

Tenant loss without replacement is what chiefly explains the great major-ity of late-medieval village desertions. And it was usually only after the tenants had gone that their holdings were enclosed and laid to pasture. Such sequences characterized, for example, the former hamlets at Brookend (Oxfordshire) and Woollashill (Worcestershire), at Wharram Percy (York-

13. Buslingthorpe (Lincolnshire) was sufficiently affected by the Black Death to be granted a 50 per cent tax relief in 1352, but had recovered almost entirely by 1377, when 63 adults (aged 14 and over) were listed in the poll-tax returns of that year. Depopulation and enclosure for sheep probably followed in the second half of the fif-teenth century, after which settlement was dispersed into scattered farmsteads (P. L. Everson, C. C. Taylor & C. J. Dunn, *Change and continuity. Rural settlement in north-east Lincolnshire* (London, HMSO for the Royal Commission on the Historical Monuments of England, 1991, pp. 84–5). *RCHME Crown copyright.*

14. A single farm and these earthworks mark the site of the Nottinghamshire village of Thorpe-in-the-Glebe, of which even the church has now vanished. As one of the smaller and more vulnerable of the pre-plague settlements, on a cold and heavy soil, Thorpe continued to lose population after the Black Death. It was cleared and enclosed for pasture during the fifteenth century, in a process largely complete by 1500. In this photograph, a central hedge now marks the line of the former village street, with house platforms and enclosures on each side. The ridge-and-furrow remnants of strip cultivation on Thorpe's arable fields, although showing only faintly here in the strong cross-light, can be made out both on the left and at the top of this photograph. *Cambridge University Collection of Air Photographs: copyright reserved.*

shire) and Eaton Hastings (Berkshire), as at Nottinghamshire's Thorpe-in-the-Glebe.[41] Thorpe was a small parish, less than half the size of its three nearest neighbours, on a clayey north-facing slope. Once surrounded by its own ploughlands before the pestilence, it was so reduced by plague mortalities and bondman migration that many of its cold and heavy fields had ceased to be cultivable by the early fifteenth century, leaving no viable alternative to enclosure. That situation has never changed, and Thorpe today is still under grass, so that a late-medieval settlement landscape survives there intact, very much as it was left on final clearance. To the west of the former village is a substantial moated site, presumably of the pre-plague Darley manor-house. The line of Thorpe's street remains clearly visible, as do the

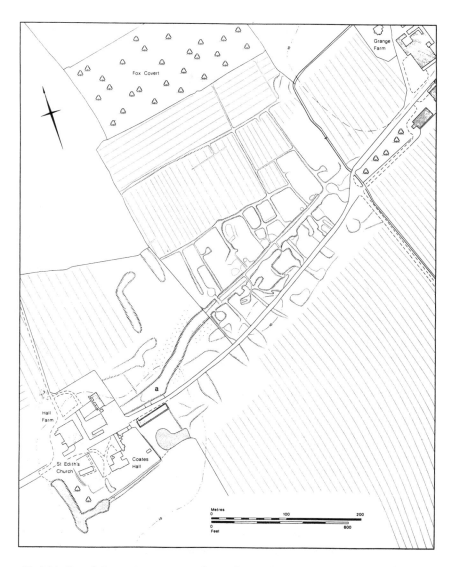

Grange
Farm

Fox Covert

Hall
Farm

St Edith's
Church

Coates
Hall

a

Metres
0   100   200

0
Feet   600

15. This Royal Commission survey shows the earthworks – a well-marked street, or hollow-way, with house-plots and ridge-and-furrow on each side – of the pre-plague village of Coates (Lincolnshire). At the west (bottom left) end of the street is the site of the former manor-house and parish church. Coates suffered badly in the Black Death and had failed to recover by 1377, when only 17 taxpayers were recorded. Abandonment and enclosure probably followed quite soon, for Coates was too small to qualify for the parish tax of 1428 (Everson, Taylor & Dunn, *Change and continuity*, pp. 185–7, 189). *RCHME Crown copyright.*

clay platforms and other earthworks of individual peasant houses, with enclosed stockyards to the side and to the rear. Well-marked late-medieval ridge-and-furrow spreads out in all directions, undamaged by the plough

16. An air view from the south of the village at Rougham (Norfolk) where John Reed – the target of peasant rebels in 1381 – made his enclosures. Settlement at Rougham before the plague had stretched out much further than it does today, particularly through the wooded pastures (top left) to the west and north-west of the parish church. *Norfolk Air Photographs Library: photo Derek A. Edwards.*

since arable farming was given up and the community was swallowed by its sheep.[42]

Before long, the common belief of Sir Thomas More and his contemporaries would be that "sheep begin now to be so greedy and wild that they devour human beings themselves and devastate and depopulate fields, houses and towns".[43] However, such wholesale enclosure was almost always a last resort in fifteenth-century England, usually yielding (as at Thorpe) a poor return. Rather than tread the encloser's entrepreneurial road, most landowners continued to cling to the hope of an eventual recovery in their rent rolls. One Johnny-come-lately who took a different view was John Reed, lord of Rougham in western Norfolk. Reed, the engrosser, was of local villein stock. More than most, he had profited from the social turmoil of the post-plague decades to accumulate a large personal fortune before 1379, when appointed a collector of the poll tax. Two years later, in the Great Revolt of 1381, Reed was the target of enraged poll-tax payers, who gathered from far around to do him mischief. His house was badly damaged and his possessions were carried away. On 17 June 1381, when rioting broke out at Rougham, Reed suffered personal losses of over £50, or the entire profits he might have drawn from several farms.[44]

Reed himself survived the riot, living to enclose another day. But there is more to Reed's story in the Revolt of 1381 than a simple moral tale of greed and envy. Reed's success as an engrosser, both before and after the Revolt, had many close parallels in the later Middle Ages.[45] Nor were England's newly prospering yeoman farmers the only ones to feel a growing self-esteem and independence. Rougham, a shrunken village with a long history of decay, still carries the scars of Reed's enclosures. But, rapacious bully though he was, even Reed could not proceed without consensus. On that one midsummer day, something like two-thirds of Rougham's villagers rose against him. Yet, after all the damage his neighbours did to his property, their punishments in Reed's court were very light.[46] Reed needed farmhands to till his fields and mind his sheep. As labour shortages deepened, with no sign of change, the children of these bondmen, without a backward glance, would pack up their belongings and migrate.

CHAPTER FOUR

Impoverished noblemen and rich old ladies

Among today's historians few have written with more intuitive under-standing of the post-plague English nobility than the late Bruce McFarlane. It was McFarlane who, in one of his last lectures, identified infertility and disease as "far more potent enemies" of the noble class than either violence in general or than the Wars of the Roses in particular. "Fail-ure in the direct male line," he told an audience which had come to hear him on those wars, "happened on the average to some quarter of [England's noble families] every twenty-five years throughout the fourteenth and fif-teenth centuries . . . [and] this high extinction rate was in every period at least as much the result of natural causes as of premature and violent deaths."[1] By 1400, McFarlane calculated, fully two-thirds of the 136 baro-nial families receiving writs of summons to Edward I's last parliaments (just a century before) were extinct in the direct male line. In other words, "the stock was already withered" well before the dynastic struggle between Lan-castrians and Yorkists surfaced at the first battle of St Albans on 22 May 1455, thereby launching the Wars of the Roses which helped reduce the remain-ing third to just 16. From the Black Death until 1500, at this excessive rate of loss, "the higher ranks of the nobility rarely deserved the epithet 'old'. The turnover was always rapid, the eminence short-lived, the survivors invari-ably few."[2]

Although the Black Death undoubtedly had a role in this collapse, plague was never the most potent killer of England's late-medieval nobility. In another McFarlane sample of lords and higher clergy, the death rate in 1349 (including natural wastage) was only 13 per cent, or considerably less than half the recorded loss of other classes. And while that death rate climbed much higher in 1361, reaching an exceptional 23.9 per cent in that year, plague mortalities fell back again substantially in later visitations, to settle well below the national average.[3] But if better housing conditions and a greater ability to flee infection helped individual noblemen to survive the plague, they were not to evade its other consequences quite as easily. It has recently been argued, for example, that "ready social mobility both into and within English landed society began with the Black Death and not, as some have claimed, with the stimulus the [Tudor] Dissolution gave to the land market".[4] And this was clearly one result of the extinction of noble families in the direct male line, causing old family lands to migrate with heiress-brides to other owners. Inter-familial marriage transfers had occurred before the pestilence, but were greatly increased by male mortalities. Already in the late 1370s and 1380s, when the nobility's demographic crisis was at its worst, only about half of England's noblemen left sons to take their places. Moreover, of the extraordinary 30 per cent of landowners who died with no surviving child of either sex, fully 60 per cent were succeeded by female collateral relatives, wiping the family name off those estates.[5]

Some of the resulting difficulties might have been avoided by legal means, through such devices as the entail or the feoffment-to-use. And these were often employed in the Late Middle Ages to safeguard the rights of younger sons, or of the children of second and subsequent marriages.[6] However, closely related heirs of any kind were in short supply in late-fourteenth-century England. Furthermore, most landowners by that time had other worries. In particular, those worries concerned the declining profitability of many great estates which nothing – not even the high-quality management of the Talbot lands at Whitchurch – could reverse. Richard Lord Talbot (of Goodrich) and Ankaret le Strange (of Whitchurch), his heiress-wife and widow, managed Whitchurch energetically for 30 years after Ankaret came into her huge inheritance in 1383. Eschewing politics, Richard personally transformed the estate's administration; tried different kinds of direct farming; switched quickly to leasing when those efforts failed; and generally improved receipts from every source. But plague returned to Whitchurch in 1391; Richard died in 1396; and the brief episode of continuing prosperity under Ankaret's sole direction ended with the Welsh raids of 1404.[7] In comparison with other common survival strategies of the late-medieval aristocracy, of which arranged marriages, going to war and entering royal service were the most important, "keen" estate management was a failure. Even the Talbots – from as early as 1390 and through good years as well as bad – sold standing timber, depleting their reserves for ready cash. "There can be no more telling evidence than this," comments Dr Pollard on those sales, "that the returns from vigorous management were recognized to be only marginal [by 1400]."[8]

Further land investment in such circumstances inevitably lost attraction, and those who in the fifteenth century continued to buy estates usually did so less for profit than for honour.[9] However, land-shyness developed only slowly in late-medieval England, and a more immediate effect of the Black Death on many manors was to bring out the best abilities in skilled administrators. Thus energetic estate officials moved quickly to reduce rents in Edward of Woodstock's Cornish duchy after 1349, filling vacant holdings on all but the least fertile manors, and restoring Duke Edward's profits within a few years of the pestilence.[10] Similarly, it was the Black Death that stimulated entrepreneurial activity at Tillingdown (Surrey), acquired by Ralph de Stafford with other great estates following his second marriage to the Clare heiress, Margaret de Audley. Tillingdown was administered from the old Clare headquarters at Tonbridge Castle, and it was from Tonbridge that John Fromond, Stafford's receiver, was despatched to this downland manor shortly after the Black Death to do what he could to restore profits. Over the next decade, arable acreages were increased at Tillingdown, buildings were re-erected, draught animals were purchased and extra labourers were hired; there were experiments in dairy farming and breeding rabbits. But the first measure Fromond took, probably reflecting past experience, was to bring sheep to the manor in 1350, to graze its surplus fields and vacant holdings. Tillingdown's demesne flock then grew to 1,700 by 1362, when a severe epidemic of sheep scab reduced it by a fifth, contributing to the decision of Earl Ralph and his council, four years later, to abandon direct farming on the manor.[11] That decision was taken unusually early, while most other demesne estates continued profitable. For at least another decade, England's estate-owning plague survivors had more to spend – on land as well as luxuries – than had commonly been their lot before the pestilence.[12] But those fortunate times were quickly over. In 1375 an exceptionally bountiful harvest, the best since the mid-century, opened a new era of falling cereal prices uncompensated for by lower wages. "The big demesne farmers who had weathered so many storms could not weather this one. For them [writes Dr Bridbury] it was the end."[13]

That end was not immediate, for direct farming continued on the more conservative estates until the 1420s and often later. Nevertheless, the contemporary profit collapse was very real. Chirkland, in north-east Wales, was only one of the many great estates of the enormously wealthy Fitzalan Earls of Arundel and Surrey. And Richard Fitzalan's officials had experienced no great difficulty after 1349 in bringing his lands back into profitability. For over 20 years, under Earl Richard's careful eye, Chirkland continued to pay well. But then the situation began to sour. Earl Richard died in 1376, leaving a Chirkland rent-roll already little altered for many years. Serious arrears began to mount in the next Earl Richard's time, while other sources of income, including the farms of tolls and mills, were drying up. Welsh resistance to the Marcher lords was growing all the time, to develop shortly into serious rebellion. But the real problem (as in England) was a chronic labour shortage: the absence of willing farmers for the Chirkland tolls and mills, or of takers of any kind for the many holdings "in the lord's hand [because] vacant for want of tenants".[14] It was that same "shortage of tenants" – so a Warwickshire jury decided in 1379 – which was the cause of John atte Well's neglect of ploughing at Blackwell, where once he "used to have three ploughs ploughing [but] now he has only two, so that the lord's land at Shipston lies without fallow ploughing, to the grave damage of the lord". In point of fact, so severely out of balance had wages and prices become, that John's options overall were much reduced. Ten years later, at Ladbroke in the same county, a calculation was made of the real profitability of arable farming. What it revealed was that costs had risen to such a level on Ladbroke's 100-acre ploughland that any hope of a return to profit had disappeared.[15]

Driven off the arable, the greatest English landowners could nevertheless survive by stocking their empty lands with sheep and cattle. And the Earls of Arundel, even before the pestilence, were already pastoralists on a very big scale. They were to double that investment in the next 50 years, and were usually well served by their officials. However, the first Earl Richard individually made his fortune less in estate management than in family alliances and in the rewards of royal office, which then gave him the ready capital for high-yield loans.[16] Competence alone offered few guarantees of profit on the land, while mounting rent arrears – at their worst on the Welsh estates of absentee landowners like the Stafford Dukes of Buckingham – continued to cause liquidity crises in many baronial fortunes, even where in the longer term they proved recoverable.[17] Margins were always tight, and profitability could quickly disappear. The Greys of Ruthin, Earls of Kent from 1465, are usually cited as prudent managers: proof that a baronial family might still flourish. And that was indeed the case in Earl Edmund's time, as it was while

George, the second earl, was still alive. But Earl George (d. 1503) was rightly pessimistic about the future. His son Richard, he predicted, would "not thrive but be a waster". Earl Richard was a gambler, paying off his growing debts with family land. Just 20 years later, when the fourth earl inherited, he "declined to assume these peerage dignities from want of fortune".[18]

Encumbered though they were, the Grey estates were still extensive on Richard's death in 1523. It was not easy for a baron to go bankrupt. "I have found no example of proved indebtedness on a really large scale," wrote Bruce McFarlane of this class. "There is no sign whatever that even a single one of the comital houses . . . came to disaster by any other road than political miscalculation."[19] But there was indeed another road; and Richard took it. His more serious offence, far worse than gambling debts, was to leave no heir. Sir Henry Grey (of Wrest), the next *de jure* Earl of Kent, was Richard's brother of the half-blood, child of Earl George's second marriage. And it was Sir Henry's flawed succession that broke the strong chain of secure inheritance and long tenure which had characterized the Greys of Ruthin across two centuries.

That exceptional run of generative fortune was a more significant factor in the rise of the Greys than any other quality – including farming competence – that they possessed. But agility in war and politics, exhibited by Earl Edmund to a rare degree, contributed also very materially to their ascent. Few late-medieval noble families emerged from all those lotteries unharmed. Among the losers were the Courtenay Earls of Devon. Edward Courtenay, the third earl, was still the dominant political force in his own county in the 1380s, with lawyers and beneficed clergy, as well as knights and squires, on his payroll. Edward prospered also, drawing a secure income from his Devon estates until the plague-induced recession of 1391 caused a dramatic decline for almost a decade in his receipts. Then "the Blind Earl" lost his sight, and for another two decades, until his death on 5 December 1419, the senior branch of the Courtenay family was largely rudderless. Three years later, the young and vigorous Earl Hugh died prematurely, and during the 11-year minority of Thomas, the fifth earl, much of what remained of the Courtenays' local patronage slipped away. In trying to rebuild the family fortunes and its one-time power base, Earl Thomas resorted to "grevous riotes" and to brigandry. He lost many friends in the West Country, made an enemy of Richard, Duke of York, and forged an ill-omened partnership with Margaret of Anjou, Henry VI's warlike queen, which committed his sons disastrously to the losing side. The next Earl

17. Arundel Castle (Sussex), the most imposing baronial fortress in the south of England, was the principal estate-centre of the hugely wealthy Fitzalan Earls of Arundel and Surrey, before the dispersal of their great fortune on the early death of the childless Earl Thomas (d.1415). A heavy-handed late Victorian rebuilding of the 1890s has replaced almost entirely the grand fourteenth-century lodgings (left centre) of one of the richest noble families of post-plague England, whose wealth nevertheless could offer no protection to their line. *RCHME Crown copyright.*

Thomas, who succeeded his father in February 1458, was captured at Towton on 29 March 1461 and was beheaded five days later. His brothers, Henry and John, both met violent deaths in the Lancastrian cause: Henry by execution in 1469 and Earl John at the battle of Tewkesbury in 1471, when in the army of Margaret of Anjou. It was a different branch of the Courtenay family which recovered the earldom in 1485 after Bosworth. The new Earl John was second cousin of Earl Thomas and great-great-grandson of Hugh Courtenay (d.1377), the second earl.[20]

There was a particular brutality in the Courtenays' swift collapse. But nothing otherwise in their story is unique. In the case of the far wealthier Fitzalan Earls of Arundel, it would take less than 40 years from the death of Earl Richard in 1376 for the great Fitzalan inheritance to be dispersed. The next earl, another Richard, was accused of conspiracy in 1397 and executed on 21 September. Earl Thomas, succeeding while still a boy, spent most of his adult life in military pursuits. He then caught a mortal fever at the siege of Harfleur and died *sine prole* (without posterity). After Earl Thomas's death on 13 October 1415 the bulk of his great fortune was divided among his sisters, while the castle and estate at Arundel itself descended by disputed entail to a second cousin.

The highest-ranking English fatality in that same campaign was Edward, Duke of York, killed at Agincourt on 25 October 1415. And it was Duke Edward's early death, again without issue, which delivered the York title to his nephew. Aged only four at the time, Richard Plantagenet was the son of Richard, Earl of Cambridge, executed for his part in the Southampton Plot earlier that summer.[21] Richard of Cambridge's shortage of funds had been a major cause of his treason. Raised to the earldom in 1414, he had been given nothing to support the empty title. Richard of York, in contrast, was enormously rich, especially after the death in 1425 of another childless uncle, Edmund Mortimer, had added the March estates to his own. Yet so competitive was the pursuit of worship in fifteenth-century England that even that huge wealth was insufficient. The "outrageous lust of princi-palitie" of which Polydore Vergil (the hostile Tudor historian) later accused Duke Richard, laying the entire blame for the Wars of the Roses at his door, was at least partly the response of "thys good Duke of Yorke" to the costs of a great household and to the unremitting demands of his annuitants.[22]

Among Duke Richard's regular expenses was the wardrobe of his Duchess Cecily, of whom it has been claimed that "her reckless extravagance [on splendid clothes] rivals the prodigality of that spectacular royal spend-thrift, Richard II".[23] But such prodigal "dispendiousness" was at least in part political, the Yorks' investment in princely state eventually proving its worth in the elevation of their son, Duke Edward, to the throne. Even as king, however, Edward IV could not proceed without economies. In 1471–2, after the short-lived restoration of Henry VI, Edward sought to mend his free-spending ways. "The kyng wull have his goodes dispended but not wasted," wrote an anonymous household officer in the preamble to Edward's *Black Book*. The royal court had spent excessively, and "if the kynges hyghnesse plese to kepe a lesse household than the foresayde grete summe sheweth of here, in this boke are devysed ix other smaller house-[holds] . . . whereof the king may choose suche as shall please hym best". In reality, Edward's choice was more restricted. The ideal household of a knight, as defined by the *Black Book*, consisted of just 16 people; of a banneret, 24; of a baron, 40; of a viscount, 80; and even the 140 *domestici* of a belted earl would scarcely suffice for a king. Nearer Edward's mark was the 240-strong household of a fifteenth-century duke, upheld in the age-old way by local patronage:

> These lordes rewarde theire knyghts, capeleyns, esquiers, yomen, and other of theyre servauntes, after theyre desertes. Some of his chapleyns with officyashippes, deanriez, prebendez, fre chapels, personages, pensions, or suche other; and for the secular men, stewardshippes, recevours, counstables, portershippes, baylywikes, wardenshippes, foresters, raungers, verders, vergers, shreves, eschetours, corouners, custumers, countrollers, serchers, surveours, beryngis of yeres giftes, wardes, mariages, corrodiez, perkers, and wareners. This causeth lordes to rule at nede.[24]

Effective though this system very often proved to be, it could never be worked without cost. It is true that many established noblemen, through judicious use of patronage, were successful in limiting their annual wage bills to under 10 per cent of all receipts.[25] But less easy to contain were men's ambitions. The upwardly mobile John Lord Howard, granted the title of Duke of Norfolk in 1483, was not by nature a high spender at any time. Even in the 1480s, having reached the top, his household was still only about 100-strong, of whom 65 drew wages. Nevertheless, between 1455 (when not yet a knight) and 1467 (while still not raised to the peerage) Howard had more than trebled the number of his attendant gentlemen from six to 21; he had increased his yeomen pensioners from 30 to 48; and had thus built himself a base for self-promotion.[26]

"All rising to great place is by a winding stair," later reflected Francis Bacon (d.1626), himself no stranger to ambition.[27] Yet "great place" was small protection in a mid-fifteenth-century society at least as close to civil war as Bacon's own. From 1450, as faction grew, Humphrey Stafford, Duke of Buckingham (d.1460), evidently felt it prudent to enlarge his retinue with men of local influence and substance. During the seven years to 1457, Duke Humphrey added another 22 annuitants to his *familia*, raising it to 17 esquires and gentlemen, 51 yeomen, 38 pages, 15 waiting women, four chaplains and a herald, not including the menial servants of the *hospicium*.[28] But rich though Duke Humphrey was, there were already clear signs before his death of some deliberate containment of household costs and of a reassessment of the real worth of the affinity. It had become usual by the mid-century, even for wealthy families like the Staffords, to keep house only on select estates, of which Maxstoke Castle (Warwickshire) and the manor of Writtle (Essex) were Duke Humphrey's favourites.[29] And although the duke increased (rather than reduced) recruitment in the last decade before his death, he evidently preferred the support and counsel of local gentry administrators and jobbing lawyers to that of the professional soldiers with which the frontier earls, the Percys of Northumberland and the Nevilles of Westmorland, necessarily still surrounded themselves in the northern Marches.[30]

Growing professionalism in household management finally paid off bountifully, in that the Staffords' receipts on their estates – everywhere but in Wales, where local rent strikes were still common – rose substantially in the latter part of the fifteenth century. The Staffords also successfully cut their running-costs by almost a half between Duke Humphrey's time and the third duke's death in 1521.[31] But misfortunes continued to pursue them. Both Duke Edward ("bounteous Buckingham") and his father, Duke Henry (d.1483), died on the scaffold. A major element in their treason – real in Henry's case, hypothetical in Edward's – was the frustration both endured through long minorities. Duke Henry was only five when he succeeded his grandfather, Duke Humphrey. And it was not until two decades later, on the death in 1480 of his grandmother, the Dowager Duchess Anne, that he at last came into his entire patrimony. Duke Edward's early life had many parallels. He was also just five when his father was executed on 2 November 1483. His mother, the Dowager Duchess Katherine, lived until 1497, re-marrying twice, with the result that when Edward's minority ended the next year, his estates were already heavily encumbered.[32]

Where noble ladies usually married early and their husbands late, the lot of the Stafford dukes was not uncommon. In Lancastrian Nottinghamshire, for example, fully two-thirds of the major landowners who died before 1460 were survived by widows, many much younger than themselves. Those were then able to re-marry, and frequently did, while retaining a widow's portion of the family estates for two or three decades or even longer. In circumstances like these it is hard not to sympathize with the despair of Richard Willoughby, son of Sir Hugh (d.1448), whose stepmother Margaret Freville lived into her nineties, surviving her former husband by almost 50 years; or with the very similar frustration of Sir Thomas Rempston, the noted war captain, whose mother's longevity kept her son in France, so that when Margaret died in 1454 – again at an advanced age – Sir Thomas himself had just four years remaining to enjoy the inheritance to which (since 1406) he had aspired.[33]

Rich old ladies, frequently surviving the natural heirs, have brought misery to every generation. But what made the problem worse for England's late-medieval nobility was a combination of demographic factors – a young bride, an older husband and a premature or flawed succession – with the emergence of legal processes which, for those centuries at least, were especially favourable to the protection of women's rights. Between Magna Carta in 1215 and the Black Death in 1348–9, a widow's common-law dower had already moved from the traditional third of her husband's property "at the church door" (on their wedding-day) to a third of his estates on his death. And as the increasing failure of male lines made substantial heiresses of many brides, they obtained further protection of their personal inheritances through a new style of marriage contract, the jointure, which conceded joint use of the merged estates until the death of one party (usually the husband) conveyed sole enjoyment to the survivor for life.[34]

It was the jointure, in particular, which brought about that "peculiar prominence of dowagers in late-medieval England" to which McFarlane was the first to draw attention.[35] And jointures, along with the new entails beginning to be drafted in this period, continued to be popular with the English nobility because they enabled rich landowners to circumvent strict primogeniture, while keeping the name attached to the land. It was not entirely unknown for the surviving partner of a deceased nobleman to renounce her rights, as did Elizabeth de Mowbray, Dowager Countess of Suffolk, who (with her eldest daughter Katherine) took the veil, so that they "ended their lives in prayer and chastity that the earldom should remain to the second brother, Sir William de la Pole, because of the name". But Elizabeth, mother of three daughters (of whom none married), was a young war widow whose husband, Michael, had been earl for just a month when killed at Agincourt on 25 October 1415. Her sacrifice was not repeated by the next earl's widow, who in any event had borne him a son. Earl William (created duke in 1448) married the already twice-wed heiress Alice Chaucer in 1430. Twelve years later Alice gave birth to John (d.1492), but then survived William's murder in 1450 for another quarter century, continuing to collect her dower not just from the estates of the de la Pole family but from those of her second husband, Thomas de Montague, Earl of Salisbury (d.1428), who had predeceased her by 47 years.[36]

Noble relicts, many of them still young, were a familiar presence in fifteenth-century England.[37] Nor was early widowhood necessarily a misfortune. Particularly well placed was Elizabeth Wydeville, the beautiful eldest daughter of the "handsomest man in England", whose widow's weeds attracted the attention of Edward IV. Three years after her first husband, Sir John Grey (a Lancastrian), was mortally wounded at St Albans in 1461, Elizabeth married the Yorkist king in a secret ceremony at the Wydeville family manor-house at Grafton. She brought the king little but her extraordinary beauty and a predatory tribe of Wydeville relatives.[38] But other war widows offered richer prizes, while there were many dowagers also who chose rather to remain single, for "how much better and more comfortable an estate we widows have than we had [formerly] in marriage".[39] The once prodigal Duchess Cecily, widow of Richard of York and mother of two kings (Edward IV and Richard III), may never have made the point quite as openly. But when eventually laid to rest next to Duke Richard at Fotheringhay College in 1495, Cecily had outlived her fractious husband by fully 35 years, free to enjoy a long and detached retirement of exemplary piety, marred only by the constant loss of kin.[40]

Duchess Cecily was a Neville, one of the 22 children of Ralph, Earl of Westmorland (d.1425), whose carefully staged alliances "made up an almost interminable series of matrimonial triumphs".[41] She was not the only Neville daughter to survive a wealthy spouse by many years. Margaret, who married twice, continued to draw a dower from the Scropes of Bolton for 43 years; her sister Matilda outlasted Peter Lord Mauley by 24 years; their half-sister Eleanor, whose second husband was Henry Percy, Earl of Northumberland, had earlier been the child bride of Richard le Despenser (d.1414), then keeping a life interest in the Despenser estates for half a century; Anne was the long-lived dowager, widow of Humphrey, Duke of Buckingham, who kept Duke Henry out of his full inheritance for 20 years after his grandfather's death in 1460; and Catherine, who married (while still a girl) John de Mowbray, Earl of Norfolk (d.1432), continued to enjoy her Mowbray jointure with three subsequent husbands, the third of whom – John Wydeville, the queen's teenage brother – she nevertheless survived by 14 years.[42]

Catherine's fourth marriage, contracted in January 1465 when she was well into her sixties, was probably imposed on her by Edward IV. It caused much scandal and was especially upsetting to her grandson, John de Mowbray, last Mowbray Duke of Norfolk, who took livery of his estates just two

18. Dame Cecily (d.1495), Dowager Duchess of York, spent much of her long widowhood here at Fotheringhay, in Northamptonshire, where she made it her business to complete her father-in-law's collegiate chantry (top centre) as a memorial to Duke Richard (d.1460), while living at Fotheringhay Castle (the big moated mound due east of the church, just below the farm buildings in this photograph). Cecily moved south in her last years to be nearer the two religious communities she most admired – the Bridgettine nuns of Syon and the Carthusian monks of Sheen – but was buried at Fotheringhay next to Duke Richard. *Cambridge University Collection of Air Photographs: copyright reserved.*

19. Margaret of York, Duchess of Burgundy, was the daughter of Duke Richard and Duchess Cecily and the sister of Edward IV. In this Flemish miniature of 1465 Margaret and her ladies are seen at prayer, the Duchess kneeling before an image of the Virgin. *The Bodleian Library, Oxford: MS Douce 365, fol. 115r.*

months later, with another dowager, his mother Eleanor, to support.[43] But while Catherine's last encounter may have brought her little pleasure, her successful, and no doubt gratifying, matrimonial career is evidence enough of the considerable distance English noblewomen had travelled since pre-plague times towards greater personal choice and independence. After the first dynastic match they could usually take a partner of their choosing. And if they preferred not to re-marry, they had much also to look forward to in a busy and useful life of estate and household management, accompanied characteristically by pious works. The great ladies of late-medieval England included some of its ablest managers. And it was often these comfortably off and supremely well-connected dowagers – Margaret of Brotherton (d.1399), Cecily of York (d.1495) and Margaret Beaufort (d.1509) – who gave the best example as forward-looking patrons of the Church.[44] "All

England had cause of weeping", eulogized John Fisher (her confessor) when Lady Margaret died, and there was much that was truly admirable in these old ladies. But as the venerable Thomas Jefferson once wrote to his old friend John Adams:

> There is a ripeness of time for death, regarding others as well as ourselves, when it is reasonable we should drop off, and make room for another growth. When we have lived our generation out, we should not wish to encroach on another.[45]

The crime of the rich old ladies of late-medieval England was not that they lived badly but too long.

CHAPTER FIVE

Knight, esquire and gentleman

In talk of peers and burgesses, priests and landless peasants, there is no room for a category mistake. The same has never been true of the English gentry, who have defied categorization from the start. Yet out of the social pressures consequent on plague came increasing clarity of definition. To the question "who are the gentry?" in fifteenth-century England there was still no single answer, for perceptions of gentility differed widely, not just across regions but between local government and the crown. Nevertheless, the man who held royal office and inherited manorial lordship was more likely to be seen as *gentil* than his associate who did neither. And while this separation had already begun in many localities well before the Black Death, it was mounting pressure from below which speeded-up the existing processes of definition. Sumptuary laws (which regulated food and dress by social status) and poll taxes (which equated rank and wealth) forced a new hierarchical precision on royal legislators. "The Statute of Additions of 1413," writes Christine Carpenter of this process, "was to be the catalyst that finally produced the extrapolation from *gentil* for all well-born people to 'gentlemen' for the lowest of the well born . . . [It was] the last stage along the road to precision of social terminology, the end of a long-drawn-out process in which the growth of royal government and the demand for definition which the king's law brought had played a considerable part; from soon after 1413 we have the classic three-fold division of knight, esquire and gentleman."[1]

Lordship over men, or the possession of land not worked by the owner himself, was central to the status of the *gentil* man. Yet so much of late-medieval England was locked into the inalienable land-banks of noble families and the Church that the few estates of good quality which came onto the market commanded premium prices. Those prices, as wages rose and rents fell, bore smaller and smaller relation to the productive worth of the land exchanged, but were nevertheless attractive to the successful lawyers and retired merchants, former estate officials and royal servants who aspired to "gentle" status by this route.[2] Accordingly, one of the continuing problems of the established gentry of late-medieval England was a status-driven market in quality land, artificially inflating its value beyond an acceptable working price and forcing the gentry (like the nobility above them) to resort to heiress-hunting for new estates. Another post-plague difficulty of less permanent effect but of particular concern to smaller landowners was their sudden wrong-footing in labour policy.

Broadly, the economy of post-plague England suited lesser landowners better than greater ones. They could respond more quickly to altering circumstances, whatever their nature, and had fewer lasting obligations to their tenantry. However, even the gentry were caught off-balance by the pestilence. Their own adaptability was partly to blame, for they had moved more completely than their neighbours, the greater landowners, into the developing cash economy of pre-plague times, and found it harder in consequence to step back. What they had done with alacrity when labour was cheap was to commute the labour services of their customary tenants, working their own demesnes with hired hands. And while that had been the ideal strategy in an overcrowded land, it was totally unsuited to the near-permanent manpower shortages of post-plague England, when labour services alone could provide some protection against the increasingly onerous burden of rising wages. Greater landowners had had many of the same problems, but had rarely become so reliant on hired labour before the Black Death, and were better equipped after it to enforce customary works and to pursue fugitive villeins for such rents and other services as might be owing. Thus whereas many of the greater landowners were to enjoy another quarter-century of profitability, meeting their first major reverses in the 1370s, there is good reason to suppose that the exceptional "Indian summer" of those last high-farming decades passed the gentry by almost completely. Caught in the vice of rising wages and falling rents, the gentry began their exposure to post-plague society with landed incomes that were shrinking all the time.[3]

Their lot would certainly have been much worse had it not been for new career opportunities. In the expansion of royal government to which the war in France contributed and that plague had speeded-up, the gentry took

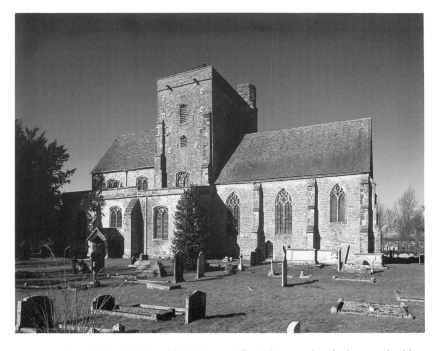

20. Sir William de Etchingham (d.1389) was still a rich man when he began rebuilding this Sussex church in the 1360s. But the work lost momentum as his rents declined, and Etchingham Church, with its abbreviated nave (left), has an austere, unfinished look in all but the great chancel, which he completed first and where he lies buried next to the altar. Sir William's brass, along with the usual "Pray for . . . " inscription, boasts: "This William caused this church to be rebuilt anew." (Nigel Saul, *Scenes from provincial life. Knightly families in Sussex 1280–1400* [Oxford, Clarendon Press, 1986], pp. 140–69). *A. F. Kersting.*

a large and growing part. And whereas relatively few knights and esquires had held royal office of any substance at the start of the fourteenth century, it was completely normal for the "county" (or upper) gentry of 1400 to serve as members of parliament, as sheriffs or as justices of the peace. Below these long-established landed families were the lesser "parish" gentry, some three times as numerous and often indistiguishable from yeomen farmers, who became the coroners, the tax-collectors and the jurors.[4] The continuing dominance of a local magnate landowner – of a Courtenay in Devonshire, of a Beauchamp in Warwickshire, or of a Fitzalan in West Sussex – might still determine the relative strength of the gentry community in any county. However, the new and improved powers of the magistracy after the Black Death, required first for the enforcement of the unpopular post-

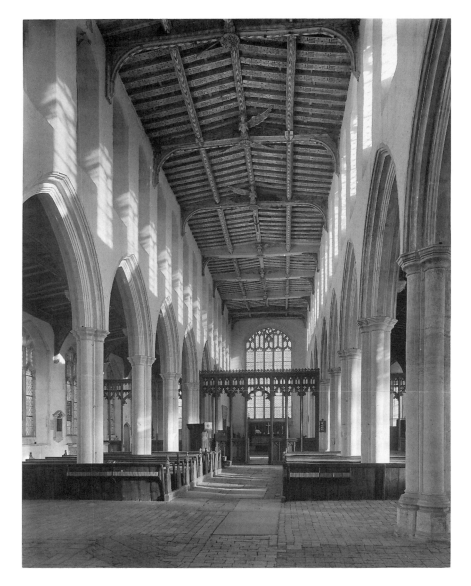

21. Blythburgh, in Suffolk, was a small coastal community which, with the help of John Hopton (d.1478), found sufficient funds in the fifteenth century to rebuild its parish church on this huge scale. *A. F. Kersting.*

plague labour laws and then for the collection of the poll taxes, gave a huge boost everywhere to the social status of the justices of the peace. Within less than five decades of the great pestilence of 1348–9 it was the county members at Westminster and their stay-at-home cousins on the bench who had plainly emerged as the "dominant political force in the shires".[5]

Office and profit go together. And taking the reins of government, even in a half-empty land, gave the gentry opportunity for some notable successes of their own. "Were there any capitalists in fifteenth-century England?" asks Christopher Dyer of a society that, just three generations later in mid-Tudor times, would swarm with every sort of entrepreneur. But while the answer is almost always negative for late-medieval property-holders of all ranks, it is the gentry who raise most of the exceptions. Usually, the problem is definition. Roger Heritage (d.1495), the wealthy lessee of many Warwickshire acres, probably never saw himself, nor was seen by any of his neighbours, as a *gentil* man. He was a yeoman farmer who worked his own land and who, while he lived in a large farmhouse of six or more rooms, furnished it with only modest show of luxury. Yet well before such equipment was usual for a yeoman of his class, Heritage already had the 11 silver spoons in his cupboard and the weight of pewter on his buffet which show him crossing, so to speak, some "white goods threshold". It was John Heritage, Roger's heir, who subsequently took to enclosure like any great lord. Another of Heritage's sons made a successful career in the Church, rising to be rector of Hackney. And the socially advantageous marital alliances of Heritage's girls – two of whom married gentry, a third a Witney merchant – are further evidence of upward mobility.[6]

Even for Roger Heritage, successful farmer though he was, the profitable working of land was no sure key to social advancement. And it was always more usual in late-medieval England for gentry to rise another way. John Hopton, for example, was one of those remote heirs – not uncommon, we may suppose, in the fifteenth century – favoured by low fertility and high death rates among his relatives. Before Hopton came into his substantial estates on 7 February 1430 no fewer than six better-qualified heirs (including his father Thomas) had died within a few years of each other to clear the way for him. And it may have been the sheer improbability of this sudden turn of fortune, with its huge unlooked-for prize, which made the young John Hopton so risk-averse. With so much gained already, Hopton had neither the motivation to marry money nor any strong incentive to increase his large estate by public office. Throughout his long life he bought little or no land, and seldom went to law if he could help it. Having no hunger for litigation nor taste for political intrigue, this amiable man of "trivial virtues and trifling vices" lived comfortably in Suffolk's Blythburgh for almost 50 years, to be buried among his neighbours in the enormous new church which all had joined together to rebuild.[7]

Paradoxically, the comparative lethargy of English gentry of John Hopton's kind probably assisted the post-plague recovery. Left to their own devices, England's small-town markets were free to find their level, able to adapt more swiftly to plague-enforced change than the more highly regulated urban economies of continental Europe.[8] Nevertheless, those same English gentry to whom John Hopton belonged included men and women of a very different temper, even among his close associates and nearest neighbours. One of them was the successful Norfolk lawyer Thomas Playter, long-term legal adviser to the Pastons, whose acquisition in the late 1460s of the manor of Sotterley (just north of Blythburgh), along with the patronage of Sotterley Church, raised him indisputably into the Suffolk gentry. Playter married a young Suffolk heiress at about that time, and their family was still growing, with another child on the way, when both were carried off, within three weeks of each other, by the "great death" of 1479.[9] By that time, plainly, the new Sotterley estate had come to rank much higher in Playter's esteem than the original family lands at Welborne (west of Norwich), which he assigned before his death to a younger son. Significantly it was at Sotterley church, not at Welborne, that this lawyer-turned-gentleman preferred to rest, there to be memorialized in full plate armour like a knight, successfully shedding his legal persona.[10]

The plague caught Playter prematurely, while his children were still young, with the result that his intentions for their future are unknown. However, we may be sure that his plans, probably taking shape well before his death, must have included negotiated marriages. Of course, some of the late-medieval English gentry married for love, and many others grew to love each other in good companionship. But the great majority of gentry marriage contracts began with land: of critical importance to all propertied families, but most particularly to those like the Pastons of north-east Norfolk who were in the early stages of building a new dynasty. The Paston story begins in 1420 with the marriage of another wealthy lawyer, William Paston I (1378–1444), to Agnes Berry, the much younger heiress daughter of a knight. Together, they lost no time in raising a family, and their eldest son, John Paston I (1421–66), was married off as soon as possible in *c.* 1440 to an associate's heiress daughter, Margaret Mautby. Then, after William's death, Agnes (d.1479) dedicated her long widowhood to energetic marriage-broking, so that two others of her five children – William II (d.1496) and

Elizabeth (d.1488) – married usefully. Only in the third generation, with the family fortunes more secure, were the children of John and Margaret Paston able at last to contemplate real love-matches. Thus Margery, the eldest daughter, successfully overcame her widowed mother's strong objections to marry Richard Calle, the Pastons' bailiff. And Sir John Paston II, the next family head, while dedicating himself at Court to the pursuit of a ripe heiress, seems to have believed (like his sister) in the possibility of true love, for he died still searching for the perfect wife, a victim of the same plague that killed the Playters.[11]

Sir John's ambition, which he might indeed have realized had he lived a little longer, was to win himself a bride "right nigh of the Queen's blood[12]." But that difficult cross-over into the nobility required a paradigm shift on both sides of the divide for which the great majority of his contemporaries were ill-prepared. A recent study of the fifteenth-century Leicestershire gentry, for one, has shown unequivocally that "marriage between gentry daughters and members of the nobility was totally unknown".[13] And while it was certainly more common for males to look aloft, most aspiring dynasts chose to marry within the group, identifying their heiresses in the daughters of their neighbours or in those of fellow justices of the peace. Thus the Berkeleys, the Woodfords and the Sherards of eastern Leicestershire looked first for marriage partners among themselves. And the joint service of Leonard Hastings and Bartholomew Brokesby on the Leicestershire commission of the peace in 1448 was almost certainly a factor in the uniting of their children five years later.[14] In one sample Leicestershire family, which he begins with the thrice-married Margaret Bugge (d.1474), Eric Acheson has been able to show that by the third generation the "Bugge network embraced Motons, Turvilles, Grymmesbys, Fouleshursts, Hotofts, the two branches of Stauntons, Shirleys, Hazilrigges, Entwysells, Wyvills, Danverses, Boyvilles, Perwyches, Brokesbys, Walshes, Sotehills and Pulteneys". To this vast and ever-widening gentry kin-group not even the Pulteneys were the last to be recruited.[15]

Endogamous marriage – confined to their class – suited the English country gentry because most were of a similar mind. And it was very evidently in marriage-broking that the great majority of gentry families found their cure for the chronic constipation of the land market.[16] Only a shortage of suitable heiresses could have held them back, and even that was less likely to damage established gentry lines – where money attracted money, as it always does – than to limit the land-hungry professional. Accordingly, in late-medieval England's growing "heiresses market" the most disadvantaged were the initially landless entrepreneurs: the careerist lawyers and govern-ment officials, the rural administrators and demesne lessees. Such self-made men, with no old money of their own, had to settle instead for wealthy widows, whose portions lasted only while they lived.[17]

That could be a long time; and the widow of several decades, sometimes re-marrying outside the family, became the albatross of many gentry lines. The Chetwynds, Cokayns and Shirleys, the Grevilles, Raleghs and Willoughbys all fell prey to hoary widows, while the Straunges of Warwickshire were killed off by them.[18] Outsize jointures, already the familiar burden of a shrinking aristocracy, were "the single cause", writes Christine Carpenter, "of serious loss of property to the [gentry] heir".[19] Nevertheless, one reason why England's upper gentry held on so tenaciously to their estates was their com-parative success with their dowagers. Their solution was to tackle the problem largely from the other end, by the ruthless enforcement of male succession. By the 1430s, in Derbyshire for example, the supply of gentry heiresses had dried up almost completely. And this had happened not because Derbyshire gentry families were growing numerous again, with more sons to inherit in the main line, but because where a daughter alone survived her father it had become the custom to exclude her from the inheritance in favour of the next collateral male.[20]

The Fitzherberts of Norbury were of an ancient Derbyshire line, more minor nobility than upper gentry. At Norbury Church, next to their castle, the tomb-chests and effigies of their meritorious dead were, and remain, a permanent reminder of noble breeding. To a Fitzherbert, accordingly, more than most, keeping the name on the land was top priority. Thus when, in 1517, the otherwise childless John Fitzherbert made his will, the last thing he desired was the succession of Elizabeth, his married daughter:

> In asmuche as the Manors of Norbury & Rossington hathe contynued in my name this CCCC yeres and more or there aboute and wold that it so shuld doo and contynue iff it pleased god Therefor I will that all the saide manors of Norbury and Rossington with thadvowson of the churche of Norbury And all the londs . . . in Norbury Rossington & Snelston Calton Quykeshall & Prestwod with . . . londe in Cubley . . . wholly to remayne . . . and come to my brother Anthony Fitzherbert serjaunt at the lawe & to the heyres males of his body lawfully begotten . . .

22. Norbury's great chancel, rebuilt in the mid-fourteenth century on a much larger scale than the rest of this small country church, became the mortuary chapel of one of Derbyshire's most prominent upper gentry families, the Fitzherberts of Norbury Castle, whose heraldic glass and whose alabaster monuments it still preserves. The two fine Fitzherbert tombs, which have been re-sited here, are of Sir Nicholas (d.1473) and Sir Ralph (d.1483) and his heiress wife, Elizabeth. Both knights use tilting-helms as pillows. *A. F. Kersting.*

Only a century before, Elizabeth might have moved without fuss into her father's role, causing neither surprise nor opposition. She now had three successive barriers to overcome. If Anthony's line failed the family's estates would go to Henry Fitzherbert, the third brother. And if Henry, in turn, died without a son, then Humphrey Fitzherbert, a Hertfordshire "cosyn", would inherit before Elizabeth and her issue. No male successor, John insisted, governing by entail from beyond the grave, must alienate Fitzherbert family land, for if he did so the next heir male – "be yt hys [the disinherited's] son or any oder collaterall Cosyn" – should take the whole estate "in hys oone Right and to hys heires male" in perpetuity.[21]

Insistence on lineage, over "CCCC yeres and more", was as natural to a Fitzherbert as drawing breath. However, few other fifteenth-century landed families were as knowledgeable about their pedigrees, and the strong historical sense of the English gentry class is now thought to have been a development of later times. Primogeniture, on the other hand, was already widely practised in gentry circles. And to this nurturing of the main stem at the expense of other heirs was presently added the new desire, fed by regular horror stories of widows who never died, to keep intact the estates of future generations by restricting the commitments of dower contracts. Before the end of the fifteenth century, in Derbyshire gentry hands the jointure had become a much less generous arrangement, usually limited to an annual value of between £10 and £20. And the customary one-third dowers of bygone times were now beginning to be converted to cash annuities.[22] These arrangements were still far from general, and with so many different sorts and conditions of gentry to be accommodated, many of them came only very tardily. Jointures of the older and more extravagant kind continued to be offered throughout the fifteenth century, especially by families like the Rouses of Warwickshire – "hovering on the fringe of the county elite" – who knew no other way to reach a settlement.[23] However, shortly before 1500, just as the economy began to move again in the gentry's favour, many legal obstructions to their prosperity fell away. In the approaching land redistributions of mid-Tudor times the gentry would be entirely ready to take their share.

That would certainly not have been the case just a few generations earlier, when the difference between receipts and expenditure on many gentry estates had become so small that any worthwhile surplus had disappeared. Congenital risk-takers still found their openings. But it was more usual for the post-plague landed gentry to survive as passive rentiers, obliged to trim their life-styles to their rents. The English upper gentry, for example, took only a minor part in the leasing of the former great demesnes, almost all of which had reached the market by the 1420s.[24] And even in Kent, where the ancient custom of partible inheritance was still causing the fragmentation of many family holdings, very few of the county gentry took up leasing on any scale, the best of the ex-demesnes all going to yeomen.[25] Understandably perhaps, it was those same Kentish gentry, under threat from wealthy Londoners, who most closed ranks against outsiders. The Lovelace family were rich London mercers who had bought their first Kentish manor as early as 1367. They then continued to invest in Kentish lands, while Lovelace heiresses found husbands among the gentry, and the family came to view themselves as "gentle". Not so their Kentish relatives; and probably the main reason why, after the death of Richard Lovelace in 1465, his estate took so long to settle was that the established county families, who might otherwise have found it natural to arbitrate between their neighbours, stood aside from the brothers' quarrel, unwilling to admit the squabbling Londoners as their chums.[26]

This separation of new and old, of the dedicated risk-takers from the cautiously risk-averse, might have grown still wider in post-plague England had the recession not lasted so long. But with rents continuing their slide after 1400, so that a family's principal source of revenue might decline again by as much as between a quarter and a half before 1450, no rentier class could have survived the slump without diversification. For the great majority of the English gentry this happened hardly earlier than the 1480s. Nevertheless, there is good evidence of individual gentry initiatives much before that time, and it is a remarkable fact that very few gentry families, if they were fortunate enough to survive in the direct male line, ever completely disappeared from the records.[27] Among several leading Nottinghamshire gentry families put at risk by their dowagers, the Willoughbys of Wollaton were prominent victims. Margaret Willoughby (d.1493) outlasted her husband, Hugh, by 45 years; and their son, Robert, who died in 1474 almost two decades before his mother, himself left a widow of 17 years, again very handsomely provided for. Both widows married a second time. Yet Hugh Willoughby, as much as two decades before his death in 1448, had already begun the long work of consolidation and enclosure at Middleton, the family's Warwickshire estate, which was then continued by Richard Bingham, Margaret's second husband. And Henry, Hugh's grandson, survived the simultaneous onslaught of two Willoughby dowagers on his fortune by drawing on the profits of Wollaton coal.[28]

Enclosure for animal husbandry (both sheep and cattle) and a more vigorous exploitation of under-used resources – of timber or building-stone, salt or slate, lead, coal or iron – were the most commonly employed strategies for survival. For the one unassailable advantage of the English gentry class was its once and always ownership of the land. The Throgmortons of Coughton, for example, were among several Warwickshire landed families – the Dalbys, the Harewells and the Catesbys were others – who were especially well placed after 1450 to fill the gaps in their existing holdings with leased demesnes. So adept as consolidators did the Throgmortons become that Robert Throgmorton was enclosing whole manors by the 1480s, to put

23. The Throgmortons of Warwickshire were comfortably-off landed gentry who were able to build a very considerable fortune in the second half of the fifteenth century on the profits of enclosure for sheep. This prodigy gatehouse (centre) at Coughton Court – flanked by two much later "Gothick" ranges – is typically *nouveau riche* Throgmorton work of the 1510s, making a bravura show towards the road. *A. F. Kersting.*

them together as a huge and profitable sheep-run next to his family's Coughton base.[29] It was in that decade again that animal husbandry became "very big business indeed" right across the Midlands. And it was then for the first time that specialist graziers like the Spensers successfully penetrated the gentry class, which they achieved not as lawyers but as agriculturalists.[30]

In less than two centuries a Spenser of Wormleighton would climb to the first rank of the English nobility as Earl of Sunderland. But as early as 1506, when the first Spenser grazier became a lord of the manor, there was already little reason why older-established English families should not prosper just as well, advantaged by landholding and social contacts. In the 1490s William Compton, son of a rustic "gentleman", would only just have made it onto the lowest rung of the Warwickshire gentry class. Nevertheless, between inheriting his father's small estate in 1493 and his death in 1528, when only 46, Sir William (as he became) skilfully used his court connections to assemble a great fortune, to purchase much new land and to build the huge brick mansion which survives him even now at Compton Wynyates.[31]

24. Sir William Compton (d.1528) was so successful as a Tudor courtier and as a consolidator of Warwickshire estates that he was able to build this huge country house on family land at Compton Wynyates before his death at the early age of 46. The multiple chimneys of Compton's new house, his use of brick instead of timber, and his great spread of window-glass (still an expensive luxury when he built) would all have been reminders of his wealth. *A. F. Kersting.*

Compton's story has many parallels in Tudor England, not least in his removal by an epidemic of the sweating sickness in 1528, which was followed, as had so often been the case ever since the Black Death, by severe succession problems: the wardship and arranged marriage of his young son Peter; Peter's own early death before coming of age; and his grandson Henry's long minority before inheriting.[32] Similarly flawed successions continued to trouble the English gentry throughout the sixteenth century. But family sizes were again rising after 1500, and the complete failure of a gentry line became less threatening. That danger had only recently begun to fade. Just 50 years before, "propensity to failure [had remained] the principal engine of social change" in Nottinghamshire gentry lines of the mid-fifteenth century.[33] And that was said of a county where the extinction rate of the upper gentry class was markedly lower than that of the contemporary baronage, and of which the gentry elite had escaped relatively lightly from the more general afflictions of over-long minorities and outsize jointures. Even so, almost a third of Nottinghamshire's leading gentry families failed in the male line during the little more than six decades of Lancastrian rule, with the obvious result that landownership in the county became increasingly concentrated in fewer hands.[34]

Those who lost most in this unceasing merry-go-round of gentry fortunes were almost always the poorer knights, who neither worked their own land nor enjoyed sufficient prominence to marry more of it. In their case too, even the comparatively rare advantage of an untroubled succession might not be sufficient to keep them prosperous. Of the 16 Nottinghamshire knightly families who are known to have survived in the direct male line from the Black Death until 1460 or later, just six held their place in the county elite, while the other ten, starved of heiresses, all moved downwards.[35] Accordingly, along with the constant upward pressure of successful professional men, there was a regular downward movement within the gentry class, as pre-plague knightly families abandoned their higher rank to settle permanently among the esquires and lesser gentlemen. In late-medieval Nottinghamshire, the St Andrews and Stauntons, the Suttons and Hercys, the Husys and Comptons, the Barrys and Thorpes, crippled by falling rents and unable to attract heiresses, all found themselves too impoverished to support their knightly rank, and stopped claiming it.[36]

With the old-style medieval baronage nearing extinction and knighthood now limited also to the much smaller group identified with the ruling gentry of each county, the essentials of a better-defined and more highly stratified social system were in place. And clearly one of the more important consequences of the post-plague recession was a re-shaping of the English governing classes at county level. The new pattern was partly owed to long-standing endogenous factors: to economic and social changes that had originated well before the Black Death. Nevertheless, the real imperative was the post-plague phenomenon of repeated family failures; for while landed families everywhere could usually ride out a recession with some success, they could not protect themselves against the slow attrition of low fertility or the sudden fatal onslaught of a pestilence. If otherwise advantaged gentry lines failed, as they continued to do in large numbers for well over a century after 1350, it was almost always for biological reasons. Often wealthier by accumulation than they had ever been before, and with more power and responsibility in their own localities, England's gentry families during the Late Middle Ages remained permanently at risk. Biology – more than war, economic recession or the everlasting folly of politicians – was what chiefly caused the continuing "unstablenesse" of their world.[37]

CHAPTER SIX

Of monks and nuns

For almost every religious community in post-plague England the big issue was keeping up numbers. The more rigorous and newly fashionable orders – the Carthusians (monks), the Bridgettines (nuns) and the Observant Franciscans (friars) – recruited successfully until the last. And there were always individual houses of the older Benedictine congregation so spacious and well endowed that new recruits were attracted by their quality. But high though that quality continued to be in many of the larger and better-conducted Benedictine houses of the Late Middle Ages, including Durham and Glastonbury, Westminster, Evesham and Christ Church (Canterbury), it was the superiors of those same houses who were to turn aside Cardinal Wolsey's reforming proposals of 1521 as unworkable. In this "tempestuous" world now nearing its end, they warned, there were not enough willing to practise the self-denial still demanded of a Carthusian, a Bridgettine or an Observant. If they (as Benedictines) were to impose such a Rule their monks would either rebel or would leap the wall, and new postulants would cease to come forward.[1]

They made too much of those dangers, for numbers at the greater houses were already rising again to within sight of their pre-plague peaks.[2] In contrast, the perils of the smaller and poorer communities were very real. When Cardinal Wolsey, just three years later, began the monastic closures that anticipated the total dissolution of the monasteries in 1536–40, the best explanation he could give for his suppressions was that the houses he closed were both "exile and small", so that "neither God was served, nor religion kept" in those places.[3] In 1536 again, it was the smaller communities, allegedly incapable of self-renewal, that were the first to be attacked, "forasmuch as manifest sin, vicious, carnal and abominable living, is daily used and committed amongst the little and small abbeys, priories, and other religious houses of monks, canons, and nuns, where the congregation of such religious persons is under the number of twelve persons". In redistributing their errant communities among the "great and honourable monasteries of religion in this realm, where they may be compelled to live religiously for reformation of their lives" a parallel consideration was the clearly perceived need to build up numbers again in the better-quality houses: for "divers and great solemn monasteries of this realm wherein, thanks be to God, religion is right well kept and observed, be destitute of such full numbers of religious persons as they ought and may keep".[4]

The belief that a religious community should never fall below 12 persons was of great antiquity. But for many lesser houses in post-plague England there was little hope of regaining that total. Among those that never did were Selborne Priory, in Hampshire, and Creake Abbey, in north-west Norfolk, both of them founded in the first half of the thirteenth century for communities of Augustinian canons. Selborne's original community was of 13 canons and their prior. And while Creake's establishment (as a former hospital for paupers) may have started somewhat smaller, it had probably risen to the canonical 12 by 1231, when the priory was elevated to an abbey. There is no direct evidence of Black Death mortalities at either house. However, both suffered losses in the post-plague recession, and although Selborne still had ten canons in 1410, Creake was down to seven by 1381 and may never have improved on that small number. Selborne, in the event, was the first to go. It had just four resident canons in 1462, five in 1471, and five again seven years later; but of those last five only the aged Thomas Ashford (calling himself "prior") was still living at Selborne in 1484, when the first suppression proceedings were begun there.[5] It was in that year also that Creake was burnt down by an arsonist; but rebuilding had begun again within the decade, and it was not fire that closed the abbey but the sweating sickness. When Creake's last abbot, Giles Sheryngton, died on 12 December 1506 he was alone at the house, "without any convent of fellow monks or of any canon to be found in the said monastery". With nobody left to elect Sheryngton's successor, his abbey escheated to the crown.[6]

Total collapses of this kind would be rare at any time. But there were at least two common causes of weakness in religious houses that could lead to an early suppression. One of those, often found in Austin houses, was the reduction of the community to such small numbers that it could no longer

25. The Augustinians of Creake Abbey, in Norfolk, were probable Black Death victims, reduced to just seven canons in 1381. The community continued to lose numbers through the fifteenth century, and was suppressed in 1506–7 on the death of the last abbot, who had been living at Creake on his own. In this recent vertical air photograph of Creake, a cropmark in the field north of the church reveals the foundations of a large L-shaped building (below), possibly contemporary with the abbey. The church itself is an empty ruin, but some of the canons' former claustral buildings have been incorporated in the post-suppression farmhouse (top). *Norfolk Air Photographs Library: photo Derek A. Edwards.*

maintain a life of religion. The other cause – seen there also, but character-istic especially of the many English nunneries founded in the twelfth and thirteenth centuries – was extreme and irremediable poverty.[7] Both condi-tions resulted from inadequate endowments, and had usually originated much before the Black Death; yet both were greatly aggravated after 1349 by plague mortalities and continuing recession. When new recruitment had been easy in pre-plague times, it had been perfectly possible to reform and re-populate even the most corrupt of houses, "God replacing sycamores by cedars".[8] But after the Black Death there would be no new nuns, for example, to re-settle Wothorpe, a little Nottinghamshire priory housing only one survivor of the plague, which merged in 1354 with Stamford Baron. Nor would anything more be heard after 1349 of their Benedictine sisters-in-religion at Foukeholme Priory (North Yorkshire), who seem also to have been eliminated by the pestilence.[9]

Wothorpe and Foukeholme were very poor communities, and their demise made little difference to the Church. But many more religious houses suffered a slower and sadder death, of the thousand cuts of a century of shrinking numbers and falling rents. Nuns, while almost always of slender means, were much the most resolute survivors. True, the little community at Rowney (Hertfordshire) gave up the struggle in 1457, too poor to continue in religion. And some other nunneries also, declared profane – St Radegund's (Cambridge) in 1496, Broomhall (Berkshire) in 1521, and Littlemore (Oxford) in 1525 – would be closed in favour of academic colleges. However, the great majority of the English nunneries held out through the recession, although often on incomes which, however modest their needs, were pathetically reduced for such establishments. Henwood, a Warwickshire priory where only three of the pre-plague community of 15 survived the Black Death, had climbed to 12 again by 1404, and was still seven-strong in 1536, sharing an income of just £21. There had been 13 nuns and two chaplains at Cheshunt (Hertfordshire) before the pestilence; by 1536, reduced to four, their income was only £14. The eight nuns remaining at Nunburnholme Priory (Yorkshire) shortly before its suppression had somehow contrived to make ends meet on as little as £8 between them.[10]

Augustinian canons could be just as poor, the six at Torksey (Lincolnshire) in 1536 subsisting on an income of only £13, or about half what would have supported the same number before the pestilence.[11] However, in contrast to the nuns (including canonesses of their own order), it was exceptional for the poorest Austin communities to retain their independence as late as the 1530s, while a fair proportion failed altogether. Most of those failures were in the second half of the fifteenth century, fallen victim to the mid-century recession. But others had gone earlier, and the eventual roll-call of Augustinian collapses before the Dissolution, along with the communities already mentioned at Selborne and Creake, included Great Massingham, Peterstone and Wormegay (Norfolk), Alnesbourn, Chipley and Kersey (Suffolk), Barton (Isle of Wight), Bicknacre (Essex), Charley (Leicestershire), Chetwode (Buckinghamshire), Cockerham (Lancashire), Cold Norton (Oxfordshire), Dodford (Worcestershire), Grafton Regis (Northamptonshire), Hastings (Sussex), Llanthony Prima (Monmouthshire), Sandleford (Berkshire) and Spinney (Cambridgeshire), all of which were either closed and religious life there discontinued, or demoted to priory cell.[12]

Other religious orders, in particular the Cistercians (who lost not a single house in the recession), had handled things better from the start. But Cistercian policy, from the time of St Bernard, had always been to insist on a sufficient endowment. And a rich community, whatever its allegiance, could survive almost any misfortune. Croxton Abbey, under the wise rule of Abbot Elias Attercliff (1491–1534), was a rich and well-conducted Premonstratensian house, having as many as 30 canons in 1500. There had probably been about the same number there before the Black Death, and when Croxton was dissolved in 1538 no fewer than 22 canons put their names to the surrender. Yet in 1348 this big Leicestershire community had been on the brink of collapse, with a huge rebuilding debt of £2,000 still owing towards the end of that year, only months before the onset of the pestilence.[13] Most of the canons at Croxton died in the Black Death, and four years later the abbey remained in such grave trouble that Edward III excused Abbot Thomas from his duties as tax-collector for the crown, on the grounds that:

> the abbey of Croxton . . . was in great part destroyed by the burning of the church and other houses [in 1326], and was afterwards deprived by the plague of those by whose knowledge and ability it was then governed, except the abbot and prior, and the abbot is so infirm and so occupied in directing the affairs of the abbey, and the prior is so engaged upon the control of divine worship and of the novices received into the convent after the plague that the abbot cannot conveniently collect the said tenth.[14]

Croxton's hastily recruited novices were too young for the priesthood, and some were still below the required age in 1363 when (after the return of the Black Death in 1361) Abbot Thomas obtained papal dispensation to ordain

12 of his younger canons at 21, "there being, on account of the pestilence, but few priests in the monasteries and churches of their order".[15] By 1377 numbers had risen again at Croxton to a more normal 29. But quality almost certainly had fallen. Henry Knighton, the Black Death's chronicler, was a local man. As a canon of the well-provided Leicester Abbey, with many parish churches in its care, Knighton had personal experience of the post-plague clergy, or at any rate (for he wrote a generation later) of the clerical intake after 1361, when his community lost another 11 canons. Back in 1350, he relates, there was already "such a great shortage of priests everywhere . . . [that] a man could scarcely get a chaplain for less than £10 or 10 marks to minister to any church, and whereas before the pestilence there had been a glut of priests, and a man could get a chaplain for 4 or 5 marks, or for 2 marks with board and lodging, in this time there was scarcely any-

26. Ingarsby Grange (the big farmhouse at the bottom of this photograph) was one of the two rich manors acquired for his community by William of Clown, Abbot of Leicester (d. 1378). Later abbots enjoyed Ingarsby's calm as a country retreat, and it was probably for this reason that they encouraged the steady depopulation of the adjoining village, eventually enclosing it entirely in 1469. Since that time the settlement site and part of its open fields (top) have remained unploughed, leaving the prominent earthworks which show up here so distinctly under snow. *Cambridge University Collection of Air Photographs: copyright reserved.*

one who would accept a vicarage at £20 or 20 marks." However, what then followed, as Knighton acknowledges, was even worse, for "within a short time a great crowd of men whose wives had died in the pestilence rushed into priestly orders. Many of them were illiterate, no better than laymen – for even if they could read, they did not understand what they read."[16]

At Leicester, Knighton's abbot was William of Clown (1345–78): a "lover of peace and quiet . . . untiring follower of good works . . . reformer of quarrels and wrongs . . . wholly a servant of God". Clown was also a famous hunter, one of the best in the land, although (reports Knighton) "he would often say in private that the only reason why he took delight in such paltry sports was to show politeness to the lords of the realm, to get on easy terms with them and win their good will in matters of business". True or false, the great and the good could deny him nothing. Abbot Clown, unlike the huge majority of monastic superiors in his day, continued to add valuable new properties to Leicester's already large portfolio, successfully appropriating the near-by parish churches at Humberstone and Hungarton, and acquiring important manors at Kirkby Mallory and Ingarsby, both also within a short ride of his abbey.[17] Thus supported by their wealth, the Augustinians of Leicester could live with occasional rotten apples like Abbot William Sadyngton (accused of necromancy at Ingarsby and other black arts), to end their days in reasonable shape, some 20-strong in 1539, united in their opposition to surrender.[18]

Abbot Sadyngton's misdemeanours were extreme by any standard. But there was nothing unusual about their context. Sadyngton shared with fellow abbots the strong desire to build, and he chose, as others did also, to meet those costs by saving on the numbers of his community. At Bishop Alnwick's visitation of 3 December 1440 one of the stories told against Sadyngton by Brother William Wykyngstone was that "oftentimes he has heard the abbot say that never in his life will he admit more than there now are to be canons, inasmuch as he says that in these days there are more than is needful". And there were others who told the same tale: "there are few who keep quire," complained Brother John (the cellarer), for after all those excused attendance "there are not more than two or three who stand in quire in their habit"; also, reported Brother Robert of the boys in his almonry, "whereas there were wont to be twenty-four, there are now but six". In face of such complaints Bishop Alnwick's response was to require Abbot Sadyngton to restore Leicester's community to at least 30 canons and 16 boys, "seeing that the said monastery is endowed with abundant and noble possessions, so that a far greater number of canons than you have at the present time shall be able to be maintained in seemly wise and without want".[19] But good counsel though that was – of more than local application – Alnwick passed over the hardly less universal complaint of William Coventry, warden of Leicester's guest-house, that "there are fifty-two serving folk, seculars, within the monastery and in the verneyerde [another] eighteen, the more part whereof are not only unprofitable but hurtful to the monastery". While properly concerned to rid the abbey of its "great crowd of useless hounds", Alnwick closed his mind to the huge under-employed army of surplus servants and sponging layfolk that was the self-inflicted burden of monastic households.[20]

One such household of 84, individually listed on the suppression of Butley Priory (Suffolk) in March 1538, supported another Augustinian community of just 12 canons. Butley, with its many rich manors and even more parish churches, was in no conceivable danger of collapse. Yet here also under-resourced building works and other financial stresses had persuaded the canons to think the unthinkable, causing them to limit their numbers to the statutory 12, or between a third and a half of pre-plague strength. Much the heaviest burden on Butley's finances was the steadily increasing pressure of household overheads. Along with its 12 canons, Butley's establishment in 1538 included two chaplains and a clerk, a schoolmaster and seven children ("kept of almes to lernyng"), two bedesmen and several other pensioners. Salaried lay officials – an under-steward, a surveyor and eight "yemen weyters" – directed a carver and three pantrymen, two cooks and a kitchen-boy, two maltsters, three bakers and brewers, six laundresses and dairy-women, a cooper, a gardener, a candlemaker, a smith, and all the other craftsmen, carters and ferrymen, shepherds, warreners and "servantes in husbondry" needed to keep the canons in religion.[21]

Many noble householders kept establishments just as large; but hardly ever on a budget as inflexible. Butley, in its final decades, could still depend on the occasional bequest, as in the will of a former priory official, William Pakeman (d.1504), who remembered everybody, even the kitchen-boy, on his death-bed.[22] But any regular flow of worthwhile gifts had dried up long before. And it was out of a fixed income, with little hope of windfall gains, that Butley's canons found the means to meet every extra cost of fire and flood, lawsuits and annuities, poor-relief and hospitality to noble patrons. One of the "yeomen waiters" at Butley in 1538 was John Crewe, who had been introduced to the community "at the appoyntment of [Charles

27. Butley Priory's substantial early-fourteenth-century gatehouse is the only material re-minder of the comfortable lifestyle which a well-off community of Augustinian canons could continue to enjoy even after the Black Death by limiting numbers to the statutory 12. Over the big double entrance are five tiers of heraldry claiming the patronage of the good and the great, from the King of England to the Holy Roman Emperor. *A. F. Kersting.*

Brandon] the Duke of Suffolk". Four years earlier Brandon had lodged his personal choristers with the canons for several months, and when he came to Butley with his duchess, Henry VIII's sister, they expected to be royally entertained.[23]

In the 1500s, with agricultural profits again rising, such demands were more easily met. But until that time, within a generation of suppression, most of England's religious houses had seen no real increase in receipts for upwards of 200 years. Arguably, they had only themselves to blame for that outcome. The monks of Westminster, concluded Barbara Harvey after a very thorough study of their estate policies, "were remarkably insensitive, as land-lords, to market forces".[24] And while others, from Battle's demesne farmers to Oseney's enclosing pastoralists, were decidedly more proactive, the usual farming strategy of the great majority of religious houses was rather to follow than to lead their laymen neighbours.[25] If the rich canons of

28. In this oblique air view of Bolton Priory (Yorkshire), Prior Mone's massive but incomplete tower, begun in 1520, can be seen at the west end (left) of the re-roofed nave. It still carries the boldly lettered commemorative inscription: "In the year of our Lord MVCXX R[ichard Mone] began this foundation, on whose soul God have mercy, Amen." *Ministry of Defence Crown copyright.*

Haughmond (Shropshire) and the still wealthier monks of Spalding (Lincolnshire) learnt to keep a closer watch on leasing contracts, it was precisely because their receipts, for far too long, had remained either stagnant or in decline.[26] At Augustinian Bolton Priory, in the remote West Yorkshire dales, an upturn in rents from as early as the mid-1470s ultimately set the scene for the completion of a long-term programme of rebuilding. But Prior Mone's over-ambitious west tower, begun in 1520, never rose higher than the adjoining roof-ridge. And Bolton on its suppression, with 19 canons to pension off, including five at the parish churches, had an income hardly larger in 1540 than in 1322, when famine, stock murrains and successive Scottish raids had already cut receipts by at least a third.[27]

Keeping solvent through a long recession posed special problems for the monks. They could neither marry nor inherit; politics were largely closed to them, as was war. Accordingly, unable to restore their incomes by the usual layman's methods, they had to turn instead to cutting costs. In 1349 the Black Death had begun their work for them by reducing numbers at many houses by over a third. And, like it or not, that work would have to be continued in later years, when the urge (however powerful) to rebuild a shrunken community was overcome by the bleak reality of its cost. Inevitably, those remaining on the establishment were over-housed. They were tempted, like all such fellowships, to treat common assets as their own, and fell deeper into the trough of private property. Of that vice St Benedict had warned with particular emphasis that it "ought utterly to be rooted out of the monastery":

> *Ne quis praesumat* [he had insisted] . . . Let no one presume to give or receive anything without the abbot's leave, or to have anything as his own, anything whatever, whether book or tablets or pen or whatever it may be; for monks should not have even their bodies and wills at their own disposal. But let them look to the father of the monastery for all that they require, and let it be unlawful to have anything which the abbot has not given or allowed.[28]

Yet in late-medieval England, as all could see, father abbot was the principal offender.

Much the richest of the Benedictine communities, on their suppression in 1539–40, were the great Anglo-Saxon foundations at Westminster and Glastonbury, both still of such high quality in the early Tudor period as to be potentially the leaders of a renewal.[29] But these also were the houses which, centuries earlier, had led the way into a pernicious separation of common goods. At Westminster, for example, a permanent division of estates between the abbot and his community had been formalized as early as 1225.[30] From that beginning it was no great leap for Westminster's obedientiaries to be assigned manors of their own, and then for every monk to have his dole (*peculium*). "Men were wont to give them clothes," complained Gilles li Muisis in 1350, after 60 years as monk and abbot, but "now they will have clothes-money and caskets and coffers, and each his own cupboard . . . It is the favour of the abbot, so say the monks nowadays; he gives money for them to be decent and to clothe them; but the Rule, by God! clearly says the contrary, and St Benedict also neither says it nor commands it."[31]

These practices had spread most widely during the previous half-century, and were certainly not new when Gilles li Muisis ("unworthy abbot of the Benedictine monastery of St Giles in Tournai") wrote his *Chronicle* and two successive accounts of the Black Death. The first had been founded on travellers' tales. In the second he wrote directly from experience. "Future generations should know," he recorded, "that in Tournai there was a staggering mortality at Christmas time, for I have heard from many people who said that they knew for a fact that in Tournai more than 25,000 had died . . . And when the mortality was so appalling in Tournai, who could conceive what was happening in all the other kingdoms and countries?"[32]

No contemporary could. However, it soon became clear to all plague survivors, including the monks, that there would be more to share out among the spared. Glastonbury Abbey was one of the great Benedictine houses at which individual cash doles, paid by the chamberer out of the profits of designated manors, were already well established before the pestilence. And Glastonbury's chamberer, like its other obedientiaries, had to manage with smaller profits from 1350. But of all the different economies forced upon him by the recession, the one cut he never made was to the *peculium*. Even before Abbot Chinnock's successful appropriation in 1393 of Longbridge Deverill Church gave another substantial lift to their allowances, the 52 monks at Glastonbury in 1377 were sharing a dole of £151 16s 11d between them. Although down by more than a quarter on their pre-plague numbers, their dole allocation had gone up by a third.[33]

Glastonbury's monks, with personal cash allowances of £3 and over, were among the highest-paid religious in the kingdom. But times were changing everywhere and, as Eileen Power once remarked of the doles paid at English nunneries, whereas "in the thirteenth century it is a fault in the Prioress to give the nuns a *peculium*; in the fifteenth century it is a fault to withhold it".[34] The same expectation of a general softening of the Rule was even more apparent in monastic diets. No institutional food has ever earned the unqualified approval of those who have to eat it. To monk and nun alike, the ox was always skinny, the roast lamb burnt, the cook either surly or incompetent.[35] Yet at Glastonbury today it is the abbots' huge late-fourteenth-century kitchen that remains most intact as the community's last memorial. And to this may be added surviving household accounts, detailing a diet which was always rich and plentiful, and that was frequently improved by feast-day treats: salmon on Lady Day, meat pasties for Corpus Christi, sucking-pigs for Dedication, lamb for Easter, pea soup and fresh fish on the Monday after Advent, and so on.[36]

"If the abbot of Westminster," wrote Simon Fish, his gadfly critic, in 1528, "should sing every day as many masses for his founders as he is bound to do by his foundation, a thousand monks were too few."[37] Yet there were seldom more than 50 monks at post-plague Westminster, and those who

29. This huge fourteenth-century stone kitchen at the Abbot of Glastonbury's lodgings, with its four great corner fireplaces and ingenious central chimney, is some indication of the importance increasingly placed on diet by many post-plague religious communities. *A. F. Kersting.*

were left to divide its great possessions between them could hardly do other-wise than live well. Once St Benedict had been as emphatic in his condem-nation of over-eating as in his rejection of private property: "gluttony must be avoided *above all things* . . . and frugality shall be observed *in all circum-*

stances. Except the sick who are very weak, let all abstain *entirely* from the flesh of four-footed animals."[38] However, meat was eaten routinely at the great majority of religious houses in late-medieval England. And while most of Westminster's monks probably avoided gluttony, they almost certainly ate more than was strictly necessary for their health, and "were surely on average rather obese".[39] How far this over-eating contributed to early death is of course unknown. Yet there are evident dangers in an excess of meat protein (kidney failure) and in too much drink (cirrhosis of the liver); and the monks of Westminster – sedentary, bored, and chilled throughout the winter by their great unheated spaces – grew fat on a diet rich in both.[40]

In this company it comes as no surprise that some 20 comfortably-off Cistercian monks at Whalley Abbey, in northern Lancashire, should have spent as much as two-thirds of their considerable revenues in 1520 on the purchase of foodstuffs and drink.[41] Forty years earlier they had spent much less, and the figures for 1520 might have been thought an aberration had they not been repeated the next year. In all probability what gave scope for this expenditure was an unusually low outlay on building repairs, for Whalley's church and claustral ranges were comparatively new, the greater part of them post-dating the Black Death. After the move from flooded Stanlaw (Cheshire) in 1296 these buildings had taken many decades to complete, and one important reason was that the process was entirely out of step with the community. In the over-populated 1280s, when the transfer to Lancashire was first approved, Stanlaw's monks had been urged to increase their numbers by fully a third, from 40 to 60. Yet that target, while influencing the scale of the new buildings at Whalley, was delayed by lawsuits before being wrecked by plague, and can never have been even remotely attainable.[42]

Battle Abbey (Sussex), founded by William of Normandy on the site of Hastings, was another of the great houses where a community of less than 20 in 1538 still occupied buildings that, in the first flush of William's victory, had been intended originally for 60. That short-fall, no doubt, was in part the result of the failure of novices to come forward. However, at a rich house like Battle, where expectations remained high in bad times as in good, such limits were more probably self-imposed. What they did nothing to dissuade was heavy drinking. Even St Benedict, unable in the sixth century to forbid wine altogether ("since monks nowadays cannot be persuaded of this"), had been forced to concede a daily allowance of the equivalent of a pint or somewhat less[43]. But the monks of Battle, from the start of new concessions at major feasts in the twelfth century, were more likely to drink wine by the gallon.[44] One of them, towards the end, was Brother John Whatlyngton, a close friend and welcome guest of William Ingram, penitentiary of Christ Church (Canterbury). Ingram kept a personal account-book (still preserved in the cathedral library) in which he entered all his costs, including the purchase of special treats for his friend. For just one of

30. The foundations of a great cruciform church can be seen in the grass to the north (left) of what remains of Whalley's one-time cloister (centre). East of the cloister, another substantial building (top) is the former abbot's house, of such quality, size and comfort when the monks were expelled in 1537 as to persuade the site's new owner to keep it as a mansion for himself. *Ministry of Defence Crown copyright*

Whatlyngton's visits Ingram bought enough wine for them both, with sucking-pig, rabbit and other meats, fish, bread and butter, to be feasted on in private in his chamber.[45]

Ingram played the generous host again in June 1521, when a prominent courtier, William Lord Mountjoy, came to Canterbury. Mountjoy (like many at Henry VIII's court) was a convinced Erasmian, the loyal patron and former pupil of the great scholar. And although Ingram made him as warmly welcome as any of his guests, there was little enough, in truth, to unite the two of them. Before Ingram's promotion to penitentiary at Canterbury in 1511 he had been keeper for some years of the cathedral's famous shrines. He was well aware of the contemporary decline of the cult of Thomas Becket, and may even have been present when Erasmus and John Colet, standing before Becket's feretory, had been openly contemptuous of the ignorance of its custodian and strongly dismissive of the shrine's commercialism.[46] Much later, Erasmus would write concerning the "paradoxical opinions" of Dean Colet, his late friend, that whereas Colet had never entirely given up hope of finding a religious community he could enter, eventually favouring the Carthusians of Sheen for his retirement, "he none the less had very little affection for monasteries, a name most of them now do not deserve; he contributed either nothing to them or very little, and even on his deathbed gave them no share. It was not that he disapproved of the orders, but that their members did not live up to their profession."[47]

In that same letter of 1521 to Justus Jonas, a Lutheran convert, Erasmus memorialized another dead friend, the Franciscan preacher Jean Vitrier. Assisted by a fine presence and a silver tongue, Vitrier's advanced opinions "carried very great weight with those whose approval was worth having". Yet, as Erasmus says,

> The regular way of life into which he [Vitrier] had slipped or had been drawn in the ignorance of youth by no means appealed to him. He used to say in my hearing that it was a life for idiots rather than religious men to sleep and wake and sleep again, to speak and to be silent, to go and to return, to eat and to stop eating, all at the sound of a bell, and in a word to be governed in everything by human regulations rather than the law of Christ.[48]

They had met in 1501 when Erasmus, once himself a plague orphan, had retreated to the country near Vitrier's friary at St Omer, fleeing the pestilence in Paris. And it was there, in safe retirement at the Château de Tournehem, that Erasmus composed his first devotional manual, the *Enchiridion militis christiani* (The handbook of a Christian soldier), deeply influenced by Vitrier's thought. Vitrier, he would later write, "never suggested to anyone that he should change his way of life, nor did he attempt anything of the sort himself; for he was ready to endure everything rather than be a cause of stumbling to any mortal man".[49] And it was in much the same spirit that Erasmus, the ex-religious, delivered his own verdict on the monastic life – ostensibly anodyne, but all the more deadly on that account: "Monasticism is not holiness but a kind of life that can be useful or useless depending on a person's temperament and disposition. I neither recommend it nor do I condemn it."[50] While moved to greater emphasis in later years, "for no gentle, peaceful voice could rouse the world from such deep lethargy",[51] Erasmus never again inserted the blade with more precision.

CHAPTER SEVEN

Like people, like priest

O f all those who perished in the first outbreak of the Black Death the class worst affected was the parish clergy. "No one, rich, middling or poor, was safe," wrote Abbot Gilles li Muisis of his own city of Tournai, but "certainly there were many deaths among the parish priests and chaplains who heard confessions and administered the sacraments, and also among the parish clerks and those who visited the sick with them".[1] In Spain at Barcelona, through the summer and autumn of 1348, vacant benefices in the diocese rose by 15 times over the previous year's total, and "at least 40 per cent" of the parish clergy died.[2] Then, as the plague moved northwards that winter, reaching another well-documented diocese in England's Coventry and Lichfield the following spring, new institutions of clergy increased tenfold, so that even when every allowance is made for normal pre-plague losses "we are still faced with a death rate of some 36 per cent, all of which can confidently be attributed to the Great Pestilence".[3]

Looked at another way, average survival rates among the parish priesthood in the plague of 1348–9 could be as high as 60 per cent. But there were huge variations between parishes. Thus, in that same Lichfield register, the 29 per cent mortality of Chester archdeaconry's parish priests may be set against 57 per cent in the archdeaconry of Derby, where at Pentrich alone, in just three weeks, four different priests held the cure.[4] Pentrich-style mortalities were highly exceptional, even in the worst-affected parishes. Yet they can help explain the comparatively rapid disappearance of any remaining surplus of unbeneficed priests such as might have built up in pre-plague conditions of overcrowding.[5] Having many continental precedents to guide him, Ralph of Shrewsbury, Bishop of Bath and Wells, was already preparing his flock, soon after the plague hit his diocese, to do without clergy of any kind:

> The contagious pestilence, which is now [10 January 1349] spreading everywhere, has left many parish churches and other benefices in our diocese without an incumbent, so that their inhabitants are bereft of a priest. And because priests cannot be found for love or money to take on the responsibility for those places and visit the sick and administer the sacraments of the church to them – perhaps because they fear that they will catch the disease themselves – we understand that many people are dying without the sacrament of penance.[6]

Bishop Ralph's remedy was to advise his people that "if when on the point of death they cannot secure the services of a properly ordained priest, they should make confession of their sins . . . to any lay person, even to a woman if a man is not available". Ultimately, he admitted, where no priest might be found to administer extreme unction to the dying "faith must suffice for the sacrament".[7]

Quality was sure to suffer in those circumstances. "We are making an exception on this occasion," said Archbishop Zouche of York on 8 September 1349, admitting a regular canon to the important vicarage of Tickhill, "to make good the lack of secular priests, who have been carried from our midst by the plague of mortality which hangs over us".[8] However, before the end of the same year it had become quite common for men in minor orders – deacons, subdeacons and even acolytes – to be raised to the priesthood and appointed to cures of souls from which in better times they had been excluded. It is said, for example, of Bishop John Gynwell of Lincoln, who some months before had taken the same line on confession and absolution as Ralph of Shrewsbury, that he used his Christmas ordination of 1349 to fill the many vacant benefices of his huge mid-England diocese with some 150 former deacons, subdeacons and acolytes.[9] And while that figure is almost certainly exaggerated, there is no doubting the fact that a high proportion of the new clergy admitted at this time were seriously underqualified for their posts.

Whether fully qualified or not, priests in the plague's shadow were in short supply and were able to charge highly for their services. "In their craftiness," complained Archbishop Islip on 28 May 1350, speaking of his own Canterbury clergy, "they aim to undermine any agreement which entails a modest remuneration and a traditionally plain standard of living."[10] And what gave them that power was the mounting demand for remembrance of the dead, so that

> priests now refuse to take on the cure of souls . . . and apply themselves instead to the celebration of commemorative masses and other private offices . . . [where] for the bare priestly name and precious little work they claim greater profits for themselves than those who have the cure of souls.[11]

Simon Islip, whose own career had benefited from two plague deaths – of the archbishop-elect, John Offord, on 20 May 1349 and of his scholarsuccessor, Thomas Bradwardine, on 26 August – was ambitious enough for himself. But his road to high office had been by way of the law and royal service, and he showed little understanding of his front-line clergy. In seeking to regulate their demands and to restore clerical incomes to pre-plague levels, the Archbishop of Canterbury had as little success as the King the following year in enforcing the Statute of Labourers.

Those priests had suffered more than enough. In the account of one doomed Franciscan, John Clynn of Kilkenny – "waiting among the dead for death to come" (which it did): "This pestilence was so contagious that those who touched the dead or the sick were immediately infected themselves and died, so that penitent and confessor were carried together to the grave. Because of their fear and horror, men could hardly bring themselves to perform the pious and charitable acts of visiting the sick."[12] Helpless waiting increased the terror and the revulsion. In Brother Clynn's Kilkenny the plague raged most fiercely during Lent 1349. But horror stories had been accumulating for many months before that time, with heavy emphasis on the fate of the carers. It was early October 1347 when the Black Death first entered Sicily at Messina, brought there by Genoese galleys; and already

> because of the scale of the mortality, many Messinese looked to make confession of their sins and to make their wills, but priests, judges and notaries refused to visit them, and if anybody did visit their houses, whether to hear confession or draw up a will, they were soon sure to die themselves.[13]

In Bobbio (Northern Italy) "one man, wanting to make his will, died along with the notary, the priest who heard his confession, and the people summoned to witness the will, and they were all buried together on the following day", while in nearby Piacenza "the physician would not visit; the priest, panic-stricken, administered the sacraments with fear and trembling . . . no prayer, trumpet or bell summoned friends and neighbours to the funeral, nor was mass performed".[14] In Padua "the bodies even of noblemen lay unburied, [and] many, at a price, were buried by poor wretches, without priests or candles".[15] A generation later, when the plague was more familiar and its terrors less extreme, it would be one Yorkshire chronicler's roseate remembrance of 1349 that "God's providence ensured that, in most places, chaplains survived unharmed until the end of the pestilence in order to perform the exequies of those who died". But even Abbot Burton had to add that "after the funerals of the laymen, [the] chaplains were swallowed by death in great numbers, as others had been before".[16]

"For a Christian man to die well and soundly," wrote the anonymous English author of a fourteenth-century *Book of the craft of dying*, "he must know how to die."[17] But the last thing the plague permitted was a good death. Sudden, brutal, disgusting and demeaning, "bodily death [the *Book* continues] is the most dreadful of all terrifying things". However, worse even than bodily death is the "spiritual death of the soul [that] is as much more horrible and detestable as the soul is more worthy and precious than the body".[18] In the Great Pestilence that spiritual death had caught too many unawares, for "very seldom does any man, even among religious and devout men, prepare himself for death in advance as he ought, for every man thinks that he will live long, and does not believe that he will die soon".[19] And what, after that catastrophe, its shocked survivors most remembered was their own perceived betrayal of dead relatives and friends, left to expire "more like animals than human beings".[20] Appalled by what had happened

> during the great pestilence which was at [King's] Lynn in 1349, in which the greater part of the people in that town died, three men seeing that the venerated Sacrament of the Body of Christ was being carried through the town with only a single candle of poor wax burning in front of it, whereas two great candles of the best wax are hardly sufficient, thought it so improper that they ordained certain lights for it when carried by night or by day in the visitation of the sick . . . and designed this devotion to last for the period of

their lives. Others, seeing their devotion, offered to join them, and thirteen of them drew up their ordinances.[21]

From 1349 onwards it was the threat of an unsecured death that most concentrated minds on guaranteed provision for the dying. And equally important, for those who faced death daily, was adequate remembrance of

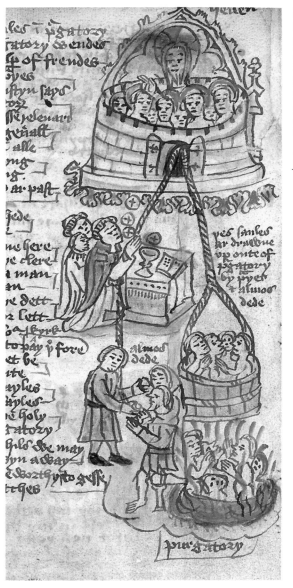

31. The power of alms-giving (bottom left) and memorial masses (centre) to lift souls from Purgatory to Heaven (top) is shown in this charming marginal drawing from a fifteenth-century Carthusian manuscript, written at Mount Grace Priory in northern Yorkshire. *By permission of the British Library, Add. MS 37049, fol. 22v.*

the dead. Keeping the dead alive in the prayers of the living was an obligation long pre-dating the Black Death. However, it had only recently been
given particular prominence by the promotion to official doctrine of that
"third place" known as Purgatory where the shriven soul, working its passage to release, might be purged (with some assistance) of remaining sins.
Fuelled by that assurance, formally given for the first time at the Council of
Lyons in 1274, faith had quickly grown in the efficacy of human intervention in relieving the pains of Purgatory, the "solemn celebration of [memo-
rial] masses . . . [being] judged highest in merit and of most power to draw

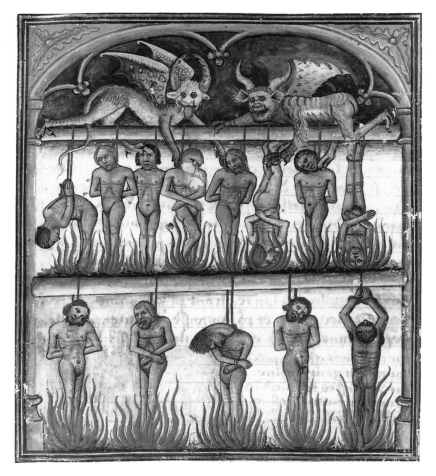

32. Thieves roasting in Hell: one of several graphic illustrations of the *Torments of Hell*
in a French illuminated manuscript of the fifteenth century. *The Bodleian Library, Oxford:*
MS Douce 134, fol. 121v.

down the mercy of God".[22] In effect, the signal had been given, fully endorsed by the Church, for a runaway inflation of spiritual benefits.

Characteristically, not one of Lynn's many parish fraternities, including the Corpus Christi gild of 1349–50, omitted provision for the souls of dead members from its ordinances. Most explicitly, the gild of St George, founded in 1376 at St Margaret's (Bishop's Lynn), was "begun in this intent: to find a priest to sing [mass] at the altar of St George in the church of St Margaret of Lynn, in the worship of God and the holy martyr, and for all the brothers and sisters that to the fraternity belong". Between them they formed a burial club to which all contributed their shares of the cost of candles and processional torches. They promised to make agreed offerings at members' funerals, to be their fellows' pall-bearers if required, and to attend each other's exequies or pay a fine. It was their gild priest's obligation to celebrate 60 memorial masses – more than double the usual number for Lynn's fraternities – for the soul of each member "so soon as he is dead", and "afterwards [he should] be had in memory with others that be dead before" of the same brotherhood.[23]

In practice few such brotherhoods were burial clubs alone. Some were covert craft associations; others (including Lynn's gild of St George) made provision for mutual insurance, "to help them which have fallen in poverty"; all fostered group solidarity in some material way, whether through collective worship, in procession, or at the feast.[24] Nevertheless, mortality and remembrance were their business. "It is not by chance," writes Caroline Barron,

> that every set of London fraternity ordinances which has survived from the fourteenth century specifies in great detail the obligations which members have towards ensuring the decent burial of dead brothers and sisters . . . [so that] in London it would seem that it was the Black Death of 1348/9 which provided both the incentive and, indirectly, the means for the formation of parish fraternities.[25]

Many English fraternities were founded well after the Black Death, and their association with plague mortalities is none too clear.[26] Yet whatever the date and declared purpose of the huge majority of parish gilds, one thing is certain. The brothers and sisters who joined together in prayer and feasting were there principally for the after-death benefits.

Greedy accumulators of those benefits included the brothers and sisters of the fraternity of St Chad, fund-raisers for Lichfield Cathedral. "These are the benefits and indulgences," notes their bishop's memorandum of *c.* 1440, "conceded to the brothers and sisters of the fraternity of St Chad in the cathedral church of Lichfield, and their benefactors." The list begins with an entitlement to 4,040 days of privilege, remitted by Bishop Chad and his successors; then follow another 12,000 days, granted by "various other Catholic bishops", with 21 years of privilege from the popes. Four masses daily are to be celebrated in the cathedral on the fraternity's behalf: "two for the living, and two for the dead". And annual quotas had been settled with every parish priest (30 masses) and with many religious houses (up to 100 masses or psalters) in the diocese. The memorandum ends: "The sum total of masses annually to be celebrated for the brothers and sisters and benefactors of the said fraternity: 2434. The sum total of psalters annually to be said for them: 452."[27]

An entire century before the Reformation set aside such beliefs, the guaranteed benefits of the brothers and sisters of St Chad's were already grossly inflated. However, they were not, even so, without parallels. Of that great warrior-king and church reformer, Henry V (d.1422), it has rather ungraciously been observed that "no one else in medieval England ever thought it necessary to invest so heavily in the purchase of paradise".[28] And whether or not such precautions were truly essential in his case, it is abundantly clear that Henry planned his personal strategy for storming Heaven with at least as much attention as any siege. Within a year of his death (the King provided) there were to be 20,000 masses sung for his soul: 5,000 for the Five Joys of Mary, 3,000 for the Holy Trinity, 1,200 for the Twelve Apostles, 900 for the Nine Orders of Angels, 300 for the Three Patriarchs, with 15 masses daily for the Five Wounds of Christ and the balance in favour of All Saints.[29] "Death", our Inland Revenue has been known to rule, "is not a chargeable occasion." But with the King's huge outstanding debts, his heavy funerary expenses and many *pro anima* bequests, Henry V's overworked executors must have viewed the cost of dying in a very different light, eventually defeated by their task.[30]

Few purchasers of soul-masses in late-medieval Europe could ever have equalled the 100,000 masses with which Bernard Ezi, sire d'Albret, planned to scale the walls of Heaven in 1358[31]. But the commissioning of soul-masses in multiples of a thousand – in Henry V's England as in Bernard Ezi's France – was not in itself unusual. For the rich and powerful everywhere, a death-bed exchange of the wealth of this world for precisely equal benefits

33. As the prayers of the poor were held to have particular value, Cardinal Henry Beaufort (d.1447) re-founded Bishop Henry of Blois's twelfth-century hospital at St Cross (Winchester) to provide accommodation for aged gentlefolk. In the centre, next to Beaufort's great gatehouse, is the bedesmen's common hall, with their kitchen behind, and their individual, separately heated lodgings on the left. The big chapel (right) dates from Bishop Henry's earlier foundation, but was left unaltered by the cardinal. *A. F. Kersting.*

in the next was an entirely respectable ambition. In flat contradiction of St Paul's words to Timothy, "we brought nothing into this world, and it is certain we can carry nothing out" (1 Timothy vi, 7), it was Cardinal Henry Beaufort's confident assumption that he could bridge the vast divide, commuting worldly goods into heavenly ones (*bona mea terrestria in celestia commutare*). However, like his nephew Henry V, this great prince of the Church, reputed by many to be "the richest prelate in Christendom", was unwilling to take any chances. Beaufort died on 11 April 1447, his soul at once protected by a barrage of 10,000 masses. Then, in generations to come, there would be the prayers "in perpetuity" of the religious houses he had helped, with dedicated memorial masses at his personal chantry in Winchester Cathedral and the unceasing tributes of his aged bedesmen of St Cross.[32]

As Beaufort had no children, he could do what he liked with his great fortune. Yet as each successive generation laid its burden on the next, the weight of obligations became unbearable. Some of this commemorative piety had entirely beneficial effects, as in the fifteenth-century English bishops' encouragement, by way of chantry-led foundations, of learning at Oxford and Cambridge.[33] However, the great majority of aristocratic chantries in late-medieval England – among them Ralph Lord Cromwell's Tattershall, Edward of York's Fotheringhay, the Beauchamps' Warwick, the Fitzalans' Arundel, the de la Poles' Ewelme, and many more – functioned almost exclusively as power-houses of prayer, as costly to maintain as Atlantic liners.[34] In these hugely expensive establishments the poor had a well-defined role. Boasts Henry V on the brink of Agincourt: "Five hundred poor I have in yearly pay, / Who twice a day their wither'd hands hold up / Toward heaven, to pardon blood."[35] Yet there was little genuine charity in such arrangements. The blood which required pardoning was that of an archbishop, Richard le Scrope of York, executed by Henry IV in brutal haste in the aftermath of the Percy Rebellion of 1405. Ten years later the murdered archbishop had already become the focus of a dangerous new cult: a stain on the conscience of the house of Lancaster which only massive works of expiation could wipe out. In practice, Henry supported his army of bedesmen neither to relieve the poor nor to care for the infirm, but to sing for his father's soul and for his own.

Henry V's duty of care for the late king's soul was of a piece with the experience of many similarly placed heirs, working off legacies of guilt. Thus, along with those everlasting widows who consumed family fortunes, the sins of the fathers lived on with their sons, obliged to right old grievances and pay off debts. "I have been all the days of my life in my country a stirrer in the world as the world asketh," confessed John Throgmorton, builder of a large family fortune, on his death-bed in 1445. But he had done too little in his lifetime to put right old injustices, leaving it to his heirs to make up for that neglect, and delivering his soul to their curacy.[36] In the mid-fifteenth century, and in Throgmorton's particular case, that faith might still have been justified. However, as the costs of parental soul-care continued to rise, heirs had little choice but to cheat on their obligations or preside over the collapse of their estates. In 1504, when Henry Lisle charged his eldest son to carry out his instructions "as he shall answer before the high judge of heaven", his reasonable assumption could well have been that the young Lisle had no such design.[37]

In point of fact, obligations to the dead had accumulated so hugely by the century's end that even dedicated fellowships were defeated by them. The London goldsmiths, for example, with 25 obits to attend, found themselves

34. When Sir Ralph Shelton died in 1487 he left clear instructions in his will that the church he was rebuilding should be completed. But the task was too much for his heirs. Shelton Church (Norfolk), walled across abruptly at the east end of the nave, still lacks a chancel (right). It was never roofed as grandly as Sir Ralph intended, and even his own founder's tomb was left unfinished. *A. F. Kersting.*

sacrificing what amounted to a working day in 12, "to the great unease and trouble of the wardens and of all the livery". They rebelled against that tyranny in 1497, amalgamating obits "a wet and a dry together", so that, at the 14 combined commemorations they were still expected to attend, a drink at least was promised at every one.[38] Business is often done on such occasions. And there is little reason to suppose that the obits of deceased gildsmen, even of those long dead, were any less well attended than the more convivial annual gatherings at the gild feast. There, numbers held up well until the end. Wymondham, a small market town in central Norfolk, is still dominated by its huge abbey church. With suppression just round the corner for their fraternity as for the monks, no fewer than 84 brothers and sisters of Wymondham's approximately 100-strong fellowship of the Nativity of Our Lady sat down to feast together on 8 September 1534; nor were such attendances in any way exceptional.[39]

The feast of Our Lady's Nativity, while enjoying a revival at just about that time, was neither the latest nor the most fashionable of Marian festivals.[40] However, Marian devotion everywhere, driven by faith in the

35. Such was the strength of Marian devotion in late-medieval England that the Virgin's imagery is found on every kind of object. This late-fourteenth-century tin-lead badge, sold at Canterbury and designed to be pinned to the cap of a pilgrim returning from Becket's shrine, measures 13.5 by 8.7 cm. It shows a *Virgin and Child* (centre), with smaller figures of *St Edward the Confessor* (left) and *St Thomas of Canterbury* (right). *Museum of London Picture Library.*

peculiar efficacy of the Virgin's intercession, was growing very rapidly in the Late Middle Ages; and Wymondham's popular fraternity was one expression of it. Both the living and the dead had found a friend. It was specifically to enlist the Virgin's help in healing the papal Schism that a new Marian festival of the Visitation (of the Blessed Virgin Mary to Elizabeth) was instituted in 1389.[41] And Henry V's purchase of 5,000 masses for the Five Joys of Mary (Annunciation, Nativity, Resurrection, Ascension and Coronation) was unusual only in its extravagance. The other face of Mary was her Sorrows. It was to the *Mater Dolorosa*, the mother acquainted with grief, that many turned for help in times of pestilence. For those touched by death, there were special prayers to the Virgin which were generally thought to be of particular efficacy against the plague (*contra pestem*). And for the others, always too many, who had seen a child die, it was especially easy to relate to a Queen of Heaven – Virgin of Humility, Mother of Mercy, Our Lady of Pity – who had herself been a witness of the Crucifixion of her son and of the long ghastly agony of his Passion.[42]

Meditations on pain and sorrow have always appealed with particular force to the bereaved, the sick and the old. And it was not just by chance that one of the most popular Marian prayers in post-plague England was the *Obsecro Te*, where Mary's humble petitioner addresses the "mother most glorious . . . consolation of the desolate" as fellow-sufferer and friend, beseeching her aid "every hour and minute of my life . . . by that great and holy compassion and most bitter sorrow of heart which you had when Our Lord Jesus Christ was stripped naked before the Cross . . . And by your Son's five Wounds, and the sorrow you had to see him wounded."[43] "There is a great deal of superstition," complained Erasmus in 1533, "in increased numbers of special Masses: the Mass of the Crown of Thorns, the Mass of the Three Nails, the Mass of the Foreskin of Christ, masses for those who travel by land and sea, for barren women, for persons sick of quartan and tertian fevers."[44] Even so, after a lifetime of reflection, Erasmus could see no reason to suppress the mass as though it were "some impiety or pestilence". Only for the most extreme reformers was there anything abhorrent in continuing to celebrate the Eucharist – where the Body and Blood of Christ are consumed by the believer – as the central act of Christian worship: a commemoration which is also a thanksgiving.

Corpus Christi, unlike some of the older Marian festivals, was a relatively late arrival in medieval England, seldom celebrated before the 1320s at earliest. However, this "glorious feast of the most precious sacrament of the flesh and blood of our Lord Jesus Christ", while still something of a novelty when the Black Death came, was at once propelled to prominence by the pestilence.[45] At the root of the new fashion was the familiar concern voiced by the 19 founding gildsmen of Corpus Christi at Coventry, "to find a chaplain to celebrate divine service daily for the good estate of the king and the founders and the brethren and sisters of the gild and for their souls when they are dead".[46] And there was clearly much that would appeal to the congenitally plague-alert in the daily propitiatory sacrifice of the mass.

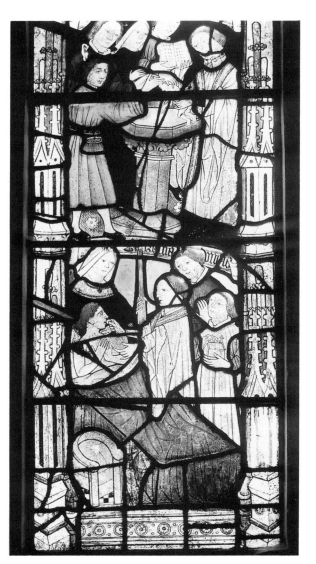

36. The *Baptism* and *Last Sacrament* panels from a fifteenth-century *Seven Sacraments* window at Doddiscombleigh Church (Devonshire). In the lower panel a priest has brought the Host to the bedside of a dying man – naked as was the custom – who receives it with hands raised in prayer. *RCHME Crown copyright.*

Another strong draw of Corpus Christi in particular, ensuring the recruitment to the new fraternities of the patrician elites of many towns, was a rising concern for the eucharistic visit and a proper way of death, so that never again should the mortally ill be without the Host at their bedsides.[47]

In late-medieval affective piety, pleas for intervention in the affairs of this world were usually combined with a bid for intercession in the next. Thus at Coventry, from 1465, there was a weekly Jesus Mass, celebrated every Friday and promising after-death benefits, founded by the gild of drapers "to the end that Almighty God, appeased by the prayers of the faithful, might deliver the said city" from pestilence.[48] And each new mass – the Mass of the Holy Name, the Mass of the Five Wounds, the Mass against the Pestilence – carried its own improbable guarantees. An early-fifteenth-century Norwich missal, for example, promises 3,000 years' indulgence for a single trental (set of 30) of Holy Name masses.[49] In the Five Wounds legend the Archangel Gabriel, sent by God, guarantees Boniface II (and all who do the same) a full recovery of health for a five-fold celebration of the Five Wounds mass.[50] No fully confessed and "truly contrite" person, as Clement VI had promised the terrified folk of Avignon in 1348, would fall victim to sudden death if he or she (penitently kneeling with candle in hand) took part in five successive masses against the Pestilence.[51]

As with the suffering Mary, it was easy to identify in post-plague England with Christ as the wounded Man of Sorrows. In *The book of the craft of dying* one of the recommended prayers recalls "the agony you suffered for me on the cross"; another "the love that caused you to be wounded and die for the well-being and salvation of mankind".[52] "I adore you, Lord Jesus Christ, wounded upon the Cross," runs the beautiful prayer *Adoro te*, often associated with Five Wounds imagery: "I beseech you, Lord Jesus Christ, that your wounds may be my remedy."[53] That *Image of Pity* – a bleeding Christ often surrounded by the instruments of his Passion (the ladder, the nails, the hammer and pincers, the sword and staff, the rods, the seamless robe, etc.) – was everywhere repeated, as a devotional aid, in the sculptures and wall-paintings of parish churches.[54] It became the stuff of many sermons, and was commandeered also for individual leave-takings, so analogous were the two death experiences.[55] In 1488 it was the desire of a London goldsmith, Sir Edmund Shaa, that two of his former apprentices should prepare rings of remembrance, as they "understand right well the making", for 16 named mourners at his funeral. The rings, of fine gold, were to be engraved with an image of the wounded Christ rising from wells of grace – of pity, mercy and

37. This fifteenth-century painted glass panel from St Peter Mancroft (Norwich) depicts the *Circumcision of Christ*. Traditionally celebrated on 1 January (the eighth day of Christmas), the Feast of the Circumcision was of very ancient origin, but was enjoying a revival in the Late Middle Ages when Erasmus declared himself uncertain of its worth. *RCHME Crown copyright.*

38. *Christ showing his Wounds*:
a late-fifteenth-century stone figure,
celebrating the Five Wounds
devotion, against the tower of
Fairford Church, in Gloucestershire.
A. F. Kersting.

39. A fifteenth-century reliquary pendant
(50 cm high) of gold set with garnets, found
recently on the foreshore at Upper Thames
Street, London. A hollow at the base still carries
a splinter (of the True Cross?) set in wax. On the
front the *Crucifixion* is depicted on a blue enamel
ground; on the back is a *Virgin and Child*.
Museum of London Picture Library.

40. A gold ring very similar to the mourning rings ordered by Sir Edmund Shaa, the London goldsmith, in 1488. Found at Coventry, this ring is engraved (as was Shaa's instruction) with *Christ Showing his Wounds*, rising from a *Well of Grace*. The British Museum: Department of Medieval and Later Antiquities.

41. Found on the Thames foreshore near London Bridge, this heavy gold ring is plain on the outside but engraved on the inside with images of popular intercessors, thought to be more effective for being worn against the skin. From this angle the central image is of *St Anne teaching the Virgin to read,* with (left) the *Holy Trinity* (God the Father, with the dove of the Holy Spirit at his right shoulder, holding the crucified Christ), and (right) *St Antony of Egypt* (identified by his tau-cross). Hidden further round the band are the *Virgin and Child* and *St Thomas of Canterbury* (dressed as archbishop). *Museum of London Picture Library.*

114

everlasting life – for (explained the preacher, taking his text from Isaiah xii.3) "the wound in the side and heart of Jesus Christ is the well of mercy, the well of life, the well of plentiful redemption".[56]

It is probable that Shaa, long before his last illness, had made other costly preparations for personal soul-care.[57] Yet he still felt obliged to take remedial action to wipe his conscience clear of past wrongdoings: of a theft of two oxen "forty years since", and of the £14 of which, at some remote date, he

42. Behind the heads of the seated parishioners at Trotton, in Sussex, was this big late-fourteenth-century *Last Judgement* on the west wall of their church, with a *Christ of Judgement* at the top and Moses (holding the Ten Commandments) just below him. Spiritual Man (whose naked soul is being welcomed into Heaven) is accompanied by roundels of the Seven Works of Mercy (right). Carnal Man and his corresponding roundels of the Seven Deadly Sins (left) are badly faded, although the rejecting angel (at Christ's right hand) is still quite clear. *A. F. Kersting.*

115

43. This much-restored *Christ of the Last Judgement* at Lutterworth Church (Leicestershire) is in its usual place over the chancel arch, but is accompanied less conventionally by a well-preserved fifteenth-century *Resurrection of the Dead* – the dead answering the call from their coffins. Other painted preaching-aids in the same church included a contemporary rendering of *The Three Living and the Three Dead,* of which the Dead have now gone and only the Living are still recognizable. *A. F. Kersting.*

had "defrauded" a deceased dean of St Paul's. Then, as was customary, he set aside sufficient funds to erect a monument for himself and to support a chantry priest to sing masses for his soul; he endowed daily masses at two other city churches, and founded an annual obit (well-provided with food and drink) at a third.[58] All this was no more than might be expected of a man of Shaa's considerable wealth. However, it was accompanied also by that wide range of charitable bequests and contributions to public works, familiar in Shaa's day, which has prompted some to see the Late Middle Ages as a golden age of religious observance and lay participation in the parishes.[59] Shaa left £20 for immediate distribution to the poor at his funeral. Other sums went to the relief of prisoners in five London jails; to the purchase of coal for the indigent; to the provision of dowries for poor maidens; to the repair of highways and the patching of London Wall; to the building of a new gatehouse at Cripplegate in that wall; and to good works in the north-west – the founding of a new grammar school at Stockport (Cheshire), near his birthplace at Dukinfield; "stuffs and alms for poor persons" in that region, and for priests there to sing for his soul.[60]

In Shaa's last arrangements, combining the "augmenting of Divine Service" with relief for the destitute, spiritual and corporal charity were complementary. And the two would blend seamlessly in a bequest to the poor by Richard Croull of York of five shirts for the Five Wounds, ten pairs of shoes for the Ten Commandments and seven pairs of hose for the Seven Works of Mercy.[61] In other wills of the period that same association reappears routinely, from John de Roucliff's gift ("to the praise of God and the use of the poor") of a penny dole to 50 York paupers, to the desire of Isabella Jacson (of that same city) that any residue of her estate should go to "works of charity, viz. in the celebration of masses and the bestowal of alms to the poor and needy".[62] Christ's vision of the Last Judgement had made the link plain, so that in charity lay the elements of a contract. "I was an hungred", said the King, "and ye gave me meat: I was thirsty, and ye gave me drink: I was a stranger, and ye took me in: naked, and ye clothed me: I was sick, and ye visited me: I was in prison, and ye came unto me." And when, astonished, the righteous asked: "when saw we thee an hungred, and fed *thee*? or thirsty, and gave *thee* drink . . . etc.", the reply had come: "Verily I say unto you, inasmuch as ye have done it unto one of the least of these my brethren, ye have done it unto me." (Matthew xxv.35–40)

Always a favourite with contemporary preachers, this often-repeated Gospel text mixed condemnation of the cursed, who "shall go away into everlasting punishment" for neglecting the poor, with promise to the blessed (among whose attributes was generosity), who shall "inherit the kingdom prepared for you from the foundation of the world" and enjoy "life eternal". There was only one Adam, Thomas Brinton taught, "who dug the earth with his spade". And it was never God's intention to breed distinctions from the start, making a man of gold (for the rich) and of clay (for the poor). On the contrary, rich and poor are mutually supportive. It is "for the rich to pay, the poor to pray" (*divitis est erogare, pauperis est orare*), for the rich are as much in need of the prayers of the poor as the poor are reliant on their charity.[63]

Caught in the middle, the parish priest was servant of both. And where so much was demanded of him in daily transactions for the soul, it was hard not to take some profit as intermediary. "O covetousness!", thundered that one-time pluralist Dean Colet from his pulpit at St Paul's: "of thee cometh this heaping of benefices upon benefices . . . of thee, all the sueing for tithes, for offerings, for mortuaries, for dilapidations, by the right and title of the church. Of thee cometh the corruptness of courts, and these daily new inventions wherewith the silly people are so sore vexed . . . all corruptness, all the decay of the Church, all the offences of the world, come of the covetousness of priests."[64] And if rather little of Colet's celebrated Convocation Sermon of February 1512 is now thought to have been fair comment on the Church overall, he was entirely right to attack it on secularization. After the priesthood's pride, its lust and its quest for personal gain, Colet identified a fourth major evil in "the continual secular occupation, wherein priests and bishops nowadays doth busy themselves, the servants rather of men than of God; the warriors rather of this world than of Christ". This misdirection of effort, while familiar for centuries, had been multiplying (Colet knew) in his own lifetime. The consequences were serious, for the "priesthood is despised when there is no difference betwixt such priests and lay people, but, according to the prophecy of Ozee [Hosea]: *as the people be, so are the priests*".[65]

Colet was born in 1466/7; he died in middle age, on 16 September 1519, the victim of three successive attacks of the sweating sickness – "a disease", noted his grieving friend Erasmus, "which is peculiarly rife in England".[66] In that one brief lifetime much had happened to change the Church, not least a surge in clerical recruitment largely unrelated to population recovery. Priests, once so numerous before the Black Death, had been in short supply since the pestilence struck, with ordinations slumping to their lowest levels in the half-century before 1450. Yet the situation had entirely changed by 1500, when ordination figures in many dioceses were running close to their pre-plague peaks.[67] Some of this new recruitment was to the benefit of all Christian folk, for "now in many places", wrote the Oxford scholar Alexander Carpenter as early as 1430, "there is greater abundance of preaching of the Word of God than was customary before our time".[68] And there must also be some case for that "increase of divine service" at parochial level on which Clive Burgess has repeatedly insisted.[69] But with as many priests in 1500 as in 1348, competing to serve only half the number of parishioners, a more likely result was alienation: the inevitable consequence of overexposure. "Dearly beloved," began the preacher of one Latin sermon preserved in a fifteenth-century anthology, "I find that many people nowadays like three things, that is to say, short penances, short masses, and short sermons (*breves penitencie, breves misse, et breves sermones*)."[70] And it was to a sophisticated, not a popular, audience that he was speaking.

When, at last, the tide of priests retreated, as it began to do in the 1520s under pressure of clerical poverty[71], the damage was already largely done.

No tinkering by reforming bishops could set the world to rights, for what was now demanded was total change. The more progressive of the clergy had predicted this long before, among them Alexander Carpenter (quoting the twelfth-century St Bernard):

> There creeps today a putrid plague through the whole body of the Church and the wider it spreads, the more hopeless it becomes; the more it penetrates, the more perilous . . . Whom, now, does she expel, or from whom does she hide herself? All are friends and all are enemies; all are kinsmen and all are adversaries; all are of her own household and none are peaceable; all are of Christ and all seek their own: they are Christ's ministers and they serve Antichrist . . . To rout them or to escape them is alike impossible. Intestine and incurable is the pestilence of the Church.

"For certain," concludes Carpenter with understandable hyperbole, almost a century before Luther fired his broadsides, "such voluptuous carnal prelates and pastors are the cause of all the error and impiety now reigning throughout the entire world."[72]

CHAPTER EIGHT

Protest and resolution

A knight and a pluralist, a prior and his rebel peasantry, faction and affinity – even an image of Our Lady of Pity – all play their parts in a tale of riot and mayhem at the little market town of Shipston-on-Stour (Worcestershire), recently offered "as an antidote to an excessively harmonious view of medieval urban society".[1] And although stories of this kind may be found in any age, the circumstances at Shipston combine to suggest that its troubles were aggravated by the Black Death. New Shipston was a late arrival among England's planted towns, founded by the Prior of Worcester in 1268, when it was granted its weekly market and annual fair. By that date, routinely, newcomers to such a borough would have been enticed there by special privileges: chiefly, the right to free transferability of land (burgage tenure), where a man might exchange, devise or sell his tenement at will. A century later, in the 1360s and 1370s, that was certainly how Shipston's townspeople were behaving. Yet they had not calculated on the vigilance of their lord. In the general seignorial reaction of the post-plague decades the Prior of Worcester became (as others did) a particularly jealous custodian of his rights. When an enquiry in 1376 revealed unauthorized land transactions, entered into by his tenants without the lord's knowledge or consent, all exchanged tenements were seized into the prior's hands and the offending parties were banned from them for ever. It was the beginning of several decades of increasingly bitter confrontations, during which all New Shipston's remaining privileges were withdrawn.[2]

In this long succession of disputes, at their fiercest between 1395 and 1406, three particular elements stand out: first, the ferocity of the prior–landowner's reaction; secondly, the matching tenacity of his tenants in

44. Greed, violence, and death in the Late Middle Ages. The right-hand panel from the front of a large elm chest of *c.*1410, carved with three scenes from Chaucer's *Pardoner's Tale*. Three young "rioutours" of Flanders have boasted that "we wol sleen this false traytour Deeth . . . er it be nyght!" However, they are directed by an old man (Death himself, who they abuse) to a great treasure, over which they quickly fall out. The youngest (left) buys bottles which he will poison; then the other two set upon him and stab him to death (centre); but drink the wine and die horribly themselves as they celebrate (right). *Museum of London Picture Library.*

clinging to their rights; thirdly, the complete breakdown of law and order in this Middle England parish, aggravated by the failure of agreed arbitration to reach a settlement equally fair to both parties. It was not long after that arbitration, and very probably as a result of continuing divisions in the community, that Nicholas Burdet, son of Sir Thomas, twice led bands of murderous ruffians to Shipston in the spring and summer of 1413. Protected, as was his lawless father, by membership of the locally powerful Beauchamp affinity, Nicholas escaped the due punishment for the beatings and two homicides of which he was plainly guilty, living to turn his violence on the French.[3]

Richard Wych, rector of New Shipston's mother-church at Tredington, was another Beauchamp associate. And it was Wych, promoter of a new image of Our Lady of Pity in Tredington's north aisle, who came to be identified by Worcester Priory as chief troublemaker. Yet by 1395, when Wych added Tredington to his many other benefices, there was a long history of unrest in the locality. There had already been serious disturbances, for example, in 1342. However, those pre-plague agitations had been poverty-linked. And the fresh waves of trouble that followed the Black Death, at Shipston as elsewhere, had a great deal more to do with prosperity.[4] Once known generally as the Peasants' Revolt, the English Rising of 1381 was not, in point of fact, a rebellion of the truly disadvantaged. For while it was triggered by economic pressures bearing especially heavily on the poor – who were caught in a rural poverty trap by government intervention to hold down wages, by landowner insistence on services once commuted, and by the manifest inequities of the poll tax – it was led from the beginning by a village elite whose demands were more overtly political.[5]

Egalitarian beliefs were always less prominent among the demands of the rebels than appeals to ancient liberties and hypothetical rights. And it was wholly in keeping with other protest movements of their times that the men of New Shipston chose to argue their case on the demonstrably bogus privilege of ancient demesne of the crown, to which they had no claim of any substance.[6] "The most illustrious King Offa," boasted the dissidents of St Albans with just as little truth, "when he assembled craftsmen, smiths, carpenters, cementers and stonemasons with their workshops to build the monastery, gave the said town to the stonemasons and other workers to live in, and honoured it with liberties and privileges provided by his royal munificence."[7] And both communities made the same link, so characteristic of the fourteenth century, between the King and his poor commoners as natural partners in a social order of which only the middlemen were vile. One such intermediary was the ecclesiastical lawyer, William Doune, who died (probably of the pestilence) in the summer of 1361. Doune had been Archdeacon of Leicester since 1354, and in that office – one of the most unpopular in the Church – had accumulated much on his conscience before his death. In Doune's careful testament Robert Scothorn, vicar of Melton Mowbray, is remembered as a particular victim: "And I pray him to forgive me therefor, for that I now bitterly consider in myself that many who are in authority do bear themselves very ill with them that are set under them, yea, they do slaughter them (*immo grassantur*), and of the number of these I have been and am one, God of his unspeakable pity be merciful to me for it!"[8]

Archdeacon Doune was probably the author of the contemporary *Memoriale Sacerdotum*, where he shows himself to be familiar with the many tricks and subterfuges of an adversarial legal system that, especially in his time, had distanced true justice from the folk. The *Memoriale* is a confessional manual for the use of parish priests. "Concerning advocates," it advises, "an advocate is at fault if on account of his ignorance or lack of expertise his client shall have lost a good case . . . Item, an advocate is at fault

45. A bishop sleeps at a time when he should have been guarding his flock against heresy. This drawing illustrates the lines in *Piers Plowman* in which the poet blames the sloth of "many bischopes" for allowing in the Lollards: "For many wakere wolues ar wroken into thy foldes." *The Bodleian Library, Oxford: MS Douce 104, fol. 44r.*

if by his sophistry he deprived his adversary of a good case. Item, if he harassed his adversary in anything, by seeking superfluous adjournment. Item, if he alleged what he knew to be false . . . etc. In these cases the advocate is obliged to pay in full the actual amount at issue to him who was damaged through his fault."[9] Recognizably the tricks of the legal profession even now, they were more than usually offensive during a period of transition, when the processes of law were changing also. In the late thirteenth century a combination of gross over-population with oppressive taxes to finance unpopular foreign wars had pushed crime-rates up to such a level as to swamp the old general eyre. And it was to be a century and more before a workable system of biannual assizes (presided over by royal judges) and quarter sessions (conducted by locally recruited justices of the peace) took its place. That system, while clearly biased in favour of the greater magnates and country gentry, was at least an improvement on recent unsuccessful attempts to enforce law and order by trailbaston visitations and royal tyranny. In the interim many had been driven to abandon the courts altogether, hearkening to the greenwood's siren call. "I have served my lord the king in peace and in war, in Flanders, Scotland, in Gascony his own land; but now I do not know how to make a living", sang the outlawed poet of the *Song of Trailbaston* (1305–6). "You who are indicted, I advise you, come to me, to the green forest . . . where there is no annoyance but only wild animals and beautiful shade; for the common law is too uncertain."[10]

In fourteenth-century England many spoke of Robin Hood who "never bent his bow".[11] But while Robin himself was a creature of myth, originating very probably at a much earlier date, it is a significant fact that his ballads were written down and were particularly popular in the second half of the century, when plague mortalities, far from easing social tensions and reducing crime, had had exactly the opposite effect. "He was a good outlaw, and did poor men much good" was the final verdict of the *Gest of Robyn Hode*. Yet to the many discontented individuals exposed during these decades to a partial law and to landowner bullying of a peculiarly insensitive kind, it was less Robin's charity that furnished a role-model than the timely example of his freedom. Robin, we are told, was of yeoman stock: "a radical figure . . . nobody's servant . . . a hero for a society in transition".[12] And with King Death in the wings, life was now too short for the more impatient spirits of Robin's emergent class to wait any longer for the social reforms that the landowners themselves, as they freely admitted in 1381, would never have allowed on their own account "even if it were their dying day".[13] Shortly before the Revolt, and not long after another general visitation of the plague, John Robynes had led his fellow-tenants at Shipston-on-Stour in an absolute refusal to hoe the prior's demesne or to answer for that contumacy in his court, on the grounds that it was "nothing but stupidity" (*non esset nisi stultitia*).[14]

Robynes's bid for individual freedom in 1377–8 has a rational note. And so also has the argument of the Duchy of Cornwall's bondmen at Climsland and Liskeard, some four years later, that an unfairly punitive local custom by which the goods of a deceased tenant lapsed entirely to the lord, was driving their disinherited children off the land. They made an effective point, for such steady haemorrhage of labour, at a time of severe shortage, was certain to worry their landowner. Nevertheless, what drove them most to protest was the unjust harshness of their lot, which was so much worse than that of other duchy tenants in the locality.[15] Unsurprisingly, it was in similar mixed-tenancy counties – among them Suffolk, where many tenants were free – that such inequities contributed to social tension. At Chevington, for example, Walter Baker was a bondman of the abbot of Bury St Edmunds on one of his holdings, while enjoying a free tenancy of another. When called to account in 1371 Baker had sold wood from his lord's copses without authorization and had carried off timber from the abbot's ruinous barn, rather than repair it as required, to build a house on the plot he called his own.[16] In the 1370s, as landowners everywhere tried to make up their growing losses, such ill discipline was becoming endemic. Thus it was at Chevington again, in 1375, that 17 of Bury's tenants refused reaping services on the demesne; and it was a Chevington court roll of 1380 that identified a local brewer, John by name, by his resonant sobriquet of "Littlejohn".[17]

Targeting those court rolls especially, the rebels of 1381 "worked to give old muniments over to the flames; and lest someone might again be found who would remember the old customs, or new ones, they killed all such".[18] Thomas Walsingham, who saw this happen at St Albans, was precentor there in 1381. And what he said applied equally to the monks' treasury at Bury and to the hundred-plus other estate archives that, during the Revolt, were either burnt or carried off by the rebels. Both St Albans and Bury had suffered similar outrages once before, in the urban risings of 1327–8. However, the leadership in pre-plague times had been taken by rich burgesses, whereas at Bury in 1381 it was a country chaplain, John Wrawe, whose turbulent mob of landless peasants and lesser tradesmen quickly lost the backing of the wealthier townspeople, to be betrayed by them the instant things went wrong.[19] Wrawe and his associates met a terrible death in the blood-bath which ended the Revolt; but while they had lost the first battle even for the "little liberty" urged by one of their spokesmen at St Albans, the war had barely begun. Over the course of the next century an increasingly stubborn resistance to bondman services of any kind so reduced their benefit to the great majority of English landowners that "the point was reached when it became wiser not to mention serfdom at all".[20] At Bury itself, the growing success of the cloth trade in the locality enabled its leading merchants to buy fresh privileges from the monks, so that "it was the shilling rather than the club that won freedom".[21]

It was the prolix monk–poet John Lydgate of Bury (c. 1370–c. 1451) who included the old proverb "Who lesith his fredam, in soth, he lesith all" in one of his earlier and more popular works, the moral fable *The Churl and the Bird*.[22] And that message was more important than any other. True, John Ball had made some converts before 1381 by his inflammatory talk of common ownership. "Things cannot go right in England and never will," Ball had preached in country churchyards across the land, "until goods are held in common and there are no more villeins and gentlefolk, but we are all one

46. John Ball (centre) preaches to Wat Tyler (left) and other rebel leaders outside London: "Let us go to the King – he is young – and show him how we are oppressed, and tell him that we want things to be changed, or else we will change them ourselves." *By permission of the British Library, MS Royal 18 E 1, fol. 165v.*

and the same."[23] "He's right!" the common folk had whispered in the fields and in their homes, repeating among themselves: "That's what John Ball says, and he's right!"[24] However, the healthy diet and fine clothes – "wines, spices, and good bread" and "velvet and camlet lined with squirrel and ermine" – chosen by John Ball to characterize the nobility alone, were all more generally available in post-plague England, so that practically everybody could aspire to some share of them. Landless labourers "deign not to dine today on worts [cabbages] a night old" had complained William Langland shortly before the Great Revolt:

No penny ale may please them, and no piece of bacon,
Unless it be fresh flesh, or fish fried or baked.[25]

Nor was Henry Knighton, writing in the 1390s, the first to observe that

127

the pride of the lower orders has so blossomed forth and grown these days in fine dress and splendid display – in the variety of fashions – that one can hardly distinguish one person from another, because of their gorgeous clothes and accessories . . . each imitates the other and strives to introduce some new fashion and to excel his superior by wearing even grander clothes.[26]

Bewildered and angered by the rapid pace of change, neither Langland (the poet) nor Knighton (the chronicler) were wholly unprejudiced observers. Yet both are supported by unimpeachable contemporary sources, while it is the recent conclusion of at least one well-respected historian of the Great Revolt that "Froissart's famous attribution of the revolt to *the ease and riches that the common people were of* may have been truer than he knew".[27] After the event, every kind of obstacle, including the slur of heresy, would be put in the way of genuine equality.[28] But the case for enfranchisement was harder to set aside, for as Edmund Lacy, Bishop of Hereford, conceded in 1419 when manumitting a former bondman:

Since from the beginning nature created all men free and of free condition, and [only] afterwards the *jus gentium* imposed upon some the yoke of servitude, we believe this to be truly an act of piety and justly deserving a reward from God, to restore those whose merits require this to their pristine freedom.[29]

Among landowners generally, when rent arrears multiplied and when rigorous insistence on bondman status grew to be more trouble than it was worth, it became easier to share that point of view. In the words of a political poet of 1401, "Lords know never what commons grieves/Till their rents begin to cease."[30]

That first began to happen around the time of the Great Revolt. And it was between then and 1450 that the more invidious ancient customs, once thought unassailable, vanished with astonishing speed. Earliest to go were the rents usually associated with unfree status: the merchets and heriots (fines at marriage and on death), pannage and herbage (payments for rights of pasture), "work silver" (for commuted labour services), and occasional grants-in-aid.[31] However, more significant overall than the suspension of individual customary charges was the fact that many landowners, either by reason of their own weakness or because they saw the merits of arbitration, were at last prepared to listen to their tenantry. Thus, a former Treasurer, Ralph Lord Sudeley, would be called in to mediate in protracted mid-century negotiations between the Abbess of Syon and her Cheltenham tenants concerning work silver payments. The abbess's tenants had been withholding those payments since 1445, yet obtained a final settlement in 1452 that, while falling well short of total abolition, reduced them by as much as a third. In securing that agreement a great nobleman was the mediator; leading Gloucestershire gentry were among the witnesses; at the abbess's cost – much higher, in the event, than the rents she preserved – her bondmen enjoyed a fair hearing.[32] Over a century later it would be a patriotic Englishman's comfortable boast, in which all his countrymen would surely have concurred, that "as for slaves and bondmen, we have none; nay, such is the privilege of our country by the especial grace of God and bounty of our princes that if any come hither from other realms, so soon as they set foot on land they become so free of condition as their masters".[33] Yet in the early 1450s, when Cheltenham's rent-objectors won their right to be heard, they were still of a generation whose grandfathers had personally witnessed the brutal suppression of the English Rising of 1381, when "many were taken and hanged in London and elsewhere", when the king's army set out to "remove the entire race of Kentishmen and Jutes from the land of the living", and when "the land grew silent at the sight of the justices, and the people trembled [at their approach]".[34]

That last tragic image was Thomas Walsingham's. However, it was the "inimitably mendacious" Jean Froissart, not present himself during any part of the Rising, who wove the best account of "these terrible troubles [that] originated in England from a strange circumstance and a trivial cause". In narrating the Revolt's collapse Froissart expertly sets his scene with a single dramatic tale of seven exemplary hangings in the big Kentish village of Ospringe, south of Faversham; and "in like manner as the king did at Ospringe, he did at Canterbury, at Sandwich, at Yarmouth, at Orwell . . . and in all other places of his realm, where any rebellion had been; and there were hanged and beheaded more than fifteen hundred".[35] Froissart's Ospringe narrative is almost certainly a fiction, his figures are pure guesswork, and his selection of the main trouble-spots has no obvious logic, for his knowledge of England's geography was elementary. But if those separate risings in Kent (Canterbury and Sandwich), in Norfolk (Yarmouth) and in Cambridgeshire (Orwell) were linked by very little, one obvious common factor was the pestilence. At Canterbury, for example, government before

47. Punishment by hanging: from a French manuscript of the late fourteenth or early fifteenth century. *The Bodleian Library, Oxford: MS Douce 332, fol. 178r.*

the plague had long been the preserve of a burghal elite, secure and wealthy, fully capable of standing up to its monk–landowners. But after 1349 that traditional stability was permanently upset by heavy plague mortalities in every class and by a replacement population of disaffected rustic immigrants, bringing "discontinuities and confusion at all levels".[36] In the absence of the buffer of an old elite, resentment focused in Canterbury on a new official class in which public duties and private gain were indistinguishable. Always too closely identified with an increasingly unpopular government, Canterbury's post-plague leaders became partisan apologists for the military's lacklustre performance in the war with France; they were the compromised enforcers of one-sided labour laws, favouring only landowners and urban employers like themselves; worst of all, they were the collectors for the crown of those hugely unpopular poll taxes and other "exceptionally severe" subsidies that, "lightly conceded in parliaments and extortionately levied from the poor people", caused the commons to rise in 1381.[37]

While it is probably true, as the same source claimed, that "these subsidies did nothing for the profit of the kingdom but were spent badly and deceitfully to the great impoverishment of the commons", the causes of social tension were more often local, provoked particularly by abuses of power. One northern community which felt the strain was the market town of

Beverley, in east Yorkshire. And there the struggle continued for more than a year from May 1381, causing Beverley's constitution to be overturned and re-written in newly populist terms.[38] Egalitarianism and the politics of envy must also have played their part in Beverley's unusually long-drawn-out rising, for unacceptable divisions had grown in the borough between the *menes comunes* (*communitas*), who aspired to power, and the *bones gents* (*probi homines*), who monopolized it. Yet what was happening concurrently at Kingston upon Hull, just down the road to the south, is surely proof enough that fair and equitable government, more than any other single issue, was the primary objective of the rebels. Hull almost entirely escaped the troubles of 1381, not because the community lacked social tensions of its own but because it had already had the good sense to come to terms with them. Less than two years before, at Michaelmas 1379, a new constitution had been agreed at Hull by *toute la commonalte* of the borough. Addressing class rivalry in the community, it provided for a new measure of popular control of the executive through the annual election of eight burgesses (none to be re-elected within three years) to supervise its principal officers: its chamberlains, bailiffs and mayor.[39] Although not a solution ever likely to endure, for it required wholly unrealistic levels of popular participation in borough government, Hull's reform was nevertheless a timely acknowledgement of the legitimate grievances of the *plebs*, especially important in the immediate run-up to the Great Revolt, when feelings of injustice and alienation flowed most strongly.

Some part of Hull's constitution survived sufficiently intact to keep peace in the borough for many decades. However, it was plague again, by cutting numbers in every town, that was the rock on which populism foundered. In 1438 the young Henry VI was to advise his Lincoln subjects that they must select their mayors and sheriffs not from the *mediocres* (the middling persons) of their city but from "the more worthy, more powerful, more good and true, more discreet and more sufficient, and more befitting to occupy and exercise" such offices.[40] Yet the *probi homines* of all but the largest boroughs in post-plague England were scarcely more numerous, when it came to such selections, than the titles of honour which described them. In towns like Beverley, and even at Hull before too long, the old governing families were soon back in power. And everywhere it was a steadily shrinking pool of eligible talent that caused repeated office-holding within a very small class and the concentration of responsibilities in fewer hands.[41] More dangerously, for there is nothing necessarily undesirable in the rule of the "more discreet and more sufficient",[42] burgess status was seriously undermined as its burdens increased beyond the compensating limits of its attractions. When called upon in 1390 to take up a burgess-ship of the failing port of Grimsby, Peter Gotson gave the robust reply that he would neither agree to become a burgess nor cease trading in the borough, whatever penalties that contumacy might bring upon him. For an outsider such as Gotson, in complete contrast to earlier times, the burgess-ship was no longer worth its price. So indeed it must have seemed to many other local people, for applications for Grimsby's freedom kept on falling.[43]

Gotson's decision in 1390, so far as we can tell, was made on financial grounds alone; his exclusion from public office was self-imposed. Sixty years later, when the men of Kent and Sussex rose again in open rebellion, the real reasons for their unhappiness were a contemporary currency crisis and persisting labour shortages, even if their demands remained overtly political.[44] In mid-fifteenth-century England, as Jack Cade's rebellion showed, popular outrage at social injustices was still present. However, where there was sufficient work and land for all, there were also more opportunities for negotiated settlement, so that violence was no longer the only option of the disaffected and talking more often took its place. In the countryside, Cade's rebellion of 1450 was followed by further rent losses on the great estates, and by the waiving of customary payments.[45] In the towns, consensual oligarchies had already re-emerged some decades before, supported by easier burgess entry terms and higher wages.[46] Prosperous Norwich had been among the few major cities in 1381 where the rebels had failed to make converts. And while Norwich itself faced political crises of its own in the 1430s and 1440s, resort to violence, even then, was very limited. In practice, Norwich's citizens soon reverted to old methods of conflict-management: by informal negotiations between the principals in a dispute, by gild-sponsored mediation between business associates, or by the arbitration of outsiders as last resort.[47]

"The law is ended as folk are friended" was a popular contemporary adage.[48] And much the best way to influence that law was to keep it within the community. Nothing demonstrates this better than the costly lengths to which even a medium-sized town like fifteenth-century Southampton would take its crusade to widen the cognizance of its courts. Right at the beginning of the century in 1401, Southampton was among the first English boroughs to obtain the right to appoint its own justices of the peace. Then followed a pioneering incorporation in 1445, with county borough status just two years later. From 1461 a recorder ("a certain man skilled in the law") would be appointed to assist Southampton's JPs. And during the next two decades the borough court's right to retain all fines for the benefit of the town was at first assumed, then queried by the Exchequer, and eventually confirmed by Edward IV in 1481, "without account of rendering any thing to us or our heirs, and without demand, molestation or impediment of us or our heirs, of the justices, escheators, sheriffs, or of any other officers, or servants of us or our heirs whatsoever".[49]

It had taken Southampton eight decades to get this far. However, well before that last concession, no outsider was safe in Southampton's courts without the favour of the recorder and the backing of "great acquaintance" in the borough.[50] Such partisan justice was the downside everywhere of the apparent torpor of the English common law. The upside was new openings for conflict-resolution, as peace-keeping devolved to the localities. The Black Death, all agree, was hugely influential in creating the circumstances in which unruly knights – the poachers rather than the gamekeepers of pre-plague society – could be converted into law-abiding gentry.[51] And what contributed most particularly to that critical transformation was a mutual concern with property protection, bolstered by frequent service on commissions of the peace. After the Black Death, gentry peace-keepers in the country, like the new men of the towns, had at first made themselves deeply unpopular in their roles as labour-law enforcers and tax collectors. But from being the chief fomenters of pre-Revolt dissent, they were to assume over the next half-century another complexion altogether as the self-interested architects of good order. By the end of the Middle Ages, wealthy gentry who would once have settled happily to stay off the peace commissions would feel insulted if not invited to be on them.[52]

Paradoxically, fifteenth-century England's gradual abandonment of violence as first resort was the result not of good laws but of bad. It may well be that the inadequacies of the common law have since attracted too much attention. And certainly, in one informed view, greater credit should now be given to the royal courts for their enabling role in setting the scene for private arbitrations, which they then fully supported and confirmed.[53] Yet the fact remains that so cumbersome and unreliable had the common law become by 1400 that almost any alternative was preferable. It was this lack of an effective central system that caused many late-medieval townspeople to accept without complaint the loaded justice of their mayoral courts and gild assemblies. In the countryside also, the gentry ruled unchallenged, for where landowner JPs spent so much of their time in protecting their own property in the name of the law, they lost any taste they might once have had for side-stepping legal processes or undermining them. Individual blue-blooded law-breakers, intimidating by force of arms, remained common enough in early-fifteenth-century England, one of the most notorious being Sir Richard Stanhope, a Nottinghamshire knight, described on his apprehension as "*un de les plus puissant et riotous persons du dit Countee*".[54] Nor would there be any shortage of catastrophic family rivalries, the result almost always of those diabolical inheritance practices that left too much to the widow and nothing of any substance to younger sons. There were the Stanhope and Zouche disorders of the 1410s, the long and bitter Berkeley lawsuit of 1417–39, the Heriz and Ampthill disputes (Cromwell *v.* Pierpoint and Holland) of the 1440s and 1450s, the Grey and Willoughby confrontations of the late 1480s and many more.[55] But only occasionally was this land-owner-led violence both spontaneous and unpremeditated. More often calculated and short-term, its ultimate objective would be a peaceable solution, seeing arbitration as the end of the road.[56]

Already in general use well before the Black Death, arbitration nevertheless increased greatly in popularity during the later Middle Ages, when especially well suited to the huge number of intra-family disputes raised by irreversible entails and outsize jointures.[57] It was a procedure that had many advantages. Arbitration was not adversarial, as was (and is) the common law. It encouraged swift decisions and held down costs by forbidding the delaying tactics so usual in the courts and by excluding further appeal. It allowed the disputing parties to decide their own "loveday", appointing arbitrators acceptable to both. Most of all, it avoided the obligatory narrow vision of an imposed royal judge, and by permitting a grievance to be seen in its entirety was more likely to arrive at its source.[58] So far, so good; and the triumph of "love" over "law" was not uncommon.[59] But where great men and their affinities still controlled the localities, bullying and intimidation were just as likely to influence the preliminaries to arbitration as to bring about corrupt proceedings in the courts. Worse, if the more powerful party in an arbitration refused to abide by a decision, the other's only resort was to those very courts which both had laboured so strenuously to avoid.

Friends in high places most often prompted that refusal. And among the perceived advantages of membership of a noble affinity was a degree of protection in the courts. Even so, it was usually in the magnate's interest to maintain law and order, so that the discipline of his affinity was very often translated into efficient law-keeping on the ground.[60] Good order depends on consensus. And that consensus in late-medieval England was always more likely to obtain within a group (whatever its rationale) than between different classes or across interests. Those who gained least from "love" were, of course, the destitute. Yet it was a mid-century mayor of Exeter, John Shillingford – neither poor nor friendless – who once complained that his opponents at Chancery, the cathedral clergy of his city, had "spatte out the uttmyst and worste venym that they cowde seye or thynke by me", and "wolde have don werce yf they cowde".[61] Resort to sleaze was in practice quite unnecessary, for the cathedral already had a good case; but when those same clergy triumphed a year later, it was less the force of their arguments that had won the day than their skill in attracting friendly arbitrators.[62]

One of those arbitrators was the fractious Thomas Courtenay, Earl of Devon (d.1458), whose family's suicidal performance in the Wars of the Roses is a paradigm of late-medieval aristocratic collapse. However, civil war was the exception in this century, affecting few outside Courtenay's class. And for the rest in post-Revolt England, if ever required to choose between the egalitarian rhetoric of a peasant rebel of 1381 (or 1450) and the self-attentive peace-keeping of a fifteenth-century gentleman JP, most would surely have settled for the latter. They would have done so with wide-open eyes. "Laws are like lop-webs [cobwebs]" runs the ancient proverb, "which take small flies and let great flies go."[63] Thus Solon the Athenian in the sixth century BC; thus the popular wisdom of fifteenth-century England; thus again the Anglo-Irish satirist, Jonathan Swift (d.1745); and so also only yesterday in Thatcher's Britain. "The thing that hath been, it is that which shall be . . . and there is no new thing under the sun." (Ecclesiastes i.9).

CHAPTER NINE

Architecture and the arts

A lways the first casualty of every recession is the building industry; and building in medieval England would never again be as extravagant as in the half-century preceding the Black Death. After the noble simplicity of thirteenth-century Early English, pre-plague Decorated got its name as a style from such vastly complex works as Exeter Cathedral, totally remodelled – in the least cost-conscious way – by five successive bishops: Walter Bronescombe (1258–80) and Peter Quinel (1280–91), Thomas Bitton (1291–1307), Walter Stapeldon (1307–27) and John Grandisson (1327–69). Of these probably the wealthiest was Walter Stapeldon, twice Treasurer of England, who personally found the funds for Exeter's great episcopal throne and much else. However, it is to the earlier Peter Quinel that the distinctive 16-shafted "Exeter pillar" is usually attributed, setting a standard of costly excellence for his successors.[1] What enabled all five bishops to invest so heavily in such works – only Grandisson ever claiming to be poor – was their long exposure to exceptional prosperity. For a century and more, rents had been rising and wages falling. There had been no lack of skilled labour, with the result that ambitious clerical patrons in every part of England, from Exeter (deep in the south-west) to Carlisle (on the remote Scottish border), had both the craftsmen and the revenues to support great projects. When the Black Death harvested the labour force in 1348–9, ushering in a new era of lower rents and higher wages, only the King could continue unaffected by it.

In those calamitous years William of Edington (d.1366) was both Bishop of Winchester and (like Stapeldon) Treasurer of England. And it is to Edington, in particular, that the credit belongs for the sound financial

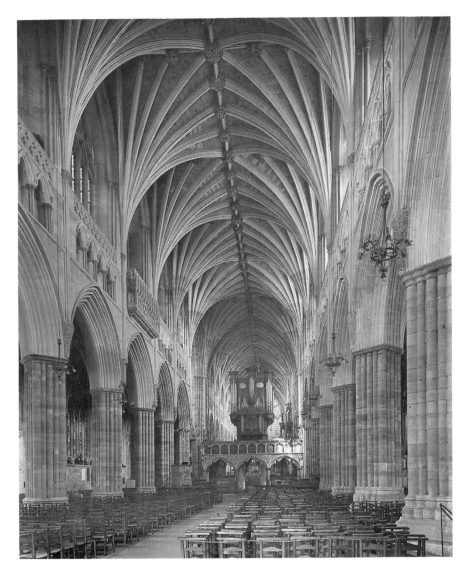

48. The English Decorated style culminated at Exeter Cathedral under the sponsorship of five wealthy bishops. In this east-facing view of the nave, Bishop Quinel's 16-shafted "Exeter pillars" show to full effect. *A. F. Kersting.*

management that enabled Edward III's government to survive intact the unprecedented collapse of normal revenues.[2] Edington, prominent in the royal service from the early 1340s, was already a rich man by 1348. And like all who could afford it including the King, he took the Black Death as an

49. William of Edington, Bishop of Winchester (1345–66), built this great church at his Wiltshire birthplace in the 1350s. He intended it originally to be a collegiate chantry, but had assigned it by 1358 to the Bonshommes – favourites of his patron, the Black Prince. Many of England's masons had either died of the plague or had been commandeered for Edward III's on-going works at Windsor Castle. Consequently, even a rich former Treasurer would have found recruitment difficult, and this may be one reason for the almost military austerity of Edington Church, in complete contrast to Exeter Cathedral. *A. F. Kersting.*

individual signal to make forward provision for his soul. Less than two years later, in March 1351, Edington began the first moves to found a collegiate chantry at the Wiltshire village of his birth, where a newly built church, financed by himself, was to be served by six chaplains and their warden. Then in 1358, "in order to free the chaplains from the cares and obligations of the secular life", he assigned his Edington chantry to a community of Bonshommes (*Boni Homines*), favourites of his patron the Black Prince. In that short time, work had evidently been pushed forward to some effect, for the brethren's church, which also served the parish, was dedicated in 1361.[3] It was a big and costly building, erected at the desire of a wealthy self-made prelate with no heirs to support and with less reason than most to count his pennies. Yet, in sharp contrast to the great majority of pre-plague church-rebuildings of comparable scale, post-plague Edington is memorably austere. Where, only a few years before, those churches had been richly decorated, multi-aisled and tall, with elegant pierced parapets and fine steeples, Edington was low of profile and heavily battlemented: more a fortress, on first appearance, than house of God.[4]

50. Patrington Church, Queen of Holderness, is arguably the best-conceived and most complete Decorated parish church of pre-plague England. Even so, work was severely disrupted here in 1349, with the result that the chancel's east window (right) is in the new style – Perpendicular – of some 50 years later, which is also when Patrington's tall steeple was finished off with its spire. *A. F. Kersting.*

Bishop Edington may have demanded this new look for some purpose of his own; and certainly the Bonshommes, when he invited them there, were not a wealthy order. However, a more likely explanation for the austerity of Edington's church is the acute contemporary shortage of skilled craftsmen of any kind – of masons and carpenters, tilers, plumbers and glaziers – to which Edward III's large-scale works at Windsor Castle had contributed.[5] Elsewhere it was that shortage, above all, which caused many building pro-grammes to be interrupted at the mid-century, while a few had to be aban-doned altogether. One such architectural casualty of the Black Death was the costly building campaign, almost at an end by 1349, at Patrington Church, in East Yorkshire. Patrington – the so-called Queen of Holderness, where Hedon Church (along the Humber shore) is the King – was the huge new parish church of a little market town at its most prosperous in the gen-eration before the pestilence. And Holderness itself, with Beverley to the north-west and Hedon just up-river, was well known at the time for its skilled masons. Yet neither the quality of Patrington's masons nor its rich friends at York – the archbishop was lord of the manor and York's precentor, Robert Thurgolts (*alias* Robert of Patrington), was a native son – could get work re-started on Patrington Church in 1350. For half a century from the Black Death, Patrington's fine steeple went without its spire. Only one of its new aisles had been vaulted by 1349, the others having to await the Vic-torians. Patrington's big Decorated chancel, among the best-equipped of its day, was eventually rounded off at the beginning of the fifteenth century with an east window that is unmistakably Perpendicular.[6]

Patrington, even so, was the lucky one. Much less fortunate was Ashbourne Church, in Derbyshire, where a highly ambitious early-fourteenth-century campaign came to a full-stop in the 1350s. Other con-temporary building programmes, also in the central Midlands, continued apparently unaffected by the Black Death. There was the choir at Tideswell, for example, to the north of Ashbourne, and the collegiate church at Tamworth to the south.[7] Nor can it be said with absolute certainty that the plague was the cause of Ashbourne's troubles. Nevertheless, what is obvious is that a large-scale remodelling, begun in *c.* 1300 and clearly intended to include the whole church west of the chancel (already rebuilt some 60 years before), stopped short on the completion of the south aisle. By 1349 Ashbourne had acquired its great crossing tower, its big aisled transepts were in place and the remodelling of the nave had begun. But then work stopped completely, and what remains today is a church which, while still very

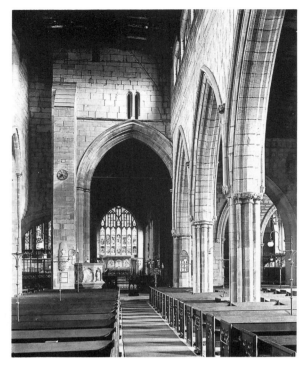

51. The mutilated interior of Ashbourne Church, in Derbyshire, is one of the best examples of an ambitious rebuilding programme which was almost certainly a casualty of the Black Death. Here a new chancel, crossing and transepts had been built before 1349, and a big new south aisle (right) had been added to the existing nave. Work stopped short at that point, so that the matching north aisle, although clearly intended, was never built. *RCHME Crown copyright.*

52. Here at Northborough (Cambridgeshire), the Delamere family's plan to rebuild the church entirely on a truly grand scale had got only as far as the big south transept (right) when the whole scheme had to be abandoned at the Black Death. *RCHME Crown copyright.*

53. Another grand rebuilding scheme which probably fell victim to the Black Death was started at Medbourne Church (Leicestershire) in about 1300, but had been abandoned half-complete well before attention switched to the west tower. Seen here from the south-west, Medbourne's tower is Perpendicular and post-plague. But the south aisle (centre) and the unusually long south transept (right) had both been completed in the pre-plague programme, there being no equivalent additions on the north. *A. F. Kersting.*

impressive, lacks its north aisle and is both seriously lop-sided and badly scarred. With no matching north arcade to hide the improvisation, a great buttress disfigures Ashbourne's crossing. A Perpendicular clerestory of the early sixteenth century, while successfully introducing a new light source, appears mean and ill-conceived in such a context.[8]

As memorably incomplete, although on a much smaller scale, is the Delamere Church at Northborough, on the Cambridgeshire–Lincolnshire border. Here a remodelling of the parish church in the early fourteenth century coincided with the building of a new manor-house just down the road. And while that rebuilding got no further than the south (mortuary) transept, it had clearly been intended to encompass the whole church, as the grandest of personal chantries.[9] That Delamere ambition failed comprehensively in 1349. Yet for many landowners and would-be patrons who survived the Black Death there were still some decades of comparative prosperity ahead , and such wholesale cancellations were the exception. Adjustment to plague mortalities took other forms. In north-west Essex, for example, there are two closely related churches that were extensively rebuilt at the mid-century. The earlier, at Stebbing, just pre-dates the Black Death; the later, at Great Bardfield, was built soon after it. Whether or not plague was the cause, Great Bardfield is much the smaller of the two parish churches, while yielding nothing in decorative detail to its companion. Both churches are equipped with the most elaborate of stone rood-screens, richly carved at the heads and clearly commissioned regardless of the cost.[10]

Great Bardfield's handsome rood-screen, its good south porch and generous clerestory, and the inventive and costly tracery of its nave windows are all believed to have been the gift of a very rich nobleman, Edmund de Mortimer (d.1381), third Earl of March. And certainly there was neither time nor place in post-plague England when the generosity of an individual donor – of Sir Hugh Calveley at Bunbury (Cheshire) in the 1380s, of Dame Elizabeth de Botreaux at North Cadbury (Somerset) in the 1420s, of John and Katharine Denston at Denston (Suffolk) in the 1470s, or of the clothiers John Barton and John Tame at Holme (Nottinghamshire) and Fairford (Gloucestershire) in the 1480s and 1490s respectively – might not lead to the complete rebuilding of a parish church. Meanwhile, already large urban churches could be expected to grow still bigger on the chantry-related generosity of their parish fraternities and on the accumulated benefactions of local testators. The wholly different experience of two Yorkshire parish churches, urban Thirsk and rural Wharram Percy, distinguishes very clearly who were the winners in fifteenth-century England and who the losers. Thirsk, the only church of a thriving market town, probably owed its lavish rebuilding to the start-up funding of Robert of Thirsk (d.1419), a wealthy cleric and royal official. Robert founded his birthplace chantry in 1415, dedicating it to St Anne, mother of the Blessed Virgin Mary. Work continued on Thirsk Church well into the 1470s, when a big new chancel, in the same richly ornamental style as the rest, brought the long rebuilding programme to its end.[11] At Wharram Percy, in contrast, high on the East Yorkshire Wolds, a little village church which had grown steadily larger during the population expansion of the late twelfth and thirteenth centuries reached its maximum extent in about 1300, when the chancel was rebuilt for a second time. As one of the upland settlements most vulnerable to recession, Wharram had been experiencing difficulties even before the Black Death. However, it survived another century before emptying out com-

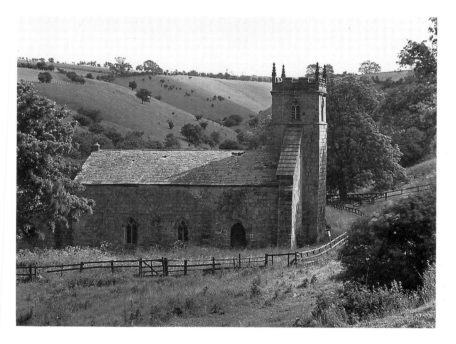

54. Wharram Percy Church grew and contracted with its village (up the slope on the right). Both had reached maximum extent in about 1300, and they suffered together in the second half of the fifteenth century, when the settlement was abandoned and its fields enclosed. Here the line of an earlier arcade can just be made out against the nave wall, with two windows from the former north aisle (gone by 1550) re-used in the blocked openings. The last service was held at Wharram in 1949, and the west tower, still intact when this photograph was taken, has since collapsed. *RCHME Crown copyright.*

pletely, losing tenants rapidly from the 1450s, when desertion was followed by enclosure. Wharram Church shrank along with its village. Before 1550 both aisles had been lost. The over-large chancel, collapsing soon afterwards, was never rebuilt on that scale.[12]

Village churches like Wharram Percy's, which acquired their aisles as the population grew and then lost them again as numbers fell, have some value as demographic barometers.[13] But that testimony can often be deceptive. The great rural church at Salle (Norfolk), for example, was entirely rebuilt in the fifteenth century, yet stands all alone in empty fields. And other equally solitary parish churches, many of them still in use, plainly owed their survival chiefly to commemorative purposes. Those purposes, clearly, had more to do with apprehensions of Purgatory than with plague. Yet it was the Black Death that had transformed the agenda. At Kersey (Suffolk), a semi-

55. Salle Church (Norfolk), all alone in its fields, is a monument to the strength of fifteenth-century piety, attracting almost unlimited building funds from a scattered rural community. Note in particular the costly pair of two-storeyed porches, each with its crenellated stair turret. The big transeptal chapels at the east end of the nave are also a rare feature, while both the west tower and the chancel (bottom) have been conceived on a scale more usually seen only at the most important urban churches of the period. *Norfolk Air Photographs Library: photo Derek A. Edwards.*

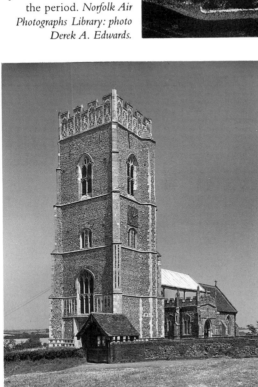

56. This monumental west tower at Kersey (Suffolk) was built in the fifteenth century, long after a pre-plague scheme to extend the church had been abandoned with only the north aisle complete. Priorities changed when Kersey's congregation was reduced, and any plan to build a matching south aisle had clearly been set aside by the time the expensive double-length south porch (right) was added in its place. *A. F. Kersting.*

industrial village which gave its name to a particular English cloth, earning money was always less of a problem than deciding how to spend it. And Kersey's rich weavers, when the Black Death came, were in the process of enlarging their parish church. As part of that programme, a new north aisle had been added in the 1330s. However, the arcade of that aisle, although almost complete, was then left unfinished, and an intended south aisle was never built. What had changed was not resources but priorities. No longer obliged to find more space for new worshippers, Kersey's testators left their money instead to what were essentially personal memorials. It was probably individual donors who financed Kersey's two handsome porches. A fine new roof was provided in the fifteenth century. From the 1430s if not before, money was being contributed, in legacies and other gifts, to the raising of that prodigy west tower which, as eventually completed in 1481, still commands the Suffolk countryside for miles around.[14]

No medieval monuments of note survive at Kersey today. However, at isolated Salle commemorative brasses still crowd the huge church, revealing the purpose of its builders. It was Thomas Rose (d.1441) and Thomas Brigg (d.1444) who, in just a few years, financed the building of Salle's north and south transepts. Thomas Boleyn, Giles Cook and Richard Dalling were among other early donors, while it was the Luces in the 1480s who, towards the end of Salle's rebuilding, gave their church its handsome Seven Sacraments font. That font, like so many other church furnishings in this plague-

57. The Seven Sacraments font which Thomas and Agnes Luce contributed to the furnishings of the new church at Salle, and which carries their "*orate pro* [pray for]. . . ." inscription. *RCHME Crown copyright.*

and purgatory-alert century, carries a familiar invocation: "Pray for the souls of Thomas Luce and [Agnes] his wife, and Robert their son chaplain, and those for whom they are bound to pray, who caused this font to be made."[15]

"Pray especially (*specialiter*) for the soul of Arthur Vernon" insists the brass of a gentleman-priest of Tong, elevating his own needs above the rest.[16] Arthur (d.1517) lies among his Shropshire kin in the Vernon Chapel, newly built in the most favoured location adjoining the chancel of this already large church. And it was not at all uncommon for prominent gentry families like the Vernons to monopolize a parish church for their memorials. The initial cost of such investments could be huge; but so also were the anticipated returns. On the big Lady Chapel added by John Clopton to Long Melford Church (Suffolk), to which it was a costly and unnecessary extension, there is a long invocation on behalf of an entire company of souls:

> Pray for the soul of John Hill, and for the soul of John Clopton Esquire, and pray for the soul of Richard Loveday, butler with John Clopton, of whose goods this Chapel is embattled by his executors. Pray for the souls of William Clopton Esquire, Margery and Margery his wives and for all their parents and children, and for the

58. Long Melford Church (Suffolk) already had a big chancel when John Clopton (d.1497) added the huge Lady Chapel (right) which blocks most of the original east window. Such chapels, while often attached to cathedral and monastic churches from an early date, were highly exceptional at parish churches. *A. F. Kersting.*

soul of Alice Clopton, and for John Clopton and for all his children and for all the souls that the said John is bound to pray for, which did this chapel new repair anno domini mcccclxxxxvi. *Christ' sit testis* . . . Let Christ be my witness that I have not exhibited these things in order that I may win praise, but so that the Spirit may be remembered.[17]

With much the same purpose, although not as elegantly expressed, the Peytons of Isleham gave their Cambridgeshire church its unusually tall clerestory, with the splendidly carpentered roof which still carries Christopher Peyton's *orate pro* inscription: "Pray for the good prosperity of Christopher Peyton and Elizabeth his wife and for the soul of Thomas Peyton esquire and Margaret his wife, father and mother of the said Christopher Peyton . . . [etc.]". Completed in 1495, just the year before John Clopton's Lady Chapel, Christopher Peyton's new roof had prominent angel supporters, each carrying an emblem of the Passion: a scourge, a crown of thorns, three nails and a mallet, pincers, a sponge and a spear.[18] That Crucifixion imagery was highly fashionable in Peyton's day, and was everywhere repeated on all kinds of church furnishings, along with other familiar images of growing cults.

59. When Isleham Church (Cambridgeshire) was rebuilt towards the end of the fifteenth century, the work was largely financed by a local gentry family, the Peytons. Christopher Peyton's expensive roof, decorated with angel supporters carrying symbols of the Passion, is inscribed and dated 1495.
A. F. Kersting.

60. A late-fourteenth-century glass panel from a Passion Cycle window, now at All Saints Pavement (York) but originally from the church of St Saviour. With the cross and the crown of thorns hanging on it, the symbols include the robe, the scourges, the three nails and hammer, the sponge, the spear, the pincers, the dice, etc. The short horizontal lines with three or four downstrokes may symbolize Christ's wounds. *RCHME Crown copyright.*

Instruments of the Passion, for example, occur again on a late-fourteenth-century window panel now at All Saints, Pavement (York) and on a bench-end at Trent Church (Dorset) of *c.* 1500; while the exquisite bench-end imagery of North Cadbury Church (Somerset), completed in 1538 just before the Reformation, includes a *Five Wounds of Christ* and a *Virgin and Child*, along with a *St Margaret of Antioch*, that robust and improbable Early Christian martyr whose cult as all-purpose intercessor flourished again in late-medieval England, with particular reference to childbirth.[19] Almost contemporary is the font at Crowcombe (Somerset), where a kneeling donor is accompanied by *Christ Showing His Wounds* and *St Anne Teaching the Virgin to Read.*[20] And it was the older-established Sacrament imagery, still as powerful as ever, that continued to inspire the craftsmen—sculptors of East Anglia's distinctive Seven Sacrament fonts, of which probably the best preserved are the Norfolk fonts at Sloley and Seething, where a *Baptism of Our Lord* completes each octagon, accompanying seven miniature tableaux of Baptism and Confirmation, Matrimony and Ordination, Penance, Mass and Extreme Unction.[21]

At Seething again, a damaged but still recognizable fourteenth-century *Life of Christ* cycle shares the church walls with a fragmentary *Three Living*

61. The bowl of a fifteenth-century Seven Sacraments font at Sloley (Norfolk), which was one of the few fonts of this distinctive East Anglian class to have escaped mutilation by Protestant reformers. *A. F. Kersting.*

and Three Dead. "As you are now," the Dead warn the Living in this ancient legend, "so once were we. As we are now, so shall ye be." Both subjects are commonly found in pre-plague paintings. Yet for each also there was to be a change of emphasis following the Black Death, hastened by the plague while not created by it. Late-medieval treatments of the *Three Living and Three Dead* are both more plentiful than before the pestilence and more shocking. They are joined also in the fifteenth century by new *memento mori* subjects – the shroud brass, the cadaver effigy, and the *Dance of Death* – treated so realistically in many cases that they must at least imply more than usual familiarity with death's corruption. Even that old and comforting history of the *Life and Miracles of Our Lord* had begun to carry a new message before 1500, hijacked by church rebuilders for intercession. It is the Virgin Mary, dedicatee of Fairford Church (Gloucestershire) and the chosen intercessor of its rebuilders, John and Edmund Tame, who appears in almost every episode of the great *Life of Christ* cycle that fills Fairford's windows, attending even such occasions as the Ascension and the Pentecost at which there is no reason to suppose that she was present. Mary takes her customary place in the big *Crucifixion* window above Fairford's altar, and is there again in the spectacular *Last Judgement* at the far end of the church which still catches the westering sun. John Tame died in 1500, before any of those windows were installed. Yet in Sir Edmund Tame's *Last Judgement,* father and

151

62. This big east window of the Corpus Christi Chapel at Fairford (Goucestershire) is one of the best preserved in John Tame's church. While the centre panel is a *Transfiguration* in which Mary does not appear, she is there on the left (where Christ shows her his Wounds) and again on the right (where he blesses the Three Marys). As installed by Sir Edmund Tame in his father's new church, the glass is more continental than English in style, and is probably Flemish work of the early sixteenth century. *RCHME Crown copyright*.

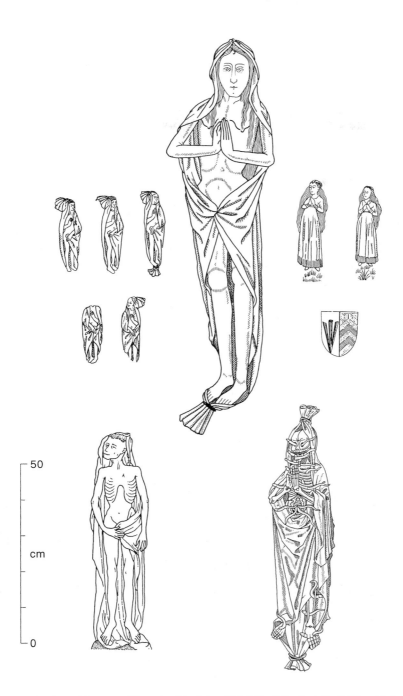

63. The shroud brasses of Tomesine Tendring (d.1485) of Yoxford (Suffolk), with her seven children, five also in shrouds; of John Brigg (d.1454) of Salle (Norfolk); and of Ralph Hamsterley (d.1518) of Oddington (Oxfordshire). Of these, Ralph Hamsterley's cadaver, consumed by worms, is much the most terrible (bottom right). It is accompanied by a Latin inscription which reads in free translation: "Here I am given to worms, and thus I try to show that, as I am laid here, so all honour is laid down." The three brasses have been drawn to the same scale. *University of Southampton Cartographic Unit.*

153

son must surely have stood among the Blessed on the right-hand side of Christ the Judge, their place secured there by huge investment in Fairford Church and by the prayers of the faithful who, for five centuries now, have heeded the admonition on John Tame's tomb: "For Jesus love pray for me. I may not pray, now pray ye, with a *pater noster* and an *ave*, that my paynys relessid may be."[22]

It was the much older mortality reminder of the *Three Living and Three Dead* that John Brigg (d.1454) chose for his shroud brass at Salle Church: "So frendis fre whatever ye be: pray for me y yow pray./As ye me se in soche degre: so schall ye be a nothir day."[23] And that identical ancient warning is included in the long verse inscription – either adapted from an epitaph by John Lydgate, the Bury poet, or the work of the subject himself – on John Baret's realistic cadaver monument in the big civic church of St Mary, Bury St Edmunds:

> Wrappid in a selure [cloth] as a ful rewli wrecche
> No more of al myn good[s] to me ward wil strecche
> From erthe I kam and on to erthe I am browht
> This is my nature, for of erthe I was wrowht;
> Thus erthe on to erthe to gedir now is knet
> So endethe each creature Q'd John Baret
> Qwerfor ye pepil in weye of charite
> Wt yor good prayeris I prey yu help me
> For lych as I am right so schal ye all be
> Now God on my sowle have m'cy & pite. Amen.[24]

John Baret died in 1467. And across his stone cadaver is that almost equally familiar *Mirror of Mortality* reminder: "He that wil sadly beholde one with his ie/ May se hys owyn merowr and lerne for to die." It was excellent advice to which Baret himself, the possessor of his own copy of *Disce Mori* (Learn to Die), had obviously paid the closest attention. Baret's long last testament, in which nothing whatever was left to chance, was drafted at least four years before his death. He was evidently a Marian through and through. But although the founder of a well-endowed chantry in the Virgin's name and the purchaser of multiple masses in her honour, Baret was a businessman also, determined to get a good return from his investment. In lieu of rent for the lodgings provided with his chaplaincy, Baret's "Seynt Marie preest" was "to prey for my soule at every meel, mete, or sopeer, and yif he gynne gracys

64. Well before John Baret died in 1467 he had probably seen and approved this cadaver monument to himself at St Mary's Church, Bury St Edmunds, for he had made every other preparation for death. In the remarkable will Baret drew up at Bury in September 1463 he had already made it clear that his monument should carry a disclaimer (now lost) of any wish for personal glory; rather, its sole purpose was "that the [Holy] Spirit should be remembered". Another of Baret's wishes, still inscribed on his monument, was that everyone who saw it "may see his own mirror and learn for to die". *University of Southampton Cartographic Unit.*

and sey *De profundis*, he to reherse my name, John Baret, opynly, that they that here it may sey, *God have mercy on his soule*, wiche greetly may releve me with heer devout preyours".[25]

Baret was no ordinary Bury burgess. He was grazier and clothier, banker and country gentleman, civic leader and ecclesiastical official.[26] His views are hardly likely to have been representative. Yet Baret's stand in religion was less out in front of the new beliefs than at their cutting edge. Baret's cadaver monument, soon to be repeated by others in his class, was one of the earliest civilian examples of a new sepulchral fashion still rare in the nobility and limited for the most part to wealthy churchmen. He could appreciate a good sermon, like many of his friends, but was more than usually well informed on new devotions:

Item I wyll that Maister Thomas Harlowe sey the sermon at my interment, if he wochesaft, and he to have vj*s* viij*d* to prey for me. And if he may not do it, be his avyce anothir to be chose at Cambridge to make the sermon and to have ye seid nobill and all heer

costes payd fore . . . Item I wille have at myn interment at my
diryge and messe v. men clade in blak in wurshippe of Jesus v.
woundys and v. wommen clad in whith in wurshippe of our lady's
fyve joyes, eche of them holdyng a torche of clene vexe . . . [etc.][27]

65. The sumptuous full-height wall-monument to Thomas Lord Morley
(d.1435), in the chancel of Hingham Church (Norfolk), is unrivalled in
its class, illustrating the strong attraction of competitive display to monument builders of the mid-fifteenth century. *A. F. Kersting.*

Baret's cadaver tomb at Bury, like John Brigg's brass at Salle, was more homily on false pride than plague reminder: "Miserable one, what reason have you to be proud? Soon you will be as we / a fetid cadaver, food for worms."[28] Quite so. The opposite of such memorials was the increasingly competitive display of many mid-century aristocratic monuments: of Thomas Lord Morley's great wall-tomb at Hingham (Norfolk); of the richly sculptured tomb-chest of the Grays of Chillingham (Northumberland); or of Earl Richard's tomb and effigy at Warwick Church, of such high quality and cost that it took many years in the making.[29] Richard Beauchamp (d. 1439) was a hero of chivalry: a champion of English arms in France. He is shown accordingly in traditional military fashion, clad in the full plate armour of his wars. In contrast Isabella, his countess, who died soon afterwards, had more freedom to establish her own death-style. Daughter of one earl and widow of another, Isabella le Despenser was already a wealthy heiress when she married Richard of Warwick. And she desired to be buried not at Warwick by

66. In this commemorative miniature from an early sixteenth-century benefactors' book of Tewkesbury Abbey, Isabella le Despenser, Countess of Warwick, kneels in prayer before a *Virgin and Child*. It had been Countess Isabella's desire that although her monument should carry the family heraldry (as here), her effigy must "be made all naked . . . myn here cast bakwardys", as was already the new convention of the day.
The Bodleian Library, Oxford: MS Top. Glouc. d. 2., fol. 27r.

Richard's side but among her own Despenser dead at Tewkesbury Abbey. Isabella began her instructions conventionally enough: "At my hede, Mary Mawdelen leyng my handes a-crosse, and seynt John the Evangelyst on the ryght syde of my hede; and on the left syde, Seynt Anton, and at my fete a skochen of myn armes departyd [impaled] with my lordys, and ij greffons to bere hit uppe; and all a-bowt my tumbe, to be made pore men and wemen in theire pore array, with their bedys in their handes . . . [but] *my Image to be made all naked, and no thyng on my hede but myn here cast bakwardys.*"[30]

Isabella's chantry chapel in the monks' choir at Tewkesbury, intended originally for her first husband, Richard, Earl of Worcester (d.1420), is still there. But her cadaver effigy has gone, and its closest parallel today is probably the shrouded figure at Ewelme Church, in Oxfordshire, at the base of Alice Chaucer's huge memorial.[31] Alice, the Chaucer heiress, had brought Ewelme to her second husband, William de la Pole (d.1450), Duke of Suffolk. Jointly, they founded a college there. And when Alice herself died in 1475 she was of such ripe age that, like Isabella, she had prepared every detail of her departure. In neither case, accordingly, did the cadaver effigy have

67. The cadaver sculpture of Sir John Golafre (d.1442), below his armoured effigy at Fyfield Church, is one of the more realistic products of this macabre late-medieval tradition. *A. F. Kersting.*

anything to do with sudden death. But the association of such effigies with unsecured death by plague was by no means lost on all contemporaries. Thus it was specifically in a "ceson of huge mortality / Of sondre disseses [and] pestilence" that the poet–author of the homiletic *Disputacione betwyx the Body and Wormes* (*c.*1440) entered a church where he saw the newly made tomb of a young noblewoman, "ful freschly forgyd, depycte, and depynte". The *Disputacione* opens with a rough ink-sketch of that tomb – fashionably

68. In this drawing, which precedes the mid-fifteenth-century *Disputacione betwyx the Body and Wormes*, a fashionably dressed young noblewoman – probably a plague victim – lies in effigy on her tomb-chest, which has been raised to show her shrouded cadaver in the coffin below, infested with worms and other creatures. *By permission of the British Library: Add. MS 37049, fol. 32v.*

dressed effigy above, worm-infested cadaver below – accompanied by this epitaph:

> Take hede unto my fygure here abowve
> And se how symtyme I was fresche and gay
> Now turned to wormes mete and corrupcone
> Bot fowle erth and stynkyng slyme and clay
> Attend therfore to this disputacione written here . . .
> To se what thou art and here aftyr sal be.

Then follows a dialogue in which Worms reason with petulant Body that far from consuming "with ane insaciabylle and gredy appetyte" Body's once fresh figure, it was their unpleasant and selfless duty to devour her putrid carrion – "while that one of thi bones with other wil hange" – as "we hafe to do / With alle that wer myghty [like yourself]".[32]

The same egalitarian message of Death's contempt for rank and wealth was carried far and wide throughout late-medieval Europe by that ever-green morality, the *Dance of Death*. "What availeth gold richesse or pearle?", wails the Empress in John Lydgate's translation of the *Dance*, "Or what availeth highe blood or Gentylnesse? / Or what availeth freshnesse or beaute? / Or what is worth highe powre or strangenesse? / Deth seith chekmat to al sich veyn noblesse."[33] Death says checkmate also to a wilting Bishop in the single *Dance of Death* panel which survives in a window at St Andrew's, Norwich.[34] And the populist's theme of Death as Leveller was taken up everywhere in fifteenth-century art, from the grand public spectacles of entire *Dances of Death* at the Holy Innocents (Paris), at La Chaise-Dieu (Auvergne), or nearer home in the cloister at St Paul's (London), to the individual *Ymage of Deth* roundels placed in the windows of Stanford on Avon Church (Northamptonshire) on the instructions of Henry Williams (d.1501), late vicar. Each roundel, Williams had prescribed in his will the year before, should show "my ymage knelying in ytt and the ymage of deth shotyng at me . . . theys to be done in smalle quarells of as gude glasse as can be goten".[35]

Henry Williams, meeting Death head-on, makes a sturdy figure. A lawyer as well as a priest, Williams was one of the fortunate few – John Barton of Holme (d.1491) was another, and Thomas Tropnell of Great Chalfield (d.1488) a third – so well tuned to their century as to seem immune from the "bludgeonings of chance". Tropnell, certainly, enjoyed a very long life,

69. Death checkmates a bishop in this panel from a big late-fifteenth-century *Dance of Death* window at St Andrew's Church (Norwich), the rest of which has been lost. *RCHME Crown copyright.*

turning successfully to the law in his later years, when he settled into his fine Wiltshire manor-house. Built in the 1470s, Tropnell's house nestles against Great Chalfield Church, which his successors may since have found a little burdensome. But for Tropnell himself the situation was ideal, for he made of

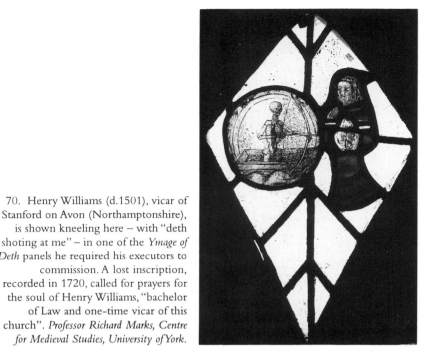

70. Henry Williams (d.1501), vicar of Stanford on Avon (Northamptonshire), is shown kneeling here – with "deth shoting at me" – in one of the *Ymage of Deth* panels he required his executors to commission. A lost inscription, recorded in 1720, called for prayers for the soul of Henry Williams, "bachelor of Law and one-time vicar of this church". *Professor Richard Marks, Centre for Medieval Studies, University of York.*

71. Thomas Tropnell (d.1488) built his comfortable stone house at Great Chalfield (Wiltshire) right next to the little parish church. Great Chalfield Manor, extensively restored at the beginning of this century, now belongs to the National Trust. *A. F. Kersting.*

72. John Barton (d.1491), a rich Nottinghamshire grazier and merchant of the Calais Staple, financed the rebuilding of Holme by Newark Church, of which he became the new "founder". Below the fully-clothed effigies of John Barton and his wife is the founder's naked cadaver, with a memorable inscription (probably Barton's own) calling upon his friends for their compassion. *RCHME Crown copyright*.

163

that church, by enlarging it greatly with a mortuary chapel of his own, an essential component of his death-plan.[36] Contemporaneously John Barton, a rich Nottinghamshire grazier, almost entirely rebuilt his own parish church at Holme by Newark. "Pray for the soul of John Barton of Holme, merchant of the Staple of Calais, builder of this church, who died 1491, and for Isabella his wife," urges Barton's inscription in Holme's big east window, above the high altar. Then, in the position of greatest honour immediately south of that altar, the founder's double monument, with his single naked cadaver effigy in the cavity below, carries this more sympathetic invocation: "Pity me, you at least my friends, for the hand of the Lord has touched me."[37]

There was once a third inscription, in a window of Barton's manor-house, which read: "I thank God and ever shall / 'tis the sheepe hath payed for all." And he was right. But Barton's fortune would have been much smaller and his flocks greatly reduced had his fields still been crowded with folk. And in post-plague England, it was entrepreneurial graziers like himself who were the most obvious beneficiaries of depopulation.[38] The greatest losers, in contrast, were corporate landowners like the monks, and noblemen fared scarcely better. In a half-empty land where labour was unobtainable and tenants hard to find, the middle man came into his own. Lesser gentry and their lawyers, clothiers and ironmasters, weavers, butchers and yeomen farmers – all lived much better than they had ever lived before, leaving behind them a remarkable legacy of fine buildings.

Nowhere is there more surviving material evidence of the growing self-assurance of this comfortably off class than in the late-medieval farmhouses of the Weald of Kent. And it is a significant fact that it was only in the latter part of the fourteenth century – after the Black Death – that the non-gentry farmhouses of the central Kentish Weald first reached the size and quality that would ensure their survival until today.[39] A 50-year break in building activity then followed, probably reflecting a weaker market for the Weald's traditional agricultural products. However, building began again in Kent in the third quarter of the fifteenth century, and it was less than two decades after Jack Cade's revolt of 1450 that good-quality houses were rising everywhere in the mid-Kent parishes of Pluckley and Smarden, East Peckham, and the more northerly Borden, which had been among the rebels' principal recruiting grounds.[40] Chips off the same block as the dissidents of 1450, the independently minded yeomen builders of these solidly constructed, medium-sized farmhouses were able for the first time to fashion new life-

73. Watermill House, in Benenden (Kent), has been sympathetically restored and is now much as it was when first built in the late fifteenth century. A typical Wealden farmhouse, it was equipped with a full-height central hall with a two-storeyed chamber block at each end, jettied at first-floor level. These comfortable houses, although concentrated in Kent, were also built through much of south and central England, where they have continued to meet the needs of farming families.
RCHME Crown copyright.

74. Of the smaller Wealden houses, fifteenth-century Yardhurst, near Great Chart (Kent), is one of the most complete. Like Watermill House, it too had a central hall, two bays wide, with another chamber bay (again with jettied upper storey) at each end, under a big hipped roof. As often happened in houses of this plan, where the improvement could be made at small expense, Yardhurst's hall was floored-over in the mid-sixteenth century to create a big private chamber above; and this also is the date of the great chimney. While the windows of the former hall and its overlying great chamber are modern, those of the chambers to right and left retain much of their original late-medieval timber tracery. *RCHME Crown copyright.*

styles for themselves that differed hardly at all from those of their rentier neighbours, the parish gentry. Improbable though it may sound, nobody now needs look further than Pluckley or East Peckham for the making of rural England's middle class.

The men of Kent, it must be said, were not typical. They enjoyed ancient tenurial privileges unknown elsewhere, and were exceptionally well placed to profit from the rural industries – in cloth, in iron and eventually in glass – that were bringing new wealth to their region.[41] Yet the fact remains that moderate affluence of this kind was spreading everywhere through the ranks of underpopulated Middle England, and that one of its manifestations was better housing. The diagnostic Wealden house of Kent and East Sussex – with open hall in the middle and jettied chamber blocks at each end, all under the same hipped roof – may be found across the central and eastern Midlands, through southern East Anglia and along the south coast into Hampshire.[42] In Essex, big H-plan farmhouses – with crossing chamber blocks and central hall – were again quite common in the fifteenth century; while in West Yorkshire, the older-style aisled-hall farmhouses of Halifax and Upper Calderdale were of at least comparable size and importance.[43] In widely scattered regions – in Devon, in Suffolk, in Warwickshire and in the Home Counties – the "Great Rebuilding" of early-modern England was already under way as much as a century before the end of the Middle Ages.[44]

That there was a general rebuilding of fifteenth-century rural England is now widely acknowledged. However, what set it apart from all subsequent rebuildings was its conservatism. Elizabethan yeomen improvers, in Kent as elsewhere, would floor-over the open halls which they had begun to find too spacious for private living. Yet only two generations earlier, when their Wealden grandfathers were building for themselves, doing without a common hall had been unthinkable. Knowing no other plan than the linear chamber–hall–kitchen arrangement of the traditional English house, late-medieval builders were always more likely to adopt it.[45] But it must also be the case that many fifteenth-century yeomen's halls were overtly aspirational, targeting a gentry life-style – in which households were extended, privacy of low priority, and hospitality habitually generous – that had changed very little for generations. The Paper Mill at Benenden, while certainly one of the larger of the surviving Wealden houses, is nevertheless typical of many good-class Kentish farmhouses of the late fifteenth and early sixteenth centuries. Yet its stylish open hall, with one-time screens passage and triple service doors, compares favourably in scale and dignity with Sir Thomas Hesketh's hall at

Rufford (Lancashire), the richly ornamented central focus of a well-off knightly household in the remote and conservative north-west.[46]

In short, while plague raised great numbers of new men into the ranks of the middle class, its effect on daily life-styles was less apparent. For if yeomen lived like gentry in late-medieval England, and gentry like noblemen of an earlier period, their accommodation (although upgraded) stayed much the same.[47]

75. This view into the hall of the late-fifteenth-century Wealden house now known as The Paper Mill (Benenden) illustrates well the great height and dignity expected of such spaces, even at a generous-sized but not extravagant farmhouse. At the lower end of the hall are the three service doors (into buttery, kitchen, and pantry) more usually found at the grander halls of long-established upper gentry and nobility. The brick chimney-stack (right) is a typical late-sixteenth-century insertion. *RCHME Crown copyright.*

76. A great display of carving, at its most ornate in the big movable screen at the lower end of Sir Thomas Hesketh's mid-fifteenth-century hall at Rufford (Lancashire), is the outstanding characteristic of a showpiece apartment, probably used as model by many of Sir Thomas's farming neighbours. *A. F. Kersting.*

The bay window and the dais canopy, the glazed oriel and the side-wall fire-place, building in brick as a prestigious new material, and the more generous provision of private chambers – all these were the characteristics of the final phase of medieval building, each adding another element to personal com-

77. Sir Richard de Abberbury, who served under both the Black Prince and Richard II, rebuilt the little castle at Donnington, near Newbury (Berkshire), of which only this gatehouse, dating to the mid-1380s, survives to full height. There was a small rectangular court behind the gatehouse, with round angle towers and narrow domestic ranges against the curtain. But Sir Richard himself probably chose to live in the big vaulted chamber on the second floor of his gatehouse, from which there are excellent views of the valley below and of the busy highway from Newbury to Oxford. *A. F. Kersting.*

fort. However, they were ameliorations of existing space rather than funda-mental changes of plan or use. And the essential geography of the medieval household altered little.

If the Black Death did indeed have a direct impact on landowner building practice, it was chiefly in the area of self-defence. Thus the ostentatious card-board castles of late-fourteenth-century England – Amberley and Donning-ton, Nunney and Wardour, Wressle, West Tanfield and Sheriff Hutton – always had more to do with restraining unruly tenants than with preventing a more professional attack. And even licensed seaboard or marcher fortresses – Sir Edward Dalyngrigge's Bodiam or Richard Lord Scrope's Bolton – were less the appointed guardians of the locality's weak and needy than the embattled private treasuries of wealthy men.[48] This swaggering self-display, of a piece with the growing heraldic pomp of contemporary tomb architec-ture, culminated in the sumptuous brickwork of such mid-fifteenth-century castle–palaces as Sir John Fastolf's Caister (Norfolk), Ralph Lord Cromwell's Tattershall (Lincolnshire) and Sir Roger Fiennes's grand extrava-ganza at Herstmonceux (Sussex).[49] They were unpopular even within the building class itself; for it was new money that built each of these self-publicizing pseudo-fortresses, inevitably attracting the heat.[50]

78. Bolton Castle, in Wensleydale (North Yorkshire), was built in the late 1370s for Richard Lord Scrope, a former Treasurer (1371–5) and at that time Chancellor of England. While having some defensive purpose against marauding Scots, Bolton was essentially a fortified country palace, where the Chancellor could keep the jewellery, plate, and other rich possessions he had accumulated during his years of royal service. Lord Scrope's private quarters were in the north-west tower (left) and in the adjoining west range; his great hall was in the north range, next to his tower; and his chapel – running through two levels – was on the second and third floors of the range to the south (right centre). Bolton's kitchens and stores were all on the ground floor, and most of the rest of the castle was given over to generous suites of well-equipped lodgings for Scrope's family, household officers, and many guests. *Cambridge University Collection of Air Photographs: copyright reserved.*

79. Licence to "enclose, crenellate, entower and embattle" the family manor-house at Herstmonceux was granted to Sir Roger Fiennes in 1441. Fiennes, an experienced soldier, had campaigned in France with Henry V and John Duke of Bedford, and his astonishing Sussex castle was clearly influenced not just by the French castles he had seen on those campaigns but by the water-girt brick fortresses of the Low Countries. *A. F Kersting.*

There is another spectacular defensive sham – again of costly brick – in the intimidatory bulk of the huge gatehouse of Thornton Abbey, in northern Lincolnshire. Licensed in 1382, just after the Great Revolt, it shows the rich Augustinian canons of this remote rural community to have been at least as determined as any of their lay neighbours to stand up to the demands of peasant malcontents. Wealthy enough to continue active building even

80. This enormous gatehouse at Thornton Abbey (Lincolnshire), pierced by many arrow-loops and originally fully crenellated, was almost certainly a direct and individual response to the Great Rising of 1381, in which prominent ecclesiastical landowners like the Abbot of Thornton had been targeted especially by the rebels. The brick barbican on the approach bridge is a sixteenth-century addition, and must – like the gatehouse itself when order was restored – have had little other purpose than decoration. *A. F. Kersting.*

after the Black Death, and still in the 1520s "one of the goodliest [Austin] houses of England", these proud canons had aligned themselves unequivocally with the most conservative of local magnates, thereby increasing the alienation of their tenantry.[51] In the immediate aftermath of the Great Pestilence, this neglect of old loyalties had mattered less than it did later: all landowners were bullies together. However, the unpopularity of the possessioner orders – the Benedictines and the Cluniacs, the Augustinians, the Premonstratensians and the Cistercians – grew more dangerous with time, slowing down recruitment and reducing the quality of intakes. Monks, like college dons, are mighty builders. And it was the monks, more than any other individual category of the pre-plague propertied sector, who showed the consequences of shrinking numbers in their architecture.

Some part of that shrinkage was self-imposed, there being well-endowed communities – among them the wealthy canons of Haughmond (Shrop-

81. In this air view of Haughmond Abbey (Shropshire), the tall precinct wall which replaced the disused west range (centre) appears especially prominent in the slanting evening sun. At the lower end of the site, beyond the smaller cloister, the abbot's lodgings and his big adjoining guest-hall (top right) were both retained for use as a post-suppression mansion, which accounts for their survival in this condition. *Ministry of Defence Crown copyright.*

shire) – which although quite able to recruit more generously were sufficient postulants to come forward, would never allow their numbers to rise again in post-plague times above the canonical minimum of 12. Thus inertia and greed, excessive financial caution and a steadily eroding emphasis on the life in common, combined at many houses to create a new architecture in which individual comfort and personal privacy were top priorities. Seen from the air today, the ruins of Haughmond Abbey show some of the more familiar consequences of that new thinking. Haughmond's big church, with its huge monastic choir and multi-ended presbytery, has been shortened appreciably towards the west, where it lacks a good stretch of its nave. The canons' improved chapter-house is still there against the cloister, but the west claustral range has disappeared altogether, with just a tall precinct wall to mark its place. The substantial new lodgings of Haughmond's last abbots dominate a second cloister to the south.[52]

At Haughmond as elsewhere, a rebuilt abbot's house of the Late Middle Ages was often the finest domestic building in its locality. It is hardly surprising, therefore, that so many of these comfortable quarters have survived intact, preserved at the Suppression by their new owners. There are good late-medieval lodgings, for example, at Whalley (Lancashire) and Thame (Oxfordshire), at Watton (East Yorkshire), Castle Acre (Norfolk), Muchelney (Somerset), Norton (Cheshire), Much Wenlock (Shropshire), Repton (Derbyshire), St Osyth's (Essex), Forde and Milton (Dorset) and many more. Whereas other late-medieval ameliorations of monastic quarters have left fewer traces, there is still much surviving evidence, both in the documents and on the sites, of the addition of new meat kitchens with their associated heated misericords, of over-large infirmary halls and dormitories partitioned into private cells, of cloisters furnished with individual study-carrels and glazed against the cold, and of purpose-built apartments for the pensioners and paying-guests on whom many of the smaller houses had become dependent.[53]

If some of these relaxations, in particular concerning diet, pre-dated the Black Death, all became more acceptable (and eventually routine) when only the greater houses found it possible to recruit fully, and when even they competed fiercely for the ablest postulants. Expansion, once so busy, was halted abruptly by the plague; so that noisy monastic building sites, where great churches were still being extended and cloisters enlarged right up to the Black Death, fell silent in 1349. When building began again – as with monks it always must – it was hardly ever on the same projects as before.

82. It was again the prior's fine lodgings in the west range – the only roofed buildings in this photograph – which were preserved at the suppression of the wealthy Cluniac house at Castle Acre (Norfolk), surrendered to Henry VIII's commissioners by the prior and just ten monks on 22 November 1537. *Norfolk Air Photographs Library: photo Derek A. Edwards.*

"There is a certain relief in change", Washington Irving once admitted, "even though it be from bad to worse." Yet for the monks of post-plague England – bored and disillusioned, unpopular, apprehensive and increasingly bereft of purpose – change could only be the beginning of the end.

What matters

For better for worse, for richer for poorer, in sickness and in health, English society changed at the Black Death. And whereas almost every later development had a pre-plague precedent of some kind, it was the arrival of bubonic plague in the autumn of 1348 – not the progressive curbing of population growth from about 1300, nor the famines and murrains of the agrarian crisis of 1315–22 which slowed it further – that "swallowed up many of the good things of civilization and wiped them out".[1] Where so much happened so quickly, its significance may easily be exaggerated. And historians of the plague period are quite right to insist on the importance of secular trends. Post-plague social conflict, for example, is probably at least as well explained in terms of closure theory – of *exclusionary closure* as the process by which one group gains (and keeps) advantage over another, while the other by *usurpationary closure* may claim it back – as by the gathering of mortality statistics.[2] Nevertheless, what chiefly stoked those tensions was a population collapse so immediate and so prolonged as to encourage even the most conservative of landowners to embrace change. In the last analysis, whether in the short term or the long, what mattered was how many people died in the Black Death.

That said, the sources can be seriously misleading. The poor are usually silent, and almost nothing can be known about their feelings. But even where the material is plentiful enough, what remains can be very one-sided. English devotional art of the Late Middle Ages is a case in point. Here an imbalance has been created by the frequent survival, both at home and abroad throughout their continental export market, of Nottingham-made alabaster panels – Our Lady of Pity was a favourite subject of the carvers –

83. Not all Nottingham alabasters were designed as full-size panels, and this exquisite little carving of *Our Lady of Pity*, once brightly painted, is only 32.4 cm high. It dates to the first half of the fifteenth century, and was probably intended to be mounted against a board (the back is flat) in a wooden housing of its own, for display in a shrine or private chapel. *City of Nottingham Museums: Castle Museum & Art Gallery.*

highly personal to their owners and easy to squirrel away in times of trouble.[3] In contrast, the carved or painted altarpiece, the theologically suspect wall-painting, or the entire late-medieval glazing scheme became the target almost immediately of Protestant zealots.[4] The business left unfinished by Edwardian and Civil War iconoclasts was then often completed by the weather. Thus little more than fragments of Sir Edmund Tame's great *Last Judgement* window at Fairford Church, in Gloucestershire, survived the storm of 26 November 1703 that blew it in.[5] And the widely imitated *Dance of Death* in the cemetery cloister at St Paul's – long thought to have been a casualty of the Great Fire of London in 1666, but probably lost much earlier – is known only from the most summary accounts:

> About this Cloyster [John Stow wrote in 1598] was artificially and richly painted the dance of Machabray, or dance of death, commonly called the dance of Pauls: the like whereof, was painted about S. Innocents cloister, at Paris in France: the metres or poesie of this daunce, were translated out of French into English, by John

84. *Souls in Torment* from what survives of the original early-sixteenth-century glass of the great *Last Judgement* window at Fairford Church, in Gloucestershire. *A. F. Kersting.*

Lidgate, the Monke of Bery, & with the picture of Death, leading all estates painted about the Cloyster: at the speciall request and dispence of Jankin Carpenter [town clerk of London and a noted philanthropist], in the Raigne of Henry the 6. In the Cloyster were buried many persons, some of worship and others of honour: the monuments of whom, in number and curious workemanship, passed all other that were in that church.[6]

Entire late-medieval decorative schemes have survived so seldom that particular importance attaches to the unusually complete record of the morality paintings commissioned by Margaret Lady Hungerford in the mid-1470s. Dame Margaret's Hungerford Chantry at Salisbury Cathedral was demolished long ago. However, it was seen before its loss by John Hutchins (d.1773), the Dorset topographer, and attracted other antiquarian interest in that century. Hutchins believed Dame Margaret's paintings to be another *Dance of Death*, "probably copied from the painting in the cloisters of Old St Paul's in London . . . a sort of spiritual masquerade". But what he saw, in point of fact, was one of the last English renderings of that baleful legend *The Three Living and the Three Dead*, complete with its usual warning message. The Hungerford Chapel, Hutchins observed, "had been beautifully painted; but by damp and neglect all the ornaments were vanishing apace":

> On the [south] wall was a curious and tolerably well-preserved picture of a Man, large as life, drest in the habit of the times, a short doublet, slasht breeches, piked shoes, a high hat and feather, a staff in his left hand, his right hand held up in terror and affright at the sight of Death, who is approaching him in a shroud; and an empty coffin at his feet. Over the Man was this inscription:
>
> *Alasse, Dethe, alasse, a blessful thyng yo were,*
> *Yf thow wolldyst spare us in our lustynesse,*
> *And cum to wretches yt bethe of hevy chere,*
> *When they ye clepe [call] to slake there dystrresse . . .*
>
> Over Death:
>
> *Grasles galante in all thy luste and pryde*
> *Reme'ber that thow ones schalte dye . . .*
> *To ye dede bodys cast downe thyne ye [eye]*
> *Behold thaym well, consydere and see,*
> *For such as thay ar, soch shalt yow be.*

At the west end of the chapel two related painted figures were partnered again – both badly faded and with Death almost gone, but with the Man "in a different dress from the other, having small shoes of moderate size, a crucifix at his belt, slashed sleeves, pantaloons, one hand on the crucifix, the other lifted up as expostulating". Also on the same wall were further faint traces of an *Annunciation* ("the Virgin looking back") and of a big *St Christopher* (again as "large as life"), present to shelter his petitioners from sudden death.[7]

85. A big fifteenth-century *St Christopher* at Breage Church (Cornwall) – seen here with a contemporary *Christ of the Trades* (often interpreted as a warning to sabbath-breakers) – is in his customary position opposite the south door, where all those departing could invoke his protection against plague or any other form of mischief. *A. F. Kersting.*

86. Like the Nottingham alabaster carving of *Our Lady of Pity*, this early-fifteenth-century York glaziers' panel of *St Anne teaching the Virgin to read* emphasizes the sweetness and tender pity of the ladies of Our Lord's family, which made their cults so appealing to late-medieval congregations. Here St Anne is teaching her daughter the opening sentence of Psalm 143: "*Domine exaudi* . . . Hear my prayer, O Lord, give ear to my supplications." (E. A. Gee, "The painted glass of All Saints' Church, North Street, York", *Archaeologia* **102**, 1969, p. 155 and plate xxb). *RCHME Crown copyright.*

Dame Margaret was no novice in religion. If she had been ignorant about current beliefs or a mere beginner in the faith, her choice of subjects might have signified less. But by the time she built her chantry and put the finishing touches to her will, Margaret had been a student of the Art of Dying for many years. In 1470, wrong-footed once again in the Wars of the Roses, she had taken refuge with the Bridgettines of Syon. And it was in their sisterhood, if not before, that she came under the spell of the new devotions – to the Five Wounds of Christ and to the Name of Jesus (still just winning recognition as a cult) – to which she subsequently assigned votive masses in her chantry. She was to learn something else from the Bridgettines as well. It had been the practice of the nuns' confessors to warn them regularly of death: to "consider in their hearts that they are of earth, and [that] unto earth they will return". They were urged "to beholde also the shortnes and unstablenes of this lyf, the hastynes of dethe, the ferefulnes of dome, [and] the bytternes of paynes" before release. In the abbey church at Syon a coffin was kept open for the nuns to throw in earth and to say a daily *De profundis* by its side.[8] That welcoming coffin, not normally a feature of such paintings, reappears below the *Living* of Dame Margaret's mortuary chapel: an ever-present reminder of the perils of an unsecured death – the one unvarying constant that, no matter what the sophistication, wealth or learning of the late-medieval chantry founder, joined them all.

When Purgatory ceased to threaten, as it did at the Reformation, and when, as late as 1700, the risks of an untimely death by plague subsided also, mortality subjects lost much of their appeal. Usually of antiquarian interest only, a late-medieval cadaver effigy or a *Dance of Death* was always less likely to survive, from the Age of Reason forward, than a more conventional military monument or milder image. The effect of plague on art is thus concealed. But whereas it is undoubtedly true, as Pamela King has rightly said of the cadaver effigy and its origins, that "as a simple explanation, the Black Death is both too early and too late", the historian of today who overhastily dismisses the pestilence as a factor in the arts is just as likely to be at fault as those who, in the past, have made too much of it.[9] Incontestably, neither the shroud brass nor the cadaver effigy was known before the pestilence. And whereas painted renderings of *The Three Living and the Three Dead* were relatively common before the plague, it was in its later post-plague treatments that the legend lost its levity, to become at once more realistic

87. *The Three Living and the Three Dead*, from an engraving (re-drawn in the last century) by the Middle Rhenish Housebook Master (fl. 1480–1500). *The Wellcome Centre Medical Photographic Library.*

and more socially aware, in the same spirit as the contemporary *Dance of Death*.[10] Everywhere, the growing elaboration of burial and commemorative rituals furnished the context for a dedicated art. Thus, the huge church at Fotheringhay (Northamptonshire), built in rural isolation just up-river from Fotheringhay Castle, had no other major purpose than to house the dynastic monuments of the newly created Dukes of York: of Duke Edmund (d.1402), the first to hold the title, and of Duke Edward (d.1415), his eldest son and heir, after which Fotheringhay became the resting-place of their successors. Edward of York, founder of Fotheringhay College, was killed at Agincourt. And it was around Duke Edward's tomb, in the now lost presbytery of his great collegiate church, that the 13 fellows, 8 clerks and 13 choristers of the foundation gathered daily after compline to sing Psalm 130 for the dead: "*De profundis* . . . Out of the depths have I cried unto thee, O

88. Fotheringhay Church had already lost its grand presbytery (right), intended to house the monuments of the Yorkist dead, some years before 1600; and the buildings of Edward of York's college – between church and river – have gone also. But the big Perpendicular nave and lavish west tower still survive in parochial use; and there are two fine Elizabethan memorials (put there by the high altar when the presbytery was demolished) to Duke Edward himself and to Duke Richard (the third duke) who took over Edward's project on his death. Duke Richard died on 30 December 1460, leaving his widow Duchess Cecily to bring the works on church and college to completion. *A. F. Kersting.*

Lord . . . I wait for the Lord, my soul doth wait . . . more than they that watch for the morning".[11]

Some of the vanished pageantry of rituals such as these is caught in a contemporary eye-witness account of the burial of Prince Arthur at Worcester. Arthur, Duke of Cornwall and Prince of Wales, died at Ludlow on 2 April 1502. And it was over three weeks later, on 25 April (St Mark's Day), that his cortege began its progress to the cathedral. "It was the foulest cold windye and rainey Daye, and the worst Waye that I have seene," wrote the anonymous recorder of these events; "Yea, and in some Places they were faine to take Oxen to draw the Charre, so ill was the Waye." But officials rode ahead from Bewdley to complete the preparations, and when the procession reached Worcester – "that Daye was faire" – the city had a carnival air. Church and civic dignitaries waited at the gates and lined the streets, "with a good Number of secular Canons in graye Amys [amices], with rich Copes: And other Curats, secular Priests, Clerks, and Children, with Surplisses in great Number, and I suppose all the Torches of the Towne". At the cathedral gate four bishops censed the coffin. The Prior of Worcester and seven high-ranking abbots, all in full pontificals, received the bier and accompanied it in formal procession up the nave. There at the high altar, at the end of its journey, Prince Arthur's coffin was placed under a rich candle-bearing canopy ("herse") that was "the goodlyest and best wrought and garnished that ever I sawe":

> There were xviii Lights, Two great Standards, a Banner of the King's Armes, a Banner of the Kinge of Spaine's Armes, a Banner of the Queen's Armes, a Banner of the Queene of Spaine's Armes, a Banner of the Prince's Armes, a Banner of the Princesse's Armes, Two of Wales, One of Kadwallader, a Bannerell of Normandye, a Bannerell of Guien [Guyenne], a Bannerell of Cornwall, a Banerell of Chester, a Banerell of Poyctowe [Poitou], and 100 Pencills [pennons] of divers Badges; also the rich Cloth of Majestie, well frindged and double rayled, covered with black Cloth, was layed under Foote, which after was the Fees of the Officers of Armes.[12]

Prince Arthur's burial service reached its dramatic climax – "this was a piteous Sight to those who beheld it" – when the coffin was lowered into its grave and when Sir William Ovedall, comptroller of Arthur's household, "sore weeping and crying, tooke the Staffe of his Office by both Endes, and

89. The great candle-bearing hearse, or catafalque, of John Islip, Abbot of Westminster (1500–1532), stands before the high altar of his abbey. Islip's coffin had been brought to its specially prepared *chapelle ardente* in solemn procession, preceded by the 24 torch-bearing poor men "in gownes and hodes" who are shown surrounding the abbot's hearse in this fine contemporary drawing from Islip's obituary roll. At the coffin's head (left) is a group of closely hooded mourners; and four processional banners are being held high on the far side of the hearse, one of them a banner of Our Lady. *By kind permission of the Dean and Chapter of Westminster.*

over his owne Head brake it, and cast it into the Grave". But then "all things thus finished, there was ordeyned a great Dinner . . . ". And with only this text for reference and the scenery gone as well, rather little would have been known of late-medieval noble burial at its most extravagant had it not been for the fortunate survival in the Westminster Abbey archives of the obituary roll of John Islip, Abbot from 1500 to 1532. Islip's roll, rehearsing the virtues of Westminster's "good old father", was one of many personal bids for intercession. It was illustrated with fine drawings in the High Renaissance manner which included a sketch of Islip's catafalque before the altar. Islip was a rich man, and his abbey was among the wealthiest in the kingdom. Accordingly, his huge candelabra-laden catafalque and great company of mourners were perhaps no more than might have been expected at the interment of a churchman of his rank.[13] Yet if just a fraction of that display had been seen at parish burials – as indeed it surely was – that would still, by modern standards, have been extraordinary. Moreover, other associated costs continued climbing. There are two regularly repeated entries in the Church Book of St Ewen's (Bristol) which chart this steady inflation. The first entry priced the annual "breakfast" at the Feast of Corpus Christi, still rarely more than 4d in the last decade of the fifteenth century, but rising quickly in the 1510s, to be capped in the 1520s at 2s. The second listed expenditure on cakes, cheese and ale at the General Mind – when parish benefactors were remembered – where again the price soared from just over 2s in the 1450s when the accounts first began, to 7s 3d in 1500.[14]

These are not huge sums, and St Ewen's (although small) was not one of the poorer Bristol parishes. Nevertheless, they form part of a long catalogue of unremitting parishioner expenditure on the upkeep, fabric and furnishings of just one church. At St Ewen's in the mid-fifteenth century it was probably the making of a great processional cross, to which individual parishioners contributed cash or "broken silver", which caused the proctors' Church Book to be opened in 1454.[15] The next year, the new cross was described, in an inventory of St Ewen's "juelx" and other ornaments, as "of sylver and overgylt. hangyng these ymagys. furst Seynt Ewen' [of Rouen]. our lady [the Virgin Mary]. seynt John [the Apostle]. Seynt Kateryn' [of Alexandria], Seynt Margaret [of Antioch]. Seynt John' the Evangelist. the iiij evangelistes. iiij patriarkes . . . [etc.]". Next after the parish cross was "the best chalyce of sylver and overgylt weyeng xxx. j quarter unces *of the gyft of John Wotton wrytten yn the fote of the same*".[16] And if we take the two together, what stands out in black and white is that it was intercession and commemoration – not the quality of divine service – that preoccupied the donors and parish chaplains of St Ewen's. For almost another century, those purposes combined to encourage increasing accumulations of church goods. But then, in just six years of Edwardian Protestant zealotry, from the death of Henry VIII on 28 January 1547 to the accession of Queen Mary on 19 July 1553, everything was swept away with the old beliefs. Great cities like Bristol have always harboured extremists, and St Ewen's was ahead of the pack. Between 1547 and 1549 the rood was taken down and all devotional images were removed; a new vernacular Bible was bought and chained in place; the parish plate was either sold or surrendered. The art of Catholic England was limewashed over.[17]

In contrast, the art of Death lived on. And its common acceptance by reformers normally opposed to imagery of all kinds strengthens the case for the recognition of sudden death as an inspiration of that art, for the plague (unlike the pope) had not been banished. That argument, for lack of data, will continue.[18] However, there are other fields of study where it is not the poverty of the material that has complicated discussion, but the categories we impose upon ourselves. Historians work in periods: we are medievalists, early modernists, or whatever. But periodization can result in tunnel vision. In one clear case of that, the origins of the so-called "rising gentry", hijacked by R. H. Tawney for Tudor England, have only recently been reclaimed by medievalists.[19] And if we look the other way, any too-swift acceptance of the belief that political sophistication developed among bondmen only *after* the Black Death would certainly take a knock if we could hear the voices more clearly of those militant villagers of Brill and North Ashby, Peatling Magna and Little Billing who, almost a century before the pestilence, had hitched their waggon to Simon de Montfort's "common enterprise".[20]

Again, the popular culture of which historians of the Late Middle Ages can see so little that it features hardly at all in their writings becomes instantly more accessible to the early-modern researcher in vernacular church-court records, where it has put a new complexion, for example, on studies of rural violence and its control. Yet those ridings and rough music, charivaris and skimmingtons – the well-documented mocking rituals of Tudor and Stuart England – undoubtedly had a much longer history. Furthermore, they may always have been condoned for the same reasons. "Central to the symbolism of charivaris," writes Martin Ingram of the 1600s, "were notions of hierarchy, inversion, reversal, rule and misrule, order and disorder – the world turned upside-down."[21] But to mock at social differences is in some way to draw their sting, and this can hardly have escaped the attention of England's comfortably-off JPs, squaring-up to traditional flash-points like Midsummer. Far better to tolerate – even legitimize – the public shaming of scolds and cuckolds, the raucous playing of musical instruments, the riotous cavalcades and presumptuous parades of arms, the noisy clash of bells and irreverent banging of pots and pans, than to risk a return to the revolutionary rhetoric of John Ball.

In the event, early-modern England – where all these inflammatory rituals were permitted expression – was a much safer place to live than almost anywhere else on the planet.[22] And how this came about had less to do with the quality of English justice (which was not at that time high) than with a pragmatic recognition of the mutual benefits of good order and of the potential profits of "responsible" protest. The two successful rebellions of the mid-Tudor period – against the levying of the Amicable Grant in 1527, and for Princess Mary against Lady Jane Grey in 1553 – undeniably proved the merits, at least to Suffolk folk, of a partnership in protest with the gentry. "What's the reason," asked Sir John Harington, why "treason dothe never prosper?" Came his reply: "For if it prosper, none dare call it treason."[23]

A genuine partnership between the classes stood little chance of success. Yet long before Harington (the Elizabethan) coined his aphorism, violence had given way to talking in post-plague England, being arguably the main achievement of royal governments. Much of that good order was owed to arbitration. And peace might never have taken hold – or not for some time yet – if the once-rebellious poor had not been dulled politically by full employment. Jobs were not the only appeaser of the post-plague disadvantaged, for what had also largely vanished was bondman status. Within scarcely half a century of the Great Revolt of 1381, most restraints on personal freedom had disappeared. Furthermore, it was in this same half-century that formerly oppressive landowners decisively changed their tune, withdrawing almost totally from direct farming. Simultaneously, once-fractious landless knights – transformed into justices of the peace and demesne lessees – were re-born as responsible country gentry. No paradigm shift had brought these things about; no sudden conviction of slavery's wickedness; no conversion on the road to Damascus. Behind every change was a labour shortage, and at the back of each shortage was the Black Death.

Late-medieval labour shortages were not, of course, the product of pestilence alone. Another new factor was the widespread (and still growing) substitution of nuclear for extended families, in which plague was at best a minor player. Even so, when Dr Razi identified the 1430s with such confidence as the exact decade during which Halesowen's extended familial system disappeared for ever, he did so for the good reason that the old kin network had become totally exhausted, so that there were no remaining relatives of deceased tenants to take their places.[24] After that time, peasant families were usually too small to be self-sustaining. And that perpetual mobility – whether up or down – would characterize equally the post-plague nobility and gentry, where again the main cause was the early death of heirs and the regular failure of intra-family succession. As Dr Payling correctly emphasizes, it was not the fire-sale of the Dissolution that first opened a way into the once-closed ranks of the English landed classes, but the merciless scything of the nobility by King Death.[25]

Nobody now denies the Black Death's status as a defining moment in late-medieval English history. But there are good reasons to tread cautiously all the same. It was famine not plague, after 1349, that remained the biggest killer in the colder, wetter and emptier northern counties. In those counties also, extended families lived on longer; while even in southern England, the Black Death's successor plagues may always have come second in population control to the growing practice of late marriage with fewer children. Gentry fell as often as they rose. More monks undoubtedly died of over-weight or of liver conditions than ever succumbed to the plague. Many towns continued to prosper through a long recession which, for them at least, had seldom begun before the very end of the fourteenth century at earliest. But with every reservation, one critical fact remains in place. England from 1400 was half-empty.

Numbers matter. However, there is greater abundance for all to share in a half-empty land, and it may be this, in the *longue durée*, that matters more. Why Goodman Robin learnt to love the pestilence was that social injustice in general, and villeinage in particular, were high on the list of the plague's victims. "In what way are those whom we call lords greater masters than ourselves?" Froissart makes John Ball ask. "How have they deserved it? Why do they hold us in bondage? If we all spring from a single father and mother, Adam and Eve, how can they claim or prove that they are lords more than us, except by making us produce and grow the wealth which they spend?"[26] He was right, of course; just as the peasants said he was. And although victory had slipped from them in 1381, the freedoms they chiefly wanted were in view.

90. Sir Ralph Wodford's cadaver slab at Ashby Folville (Leicestershire) was probably made for him some years before his death in 1498. In addition to the long memorial inscription round the edge of his slab there are four instructional legends, beginning (top) with the verses from Job 19:25–6 – "*Credo* . . . I know that my redeemer liveth, and that he shall stand at the latter day upon the earth. And though after my skin worms destroy this body, yet in my flesh shall I see God." Below this, at waist-level, are two "*Disce mori* (Learn to die)" scrolls. A fourth vernacular inscription, under the hound at Wodford's feet, is his version of the biblical "Then shall the dust return to the earth as it was: and the spirit shall return unto God who gave it". (Ecclesiastes xii:7) *A. F. Kersting.*

Also promoting their self-worth was the popular emphasis on equality in death. "Of erthe I am formed and maked," rhymed Sir Ralph Wodford, of Ashby Folville (Leicestershire), on his expensive cadaver slab, "To erthe I am turned all naked."[27] Says Death to the Emperor, in John Lydgate's *Dance of Death*:

Sir Emperowre / lorde of al the grounde
Soveren Prince / ande hyest of noblesse
Ye most forsake / of golde yowre appil [orb] rounde
Sceptre and swerde / & all yowre hie prouesse
Be-hinde leve / yowre tresowre & richesse
And with othir[s] / to my daunce obeie
Agens my myght / is worth noon hardynesse
Adames children / alle thei mosten deie.[28]

Die they certainly would; and in huge numbers. Nothing could take away that pain. But just as Tudor England had become a safer place to live than other countries, it enjoyed more freedoms also, and would subsequently become the cradle of commercial and industrial revolutions. Great weight has been placed on a Judeo-Christian work ethic, reinforced by Protestant values, as preparation for both revolutions. And it is perfectly true that, in conditions of full employment, the labouring poor of late-medieval England had little real incentive to work hard. "They [builders] waste much part of the day", ran a contemporary complaint with a still familiar ring, "in late coming to work, early departing therefrom, long sitting at their breakfast . . . and longtime of sleeping afternoon".[29] However, the greatest of all the poor's benefits were the choices they now enjoyed – of another lord, of another job, of whether to stay in the country or migrate to the towns, of how long to remain if they did go away, and of when to set up house and start a family. If winning freedom of choice is what revolutions are all about, I prefer to put my money on the Black Death.

Notes

Individual volumes in Nikolaus Pevsner's *The buildings of England* series (Harmondsworth, Penguin Books Ltd) – not always the current edition – are given thus: *Derbyshire,* 1953; *Wiltshire,* 1963, etc. National Trust, English Heritage and other guides are similarly cited by place-name and date (not always known) thus: *Great Chalfield Manor, Wiltshire,* 1980; *Holme by Newark Church* guide.

Chapter 1: Mortalities

1. A. R. Bridbury, "The Black Death", *Economic History Review* **26**, 1973, p. 591.
2. For this, see most recently W. M. Ormrod, "The English government and the Black Death of 1348–49", in *England in the fourteenth century. Proceedings of the 1985 Harlaxton symposium,* W. M. Ormrod (ed.) (Woodbridge, Boydell Press, 1986), pp. 175–88.
3. Bruce Dickins, "Historical graffiti at Ashwell, Hertfordshire", in *English medieval graffiti,* V. Pritchard (Cambridge, Cambridge University Press, 1967), pp. 181–3.
4. Andrew B. Appleby, "The disappearance of plague: a continuing puzzle", *Economic History Review* **33**, 1980, pp. 161–73.
5. Giovanni Boccaccio, *The Decameron,* trans. G. H. McWilliam (Harmondsworth, Penguin Books, 1972), pp. 50–51; for a modern account of the plague's origins, see Michael W. Dols, *The Black Death in the Middle East* (Princeton, Princeton University Press, 1979), particularly "The transmission of the Black Death: chronology and geographical distribution", pp. 35–67.
6. Quoted by John Henderson, "The Black Death in Florence: medical and communal responses", in *Death in towns. Urban responses to the dying and the dead, 100–1600,* Steven Bassett (ed.) (Leicester, Leicester University Press, 1992), p. 145.
7. Boccaccio, *Decameron,* p. 57.
8. *ibid.,* p. 56.
9. William M. Bowsky (ed.), *The Black Death. A turning point in history?* (New York, Holt, Rinehart & Winston, 1971), pp. 13–14; also quoted by Philip Ziegler, *The Black Death* (London, Collins, 1969), p. 58.
10. Rosemary Horrox (trans. and ed.), *The Black Death* (Manchester, Manchester University Press, 1994), p. 77.

11. For this generally favourable assessment of Henry Knighton, see Antonia Gransden, *Historical writing in England II. c. 1307 to the early sixteenth century* (London, Routledge & Kegan Paul, 1982), pp. 159ff.

12. Horrox, *The Black Death*, pp. 79–80.

13. Gransden, *Historical writing*, p. 361.

14. *ibid.*, pp. 366–7; Horrox, *The Black Death*, p. 68.

15. Gransden, *Historical writing*, p. 361.

16. The death of millers ("the mill stood vacant for lack of a tenant", etc.) was one of the consequences of the second pestilence noted by Mavis Mate, "Agrarian economy after the Black Death: the manors of Canterbury Cathedral Priory, 1348–91", *Economic History Review* **37**, 1984, pp. 351–2.

17. *ibid.*, p. 354; and for the more general picture, see Bridbury, "The Black Death", pp. 583–4.

18. John Hatcher, "Mortality in the fifteenth century: some new evidence", *Economic History Review* **39**, 1986, pp. 19–38.

19. *ibid.*, pp. 31–8; Hatcher is careful to warn his readers of the possibly exceptional nature of the Christ Church death-rates. However, Barbara Harvey's more recent calculations of contemporary mortalities at Westminster Abbey have yielded remarkably similar figures overall, although she too has reservations about how widely those results might apply outside the precinct (*Living and dying in England 1100–1540. The monastic experience* (Oxford, Clarendon Press, 1993), p. 122 and the rest of the discussion in ch. 4). For the case for male crude death rates as high as 55 per 1,000 in late-medieval England, which then fell sharply after 1500, see David Loschky & Ben D. Childers, "Early English mortality", *Journal of Interdisciplinary History* **24**, 1993, pp. 85–97.

20. Barbara Harvey, *Westminster Abbey and its estates in the Middle Ages* (Oxford, Clarendon Press, 1977), pp. xii, 66–7, 144; also Barbara Harvey, *Living and dying*, p. 74 and *passim*.

21. David Knowles, *The religious orders in England. Volume II. The end of the Middle Ages* (Cambridge, Cambridge University Press, 1979), pp. 10–11.

22. L. R. Poos, "The rural population of Essex in the later Middle Ages", *Economic History Review* **38**, 1985, pp. 529–30.

23. *ibid.*, p. 524 and notes 21–2.

24. Richard Lomas, "The Black Death in County Durham", *Journal of Medieval History* **15**, 1989, pp. 129–30; and see the same author's *North-East England in the Middle Ages* (Edinburgh, John Donald, 1992), p. 160. The mortalities, it should be noted, are of the priory's former tenants, not of entire communities.

25. Christopher Dyer, *Lords and peasants in a changing society. The estates of the bishopric of Worcester, 680–1540* (Cambridge, Cambridge University Press, 1980), p. 238.

26. Zvi Razi, *Life, marriage and death in a medieval parish. Economy, society and demography in Halesowen 1270–1400* (Cambridge, Cambridge University Press, 1980), pp. 101–9.

27. *ibid.*, pp. 110–13. For valuable recent contributions to the debate about the depth and permanence of the "crisis" see Bruce M. S. Campbell (ed.), *Before the Black Death. Studies in the "crisis" of the early fourteenth century* (Manchester, Manchester University Press, 1991).

28. Ray Lock, "The Black Death in Walsham-le-Willows", *Proceedings of the Suffolk Institute of Archaeology and History* **37**, 1992, pp. 319–20.

29. *ibid.*, pp. 323–6.

30. Bruce M. S. Campbell, "Population pressure, inheritance and the land market in a fourteenth-century peasant community", in *Land, kinship and life-cycle*, Richard M. Smith (ed.) (Cambridge, Cambridge University Press, 1984), p. 89.

31. *ibid.*, p. 120.

32. *ibid.*, pp. 96–7.

33. *ibid.*, pp. 122–5.

34. Horrox, *The Black Death*, pp. 285–6; also P. D. A. Harvey (ed.), *The peasant land market in medieval England* (Oxford, Clarendon Press, 1984), p. 332. For some not much later agreements of the same kind, see Simon A. C. Penn & Christopher Dyer, "Wages and earnings in late-medieval England: evidence from the enforcement of the labour laws", *Economic History Review* **43**, 1990, p. 371.

35. Quoted by Dols, *The Black Death in the Middle East*, p. 67.

36. For a useful but notably cautious review of the evidence, see Richard M. Smith, "Demographic developments in rural England, 1300–48: a survey", in Campbell, *Before the Black Death*, pp. 25–77.

37. Poos, "The rural population of Essex", p. 521; that conclusion is re-stated in the same author's *A rural society after the Black Death: Essex 1350–1525* (Cambridge, Cambridge University Press, 1991), pp. 106–7; and see also Razi, *Life, marriage and death*, p. 45, for an identical 15 per cent population loss at Halesowen.

38. Bridbury, "The Black Death", pp. 590–91; for climatic change, see Mark Bailey, "*Per impetum maris*: natural disaster and economic decline in eastern England, 1275–1350", in Campbell, *Before the Black Death*, pp. 184–208.

39. Campbell, "Population pressure", pp. 107, 127.

40. Barbara Harvey, "Introduction: the 'crisis' of the early fourteenth century", in Campbell, *Before the Black Death*, p. 24; and see the same author's "The population trend in England between 1300 and 1348", *Transactions of the Royal Historical Society* **16**, 1966, pp. 23–42. Barbara Harvey's emphasis on the critical importance of the onset of plague, this time evidenced in the post-plague transformation of the lot of the labouring poor, is repeated by John Hatcher, "England in the aftermath of the Black Death", *Past & Present* **144**, 1994, pp. 3–35. Other emphatic reassertions of the severity of the Black Death's impact on urban populations have included Samuel K. Cohn's *The cult of remembrance and the Black Death. Six Renaissance cities in central Italy* (Baltimore, Johns Hopkins University Press, 1992) and Richard Britnell's "The Black Death in English towns", *Urban History* **21**, 1994, pp. 195–210. The whole debate, from over-emphasis to under-emphasis and back to emphasis again, is usefully summarized by Horrox, *The Black Death*, pp. 229–36.

41. Razi, *Life, marriage and death*, pp. 135, 151.

42. Poos, *A rural society after the Black Death*, pp. 110, 120–29.

43. Mate, "Agrarian economy after the Black Death", pp. 342, 353; and see also the same author's "Labour and labour services on the estates of Canterbury Cathedral Priory in the fourteenth century", *Southern History* **7**, 1985, p. 64.

44. Marjorie Keniston McIntosh, *Autonomy and community. The royal manor of Havering, 1200–1500* (Cambridge, Cambridge University Press, 1986), p. 77.

45. J. N. Hare, "Durrington: a chalkland village in the later Middle Ages", *Wiltshire Archaeological Magazine* **74/5**, 1981, pp. 140–41.

46. P. D. A. Harvey, *A medieval Oxfordshire village. Cuxham 1240 to 1400* (Oxford, Oxford University Press, 1965), pp. 137–9.

47. Elizabeth M. Elvey, "The abbot of Missenden's estates in Chalfont St Peter", *Records of Buckinghamshire* **17**, 1961–5, p. 33.

48. Cicely Howell, *Land, family and inheritance in transition. Kibworth Harcourt 1280–1700* (Cambridge, Cambridge University Press, 1983), pp. 42–4; for some more recent calculations of population change at Kibworth Harcourt, based on tithing-penny payments, see David Postles, "Demographic change in Kibworth Harcourt, Leicestershire, in the

later Middle Ages", *Local Population Studies* **48**, 1992, pp. 41–8.

49. John McDonnell, "Medieval assarting hamlets in Bilsdale, North-East Yorkshire", *Northern History* **22**, 1986, pp. 269–79.

50. Mark Bailey, *A marginal economy? East Anglian Breckland in the later Middle Ages* (Cambridge, Cambridge University Press, 1989), ch. 4: "Growth, crisis and change: economic performance 1300–1399".

51. *ibid.*, p. 290.

52. *ibid.*, p. 317.

53. *ibid.*, pp. 312–13.

54. David Dymond & Roger Virgoe, "The reduced population and wealth of early fifteenth-century Suffolk", *Proceedings of the Suffolk Institute of Archaeology and History* **36**, 1986, p. 80.

55. E. M. Carus-Wilson & Olive Coleman, *England's export trade 1275–1547* (Oxford, Clarendon Press, 1963), pp. 152–3.

56. Dymond & Virgoe, "The reduced population and wealth", p. 80.

57. A. R. Bridbury, *Economic growth. England in the later Middle Ages* (Hassocks, Harvester Press, 1962); for that growth in the cloth trade, see the same author's *Medieval English clothmaking. An economic survey* (London, Heinemann, 1982), *passim*.

58. Bridbury, "The Black Death", p. 591.

59. Harvey, *Living and dying*, pp. 129–35.

60. *ibid.*, p. 122.

61. *ibid.*, p. 124.

62. *ibid.*, p. 128.

63. *ibid.*, pp. 123, 129.

64. Gervase Rosser, *Medieval Westminster 1200–1540* (Oxford, Clarendon Press, 1989), pp. 175–80.

65. Harvey, *Living and dying*, p. 145. But see chapter 3 below ("Villages in stasis") for those other variables, which could be at least as important in the countryside.

Chapter 2: Shrunken towns

1. S. H. Rigby, *Medieval Grimsby: growth and decline* (Hull, University of Hull Press, 1993), p. 146. Dr Rigby, in this comment, is looking back over a long argument in which he has himself played a significant part; for his contest with Dr Bridbury, see especially the papers in *Economic History Review* **39**, 1986, pp. 411–26. There has been no evident change of view in A. R. Bridbury's recent *The English economy from Bede to the Reformation* (Woodbridge, Boydell Press, 1992) in which he reprints unaltered his 1986 paper "Dr Rigby's comment: a reply" (pp. 293–8) and argues again that urban decline has been grossly exaggerated (pp. 38–41).

2. *ibid.*, p. 131. For "spaciousness and promise", see A. R. Bridbury, "English provincial towns in the later Middle Ages", *Economic History Review* **34**, 1981, p. 24. But for another summary of urban mortalities and a new assessment of the impact of the Black Death which gives the 1348–9 plague more prominence than Bridbury has ever done, see Richard Britnell's "The Black Death in English towns", *Urban History* **21**, 1994, pp. 195–210.

3. S. H. Rigby, "'Sore decay' and 'fair dwellings': Boston and urban decline in the later Middle Ages", *Midland History* **10**, 1985, pp. 54–5.

4. Sylvia L. Thrupp, *The merchant class of medieval London [1300–1500]* (Ann Arbor, University of Michigan Press, 1948), pp. 199–200. Sylvia Thrupp's startling figures from medieval London have frequently been disputed since she wrote, yet have found recent support in the capital's wardship records of 1309–1497, which show child mortality rising steeply (even among the orphans of better-off citizens) after the Black Death, to continue that rise after 1400, more than doubling before the end of the fifteenth century (Barbara Hanawalt, *Growing up in medieval London. The experience of childhood in history* (New York, Oxford University Press, 1993), pp. 56, 223).

5. R. H. Britnell, *Growth and decline in Colchester, 1300–1525* (Cambridge, Cambridge University Press, 1986), p. 22 and *passim.*

6. *ibid.*, pp. 202–5.

7. *ibid.*, pp. 212–17.

8. Rigby, "'Sore decay' and 'fair dwellings'", p. 55; and for Boston's tax-rates, compared with more fortunate boroughs, see A. R. Bridbury, *Economic growth. England in the later Middle Ages* (Hassocks, Harvester Press, 1975), 2nd edn, pp. 81, 112–13.

9. As does Susan Reynolds, *An introduction to the history of English medieval towns* (Oxford, Oxford University Press, 1977), p. 158; and see also her "Decline and decay in late medieval towns: a look at some of the concepts and arguments", *Urban History Yearbook 1980*, pp. 76–8.

10. Derek Keene, *Survey of medieval Winchester* (Oxford, Clarendon Press, 1985), pp. 116–17.

11. *ibid.*, pp. 93–4, 367–8.

12. *ibid.*, p. 308.

13. *ibid.*, pp. 97–8.

14. *ibid.*, pp. 246–8.

15. Gervase Rosser, *Medieval Westminster 1200–1540* (Oxford, Clarendon Press, 1989), pp. 80–81, 171–2; also Dr Rosser's "London and Westminster: the suburb in the urban economy in the later Middle Ages", in *Towns and townspeople in the fifteenth century*, John A. F. Thomson (ed.) (Gloucester, Alan Sutton, 1988), pp. 55–6.

16. A. F. Butcher, "Rent, population and economic change in late-medieval Newcastle", *Northern History* **14**, 1978, pp. 75–6. Both Newcastle's recession in the second half of the fifteenth century and its comparatively rapid return to prosperity in the early sixteenth century have been confirmed recently (using national Customs accounts) by J. F. Wade, "The overseas trade of Newcastle upon Tyne in the late Middle Ages", *Northern History* **30**, 1994, pp. 31–48. However, Wade also sees evidence of "enduring vitality" in the late-medieval Newcastle trading community, being more than sufficient to keep it alive and in reasonable health through the recession.

17. A. F. Butcher, "Rent and the urban economy: Oxford and Canterbury in the later Middle Ages", *Southern History* **1**, 1979, pp. 42–3; for the bishops as founders of colleges, see Helen Jewell, "English bishops as educational benefactors in the later fifteenth century", in *The church, politics and patronage in the fifteenth century*, Barrie Dobson (ed.) (Gloucester, Alan Sutton, 1984), pp. 146–67.

18. David Gary Shaw, *The creation of a community. The city of Wells in the Middle Ages* (Oxford, Clarendon Press, 1993), p. 102.

19. *ibid.*, pp. 45–9.

20. *ibid.*, pp. 50–54, 128.

21. *ibid.*, pp. 54–63.

22. I owe this point to P. D. A. Harvey's "Non-agrarian activities in the rural communities of late-medieval England", paper presented at Prato, Italy, 1982, p. 11.

23. D. M. Palliser, "Urban decay revisited", in *Towns and townspeople in the fifteenth century*,

John A. F. Thomson (ed.) (Gloucester, Alan Sutton, 1988), pp. 11–12; see also R. H. Britnell, "The proliferation of markets in England 1200–1349", *Economic History Review* **34**, 1981, pp. 209–21.

24. Christopher Dyer, "The consumer and the market in the later Middle Ages", *Economic History Review* **42**, 1989, p. 325; and see also the same author's comments on the economic resilience and swift rebuilding of the minor market town of Shipston after the fire of 1478 (The great fire of Shipston-on-Stour *Warwickshire History* **8**, 1992–3, pp. 189–91). Another clear success story was the little "primary" town of Loughborough, in north-west Leicestershire, discussed by David Postles, "An English small town in the later Middle Ages: Loughborough", *Urban History* **20**, 1993, pp. 7–29; other small towns in Leicestershire, such as Melton Mowbray and Castle Donington, were in decline (*ibid.*, pp. 26–9). Similarly, Hertfordshire's Buntingford rose after the Black Death at the expense of its near-neighbour Standon, to the south, which was already in some difficulty in the 1370s. However, even Buntingford's "success story" had worn thin by the second half of the fifteenth century, by which time Standon was in really grave trouble (Mark Bailey, "A tale of two towns: Buntingford and Standon in the later Middle Ages", *Journal of Medieval History* **19**, 1993, pp. 351–71).

25. R. H. Britnell, *The commercialisation of English society 1000–1500* (Cambridge, Cambridge University Press, 1993), p. 171.

26. Anthony Saul, "English towns in the late Middle Ages: the case of Great Yarmouth", *Journal of Medieval History* **8**, 1982, pp. 75–88; see also the same author's "Great Yarmouth and the Hundred Years War in the fourteenth century", *Bulletin of the Institute of Historical Research* **52**, 1979, pp. 105–15, and "The herring industry at Great Yarmouth *c.*1280–*c.*1400", *Norfolk Archaeology* **38**, 1981, pp. 34–43. Grimsby (also on the east coast but further north) was similarly in growing trouble in the half-century before the Black Death, paying substantially less tax in 1334 than it had done in 1297 (Stephen Rigby, "Urban society in early fourteenth-century England: the evidence of the lay subsidies", *Bulletin of the John Rylands University Library of Manchester* **72**, 1990, p. 184).

27. Mark Bailey, "Coastal fishing off south-east Suffolk in the century after the Black Death", *Proceedings of the Suffolk Institute of Archaeology and History* **37**, 1990, pp. 102–14.

28. Christopher Dyer, *Standards of living in the later Middle Ages. Social change in England c.1200–1520* (Cambridge, Cambridge University Press, 1989), pp. 157–9.

29. C. H. Williams (ed.), *English historical documents 1485–1558* (London, Eyre & Spottiswoode, 1967), pp. 954–5.

30. For reservations about these lists, see Robert Tittler, "For the 'Re-edification of Townes': the rebuilding statutes of Henry VIII", *Albion* **22**, 1990, pp. 591–605; also Alan Dyer, *Decline and growth in English towns 1400–1640* (London, Macmillan, 1991), pp. 43–5.

31. Bridbury, *The English economy*, p. 39. For a straightforward verdict on the plague of 1348–9 as a "turning-point in urban history", see Britnell, "The Black Death in English towns", p. 210.

32. *ibid.*, p. 41.

33. For "towns", substitute "families" (Tolstoy, *Anna Karenina*, ch. 1).

34. Charles Phythian-Adams, "Urban decay in late-medieval England", in *Towns and societies: essays in economic history and historical sociology*, Philip Abrams & E. A. Wrigley (eds) (Cambridge, Cambridge University Press, 1978), pp. 159–85; and the same author's *Desolation of a city. Coventry and the urban crisis of the Late Middle Ages* (Cambridge, Cambridge University Press, 1979), *passim*. For the alternative view, see Jennifer I. Kermode, "Urban decline? The flight from office in late-medieval York", *Economic History Review* **35**, 1982, pp. 179–98.

35. Jennifer I. Kermode, "Merchants, overseas trade, and urban decline: York, Beverley, and Hull *c.*1380–1500", *Northern History* **23**, 1987, pp. 51–73; and see for supporting material on Hull's troubles, Rosemary Horrox (ed.), *Selected rentals and accounts of medieval Hull, 1293–1528,* Yorkshire Archaeological Society Records Series **141**, 1981, introduction. For the argument that even short-term mortality crises in the relatively small mercantile communities of these northern towns could permanently damage investment capability and thus hasten urban decline, see again particularly Kermode, "Merchants, overseas trade, and urban decline", pp. 68–9.

36. Pamela Nightingale, "Monetary contraction and mercantile credit in later medieval England", *Economic History Review* **43**, 1990, pp. 560–75. See also John Day, "The great bullion famine of the fifteenth century", *Past & Present* **79**, 1978, pp. 3–54, and Peter Spufford, *Money and its use in medieval Europe* (Cambridge, Cambridge University Press, 1988), pp. 356–62 (for the second and even graver bullion famine, starting in the late 1430s and at its worst between 1457 and 1464, when "the economy of Europe ground to a halt at every level, from the humblest purchases of bundles of leeks, up to the great merchants, whose galleys had to row away with goods unsold").

Chapter 3: Villages in stasis

1. For a useful general discussion of the origin, characteristics and disappearance of plague, see especially Leslie Bradley, "Some medical aspects of plague", in *The plague reconsidered. A new look at its origins and effects in 16th and 17th century England*, Local Population Studies Supplement, 1977, pp. 11–23; and see also Keith Manchester, "The palaeopathology of urban infections", in *Death in towns. Urban responses to the dying and the dead, 100–1600*, Steven Bassett (ed.) (Leicester, Leicester University Press, 1992), pp. 8–14. But for some remnant cautions against accepting the plague too readily as a mainly urban phenomenon, see Richard Britnell, "The Black Death in English towns", *Urban History* **21**, 1994, pp. 202–3.

2. Christopher Dyer, *Standards of living in the later Middle Ages. Social change in England c.1200–1520* (Cambridge, Cambridge University Press, 1989), pp. 157–60; also the same author's "Changes in diet in the Late Middle Ages: the case of harvest workers", *Agricultural History Review* **36**, 1988, pp. 21–37. An almost immediate post-plague improvement in the lot of the labouring poor is the theme of John Hatcher's recent "England in the aftermath of the Black Death", *Past & Present* **144**, 1994, pp. 3–35; and for the monetary evidence of a substantial rise in *per caput* incomes right across the late-medieval economy, see N. J. Mayhew, "Population, money supply, and the velocity of circulation in England, 1300–1700", *Economic History Review* **48**, 1995, pp. 249–50.

3. Christopher Dyer, "English peasant buildings in the later Middle Ages", *Medieval Archaeology* **30**, 1986, pp. 28–9 and *passim*; for other evidence of substantial houses, costing up to £10 each and built by Edington Priory for its tenants at Coleshill, see P. D. A. Harvey (ed.), *The peasant land market in medieval England* (Oxford, Clarendon Press, 1984), p. 174.

4. L. R. Poos, *A rural society after the Black Death: Essex 1350–1525* (Cambridge, Cambridge University Press, 1991), pp. 121–7; E. A. Wrigley & R. S. Schofield, *The population history of England 1541–1871. A reconstruction* (Cambridge, Cambridge University Press, 1989), 2nd edn, especially ch. 10: "The economic setting of long-term trends in English fertility and mortality". But for a recent defence of mortality as the principal agent of population control, see Peter Razzell's combative *Essays in English population history* (London,

Caliban Books, 1994), ch. 7: "The growth of population in eighteenth-century England: a critical reappraisal".

5. Roger Schofield, "The impact of scarcity and plenty on population change in England, 1541–1871", in *Hunger and history. The impact of changing food production and consumption patterns on society*, Robert J. Rotberg & Theodore K. Rabb (eds) (Cambridge, Cambridge University Press, 1985), pp. 89–91.

6. For recent developments of this argument, see Ralph A. Houlbrooke's *The English family 1450–1700* (London, Longman, 1984) and Alan Macfarlane's *Marriage and love in England. Modes of reproduction 1300–1840* (Oxford, Basil Blackwell, 1986). Elements of both extended and nuclear family systems, co-existing at pre-plague Brigstock (Northamptonshire) in the 1320s, were intriguingly examined by Judith M. Bennett in "The ties that bind: peasant marriages and families in late-medieval England", *Journal of Interdisciplinary History* **15**, 1984–5, pp. 111–29; she then further elaborated her case in *Women in the medieval English countryside. Gender and household in Brigstock before the plague* (New York and Oxford, Oxford University Press, 1987), ch. 3: "Rural households before the plague". Compare also the Fenland evidence for pre-Black Death nuclear families, all but taken for granted by H. E. Hallam in his "Age at first marriage and age at death in the Lincolnshire Fenland, 1252–1478", *Population Studies* **39**, 1985, pp. 56–7 and *passim*.

7. See, for example, Richard M. Smith, "Fertility, economy and household formation in England over three centuries", *Population and Development Review* **7**, 1981, pp. 595–622.

8. Mahmood Mamdani, *The myth of population control. Family, caste, and class in an Indian village* (New York, Monthly Review Press, 1972), p. 14.

9. Macfarlane, *Marriage and love*, p. 64 (my initial source also for Dr Mamdani's trenchant and much-quoted study).

10. Zvi Razi, "The myth of the immutable English family", *Past & Present* **140**, 1993, p. 9; but for some earlier criticism of Dr Razi's use of the Halesowen nuptiality data, see L. R. Poos & R. M. Smith, "'Legal windows onto historical populations'? Recent research on demography and the manor court in medieval England", *Law and History Review* **2**, 1984, pp. 128–52.

11. Alan R. H. Baker, "Evidence in the *Nonarum Inquisitiones* of contracting arable lands in England during the early fourteenth century", *Economic History Review* **19**, 1966, pp. 518–32.

12. Zvi Razi, "The struggle between the abbots of Halesowen and their tenants in the thirteenth and fourteenth centuries", in *Social relations and ideas. Essays in honour of R. H. Hilton*, T. H. Aston, P. R. Coss, Christopher Dyer & Joan Thirsk (eds) (Cambridge, Cambridge University Press, 1983), pp. 163–4.

13. Razi, "The myth of the immutable English family", p. 33; for the same author's earlier emphasis on family continuity at Halesowen before 1430, and for some reasons for Halesowen's special attractions up to that date, see Razi's "The erosion of the family-land bond in the late fourteenth and fifteenth centuries: a methodological note", and Christopher Dyer's "Changes in the link between families and land in the west midlands in the fourteenth and fifteenth centuries", both in *Land, kinship and life-cycle*, Richard M. Smith (ed.) (Cambridge, Cambridge University Press, 1984), pp. 295–311.

14. Razi, "The myth of the immutable English family", pp. 38–42.

15. *ibid.*, pp. 36–7.

16. Conservatism at Halesowen is emphasized by Zvi Razi, "Family, land and the village community in later medieval England", *Past & Present* **93**, 1981, pp. 3–36; for activity in the peasant land market causing an early disappearance of standard holdings, see Harvey, *The peasant land market*, pp. 338–56 and *passim*.

17. The advice is William Whateley's, quoted by Alan Macfarlane, *The origins of English individualism* (Oxford, Basil Blackwell, 1978), p. 75.
18. Richard M. Smith, "Geographical diversity in the resort to marriage in late medieval Europe: work, reputation, and unmarried females in the household formation systems of northern and southern Europe", in *Woman is a worthy wight. Women in English society c. 1200–1500*, P. J. P. Goldberg (ed.) (Stroud, Alan Sutton, 1992), pp. 26–7 and *passim*; the same arguments are again rehearsed by Dr Goldberg (a former student of R. M. Smith) in *Women, work, and life cycle in a medieval economy. Women in York and Yorkshire c. 1300–1520* (Oxford, Clarendon Press, 1992), ch. 5: "Marriage in town and country". For good evidence of late marriage in the English Fenland both before and after the Black Death – growing markedly later, however, in post-plague times – see Hallam, "Age at first marriage", pp. 59–60 and *passim*. Three children per village family was the mean at early-sixteenth-century Hunstanton, when population had begun to recover. Yet the local gentry, the Lestranges, had many more. Thus Dame Anne (b. 1494), who was married at the early age of seven and whose procreative life began with the birth of her first child in 1511, went on to have another 12 children; her son (Nicholas) had five, her grandson (Hamon) "at least seven". In contrast, the majority of Hunstanton families "had only between three and five children during this period, two to four of whom survived their early childhood". (Cord Oestmann, *Lordship and community. The Lestrange family and the village of Hunstanton, Norfok, in the first half of the sixteenth century* (Woodbridge, Boydell Press, 1994), pp. 170–71).
19. For a splendidly direct and unaffected discussion of these problems, see Beatrice Gottlieb, *The family in the western world from the Black Death to the Industrial Age* (New York, Oxford University Press, 1993), pp. 121–4. The high importance of prolonged periods of infertility during breastfeeding as a factor in population restraint, particularly among the poorer mothers who both suckled their own children and may also have been employed as wet-nurses by the rich, is rightly emphasized by Dorothy McLaren, "Marital fertility and lactation 1570–1720", in *Women in English society 1500–1800*, Mary Prior (ed.) (London, Methuen, 1985), pp. 22–53. On another track, the fact that marital difficulties ending in total breakdown could have made only the most minor contribution to post-plague family limitation – being restricted to a tiny percentage (0.3%) of his late-fourteenth-century Hereford marriage sample – is convincingly shown by Andrew Finch, "*Repulsa uxore sua*: marital difficulties and separation in the later Middle Ages", *Continuity and Change* **8**, 1993, pp. 11–38.
20. See, for example, Ann Kussmaul's *Servants in husbandry in early modern England* (Cambridge, Cambridge University Press, 1981), ch. 6: "Cycles: 1540–1790"; also the same author's *A general view of the rural economy of England 1538–1840* (Cambridge, Cambridge University Press, 1990), ch. 7: "Change, consolidation, and population".
21. P. J. P. Goldberg, "Marriage, migration, and servanthood: the York cause paper evidence", in Goldberg, *Woman is a worthy wight*, pp. 1–15; and see also the same author's *Women, work, and life cycle*, ch. 4: "Servants and servanthood". For some useful cautions concerning the sometimes over-confident presentation of Dr Goldberg's stimulating ideas, see Judith M. Bennett's review of *Women, work, and life cycle*, emphasizing the comparative poverty of the York sources on which he places so much weight (*Albion* **25**, 1993, pp. 676–8).
22. Kussmaul, *Servants in husbandry*, pp. 81–2.
23. P. J. P. Goldberg, "Urban identity and the poll taxes of 1377, 1379, and 1381", *Economic History Review* **43**, 1990, pp. 212–13. Barbara Hanawalt certainly makes this assumption when she writes about such country people: "They are probably in their twenties when

they contract this first marriage, and they probably have some land, even if it is only a few acres, or they have a trade or employment as manorial servants." (*The ties that bound. Peasant families in medieval England* (New York, Oxford University Press, 1986), p. 204). But Caroline Barron has also sounded a new note of caution about too-confident generalization from the poll tax figures, pointing to the "unusually high proportion of males" at cloth-working Worcester where in 1377 "of the 232 single people aged fourteen or over, 59 per cent were male and [only] 41 per cent were female", concluding that "winds of change blew differently in different parts of the country, and there is no reason why towns in late-fourteenth-century England should all display the same social structure" ("The fourteenth-century poll tax returns for Worcester", *Midland History* **14**, 1989, pp. 1–19).

24. Smith, "Fertility, economy and household formation", p. 604. For the shift to pastoral farming, see especially B. M. S. Campbell, "Land, labour, livestock, and productivity trends in English seignorial agriculture, 1208–1450", in *Land, labour and livestock: historical studies in European agricultural productivity*, Bruce M. S. Campbell & Mark Overton (eds) (Manchester, Manchester University Press, 1991), pp. 153–9 and table 6.1. But, as Simon Penn and Christopher Dyer point out, the advantage in the Late Middle Ages was more often with the labourer than with his employer, the preferences of whom "may not have counted for much in the real world of negotiation with potential servants" ("Wages and earnings in late-medieval England: evidence from the enforcement of the labour laws", *Economic History Review* **43**, 1990, p. 369).

25. For a discussion of these, see Kussmaul, *Servants in husbandry*, ch. 5: "Entry into and exit from service"; and see Smith, "Geographical diversity in the resort to marriage", p. 41 (where the contrast is made with Tuscany).

26. Harvey, *The peasant land market*, pp. 296–7; for much the same sequence on the Bishop of Worcester's manors, including the revival of the family–land bond in the early sixteenth century, see Christopher Dyer, "Changes in the size of peasant holdings in some west midland villages 1400–1540", in Smith, *Land, kinship and life-cycle*, pp. 283–5.

27. Harvey, *The peasant land market*, p. 157.

28. *ibid.*, pp. 316, 351.

29. Razi, "The myth of the immutable English family", pp. 42–3.

30. Harvey, *The peasant land market*, pp. 234, 238–9.

31. *ibid.*, pp. 198–9.

32. E. D. Jones, "Villein mobility in the later Middle Ages: the case of Spalding Priory", *Nottingham Medieval Studies* **36**, 1992, pp. 151–66.

33. R. K. Field, "Migration in the later Middle Ages: the case of the Hampton Lovett villeins", *Midland History* **8**, 1983, p. 42.

34. P. J. P. Goldberg, "Female labour, service and marriage in the late-medieval urban North", *Northern History* **22**, 1986, pp. 35–7; and see also the same author's "Women in fifteenth-century town life", in *Towns and townspeople in the fifteenth century*, John A. F. Thomson (ed.) (Gloucester, Alan Sutton, 1988), pp. 113–14; for the argument re-stated, see Goldberg's *Women, work, and life cycle*, pp. 299–300, 337–9.

35. Simon A. C. Penn, "Female wage-earners in late-fourteenth-century England", *Agricultural History Review* **35**, 1987, pp. 1–14.

36. For a particularly useful discussion of the role of late-medieval nuptiality in population restraint, see L. R. Poos, *A rural society after the Black Death: Essex 1350–1525* (Cambridge, Cambridge University Press, 1991), pp. 143–57; and see also Chris Wilson & Robert Woods, "Fertility in England: a long-term perspective", *Population Studies* **45**, 1991, p. 406. Dr Goldberg's survey of the York probate evidence, enabling him to estab-

lish years of high mortality in the diocese, has also led him to this conclusion ("Mortality and economic change in the diocese of York, 1390–1514", *Northern History* **24**, 1988, pp. 38–55). For ageing generally, see Zvi Razi, *Life, marriage and death in a medieval parish. Economy, society and demography in Halesowen 1270–1400* (Cambridge, Cambridge University Press, 1980), pp. 150–51; also Richard M. Smith, "Fertility, economy, and household formation in England over three centuries", *Population and Development Review* **7**, 1981, pp. 608–11, and Wrigley & Schofield, *The population history of England*, pp. 215–19 and 443–50. For the general point about the primacy of choice and the relative unimportance of the exogenous factors, see Geoffrey Hawthorn, *Plausible worlds* (Cambridge, Cambridge University Press, 1991), ch. 2: "Plague and fertility in early-modern Europe".

37. Christopher Dyer, "Deserted medieval villages in the West Midlands", *Economic History Review* **35**, 1982, p. 31.

38. David Aldred & Christopher Dyer, "A medieval Cotswold village: Roel, Gloucestershire", *Transactions of the Bristol & Gloucestershire Archaeological Society* **109**, 1991, p. 157.

39. *ibid.*, pp. 160–61. For the circumstances in which a vulnerable hamlet like Roel might first have been settled, see Della Hooke (ed.), *Medieval villages. A review of current work* (Oxford, Oxford University Committee for Archaeology, 1985), which includes Dr Hooke's own paper on "Village development in the West Midlands", pp. 125–54.

40. Bronac Holden, "The deserted medieval village of Thomley, Oxfordshire", *Oxoniensia* **50**, 1985, pp. 215–38; John Brooks, "Tubney, Oxfordshire: medieval and later settlement", *Oxoniensia* **49**, 1984, pp. 121–31.

41. T. H. Lloyd, "Some documentary sidelights on the deserted Oxfordshire village of Brookend", *Oxoniensia* **29–30**, 1964–5, pp. 116–28; Christopher Dyer, "The deserted medieval village of Woollashill, Worcestershire", *Transactions of the Worcestershire Archaeological Society* **1**, 1965–7, pp. 55–61; John Brooks, "Eaton Hastings: a deserted medieval village", *Berkshire Archaeological Journal* **64**, 1969, pp. 1–8; J. G. Hurst (ed.) *Wharram. A study of settlement on the Yorkshire Wolds*, Society for Medieval Archaeology Monographs **8**, 1979, pp. 6–16; Alan Cameron & Colin O'Brien, "The deserted medieval village of Thorpe-in-the-Glebe, Nottinghamshire", *Transactions of the Thoroton Society* **85**, 1981, pp. 56–67.

42. Cameron & O'Brien, "The deserted medieval village of Thorpe", pp. 56–60 and figs 1–2.

43. Edward Surtz & J. H. Hexter (eds), *The complete works of St Thomas More. Volume 4* (New Haven, Yale University Press, 1965), pp. 64–7 (I have slightly abbreviated this passage). But while anti-enclosure riots increased markedly in the 1530s and 1540s, they were directed for the most part at other common abuses of landowner power, while enclosure itself remained much less of a problem in the sixteenth than in the seventeenth century (Roger B. Manning, *Village revolts. Social protest and popular disturbances in England, 1509–1640* (Oxford, Clarendon Press, 1988), ch. 2: "Enclosure riots, 1509–1548").

44. Alan Davison, "Six deserted villages in Norfolk", *East Anglian Archaeology* **44**, 1988, pp. 55–7.

45. For Roger Heritage (d.1495), one of these, see Christopher Dyer, "Were there any capitalists in fifteenth-century England?", in *Enterprise and individuals in fifteenth-century England*, Jennifer Kermode (ed.) (Stroud, Alan Sutton, 1991), pp. 10–16.

46. Davison, "Six deserted villages in Norfolk", p. 57. In point of fact, Reed had little choice; as Penn and Dyer write of the growing assertiveness of agricultural workers in the Late Middle Ages, "their demands for improvements, strengthened by threats to move elsewhere if unsatisfactory rewards were offered, run as a continuous thread

through all our sources, from the manorial accounts, through the court cases, to the comments of contemporary moralists ("Wages and earnings in late-medieval England", p. 372). A recent verdict on post-plague conflict in many villages is that it could often have strengthened rural communities rather than weakening them (Christopher Dyer, "The English medieval village community and its decline", *Journal of British Studies* **33**, 1994, pp. 407–29).

Chapter 4: Impoverished noblemen and rich old ladies

1. K. B. McFarlane, "The Wars of the Roses", *Proceedings of the British Academy* **50**, 1964, pp. 115–17. For a table of fifteenth-century peers "dying by violence, not leaving a son as the heir", see Joel T. Rosenthal, *Patriarchy and families of privilege in fifteenth-century England* (Philadelphia, University of Pennsylvania Press, 1991), p. 115.
2. K. B. McFarlane, *The nobility of later medieval England* (Oxford, Oxford University Press, 1973), pp. 143, 172–6. For the nobility's active participation in the first battles of the civil war, when most of the casualties were incurred, and for its much smaller role in the final struggle at Bosworth, see the calculations of Colin Richmond, "The nobility and the Wars of the Roses, 1459–61", *Nottingham Medieval Studies* **21**, 1977, pp. 71–86.
3. McFarlane, *The nobility*, pp. 168–71.
4. S. J. Payling, "Social mobility, demographic change, and landed society in late medieval England", *Economic History Review* **45**, 1992, p. 70; and see also Simon Payling's *Political society in Lancastrian England. The greater gentry of Nottinghamshire* (Oxford, Clarendon Press, 1991), especially pp. 49–55. For the argument, based on the Norfolk evidence, that the Dissolution was itself materially assisted by the collapse of patronal lines, leaving the monks with few influential friends to put the case for their survival, see Benjamin Thompson, "Monasteries and their patrons at foundation and dissolution", *Transactions of the Royal Historical Society* **4**, 1994, pp. 103–25.
5. Payling, "Social mobility, demographic change", pp. 54–6.
6. *ibid.*, pp. 56–65.
7. A. J. Pollard, "Estate management in the later Middle Ages: the Talbots and Whitchurch, 1383–1525", *Economic History Review* **25**, 1972, pp. 553–66.
8. *ibid.*, p. 562. Dr Pollard identifies a particular collapse in the fortunes of the northern nobility in the mid-fifteenth century, this being one of the principal causes, he suggests, of the Wars of the Roses ("The north-eastern economy and the agrarian crisis of 1438–1440", *Northern History* **25**, 1989, pp. 88–105).
9. Payling, "Social mobility, demographic change", pp. 68–70.
10. John Hatcher, *Rural economy and society in the duchy of Cornwall 1300–1500* (Cambridge, Cambridge University Press, 1970), pp. 116–21.
11. Mary Saaler, "The manor of Tillingdown: the changing economy of the demesne 1325–71", *Surrey Archaeological Collections* **81**, 1991–2, pp. 19–40.
12. Chris Given-Wilson, *The English nobility in the Late Middle Ages. The fourteenth-century political community* (London, Routledge & Kegan Paul, 1987), ch. 6: "Property, the family, and money".
13. A. R. Bridbury, "The Black Death", *Economic History Review* **26**, 1973, pp. 584–6.
14. Llinos Beverley Smith, "Seignorial income in the fourteenth century: the Arundels in Chirk", *Bulletin of the Board of Celtic Studies* **28**, 1979, pp. 450–51; for the wealth of the Arundels, see C. Given-Wilson, "Wealth and credit, public and private: the earls of

Arundel 1306–1397", *English Historical Review* **106**, 1991, pp. 1–26.

15. Christopher Dyer, *Warwickshire farming 1349–c. 1520. Preparations for agricultural revolution*, Dugdale Society Occasional Papers **27**, 1981, pp. 15–16.

16. Given-Wilson, "Wealth and credit", p. 21.

17. Carole Rawcliffe, *The Staffords, earls of Stafford and dukes of Buckingham 1394–1521* (Cambridge, Cambridge University Press, 1978), ch. 6: "The finances of the Staffords, 1400–1473"; also T. B. Pugh (ed.), *The marcher lordships of South Wales 1415–1536. Select documents* (Cardiff, University of Wales Press, 1963), pp. 149–53, 161–2, 164; and for the general problem of arrears, largely on ecclesiastical estates, see Christopher Dyer, "A redistribution of incomes in fifteenth-century England?", *Past & Present* **39**, 1968, pp. 11–33. However, for the case against the seriousness of arrears, see R. R. Davies, "Baronial accounts, incomes, and arrears in the later Middle Ages", *Economic History Review* **21**, 1968, pp. 211–29.

18. For the good management and prosperity of the Greys, see R. I. Jack's introduction to his edition of *The Grey of Ruthin Valor* (Sydney, Sydney University Press, 1965); and see also *The complete peerage* (under "Earls of Kent").

19. McFarlane, *The nobility*, pp. 48–9.

20. Martin Cherry, "The Courtenay earls of Devon: the formation and disintegration of a late-medieval aristocratic affinity", *Southern History* **1**, 1979, pp. 71–97; and the same author's "The struggle for power in mid-fifteenth-century Devonshire", in *Patronage, the crown, and the provinces in later medieval England*, Ralph A. Griffiths (ed.) (Gloucester, Alan Sutton, 1981), pp. 123–44; also J. A. F. Thomson, "The Courtenay family in the Yorkist period", *Bulletin of the Institute of Historical Research* **45**, 1972, pp. 230–46.

21. For Richard of Cambridge's role in the Southampton Plot, see T. B. Pugh, *Henry V and the Southampton Plot of 1415*, Southampton Records Series **30**, 1988, pp. 88–102; and see also the same author's "The Southampton Plot of 1415", in *Kings and nobles in the later Middle Ages. A tribute to Charles Ross*, Ralph A. Griffiths & James Sherborne (eds) (Gloucester, Alan Sutton, 1986), pp. 62–89.

22. These entirely contrary views of Duke Richard, together with much material on his financial health, are thoroughly explored by T. B. Pugh, "Richard Plantagenet (1411–60), duke of York, as the king's lieutenant in France and Ireland", in *Aspects of late-medieval government and society: essays presented to J. R. Lander*, J. G. Rowe (ed.) (Toronto, University of Toronto Press, 1986), pp. 107–41. Richard of York's principal servants and annuitants are usefully listed by P. A. Johnson, *Duke Richard of York 1411–1460* (Oxford, Clarendon Press, 1988), pp. 228–41. His responsibility for the wars is discussed by Ralph A. Griffiths, "Duke Richard of York's intentions in 1450 and the origins of the Wars of the Roses", in the same author's *King and country. England and Wales in the fifteenth century* (London, Hambledon Press, 1991), pp. 277–304.

23. Pugh, "Richard Plantagenet", p. 112.

24. A. R. Myers (ed.), *The household of Edward IV. The Black Book and the Ordinance of 1478* (Manchester, Manchester University Press, 1959), p. 98. For the effectiveness of this system in late-medieval England, where "the universal assumption was that power filtered down from the crown through the nobility to the gentry, and upwards through the same hierarchy in reverse", and where "the hierarchical mode, with the key role it gave to the nobles, was a simple fact of life", see Christine Carpenter, "Who ruled the Midlands in the later Middle Ages?", *Midland History* **19**, 1994, p. 12 and *passim*. Dr Carpenter makes a clear contrast with the vanishing role of the aristocracy under the Tudors.

25. T. B. Pugh, "The magnates, knights and gentry", in *Fifteenth-century England 1399–1509. Studies in politics and society*, S. B. Chrimes, C. D. Ross & R. A. Griffiths (eds)

(Manchester, Manchester University Press, 1972), pp. 101–5; also Christine Carpenter, "The Beauchamp affinity: a study of bastard feudalism at work", *English Historical Review* **95**, 1980, p. 531.

26. Anne Crawford (ed.), *The household books of John Howard, duke of Norfolk, 1462–1471, 1481–1483* (Stroud, Alan Sutton, 1992), vol. 1, pp. xvi–xvii and vol. 2, pp. 468–70. Late-medieval baronial households and their many extensions and annexes – "tenants, officials and counsellors, extraordinary retainers, livery, and miscellaneous servants and well-wishers" – are usefully discussed by Michael Hicks, *Bastard feudalism* (London, Longman, 1995), ch. 2: "Varieties of bastard feudalism", and pp. 137–46.

27. John Pitcher (ed.), *Francis Bacon. The essays* (Harmondsworth, Penguin Books, 1985), pp. 92–3.

28. Rawcliffe, *The Staffords*, pp. 68–9.

29. Mary Harris & J. M. Thurgood, "The account of the great household of Humphrey, first duke of Buckingham, for the year 1452–3", *Camden Miscellany* **29**, 1984, p. 5.

30. Rawcliffe, *The Staffords*, pp. 75–7; also Carole Rawcliffe & Susan Flower, "English noblemen and their advisers: consultation and collaboration in the later Middle Ages", *Journal of British Studies* **25**, 1986, pp. 157–77.

31. Rawcliffe, *The Staffords*, pp. 132–3; but for their continuing difficulties in Wales, see Barbara J. Harris, "Landlords and tenants in England in the later Middle Ages: the Buckingham estates", *Past & Present* **43**, 1969, pp. 146–50; and see also Pugh, *The marcher lordships*, especially pp. 145–83.

32. Rawcliffe, *The Staffords*, ch. 2: "The second and third dukes of Buckingham, 1460–1521"; for Duke Edward, see Barbara J. Harris, *Edward Stafford, third duke of Buckingham, 1478–1521* (Stanford, Stanford University Press, 1986).

33. Payling, *Political society in Lancastrian England*, pp. 56–62.

34. For these developments, see Rowena E. Archer, "Rich old ladies: the problem of late medieval dowagers", in *Property and politics: essays in late medieval English history*, Tony Pollard (ed.) (Gloucester, Alan Sutton, 1984), pp. 16–19; also Jennifer C. Ward, *English noblewomen in the later Middle Ages* (London, Longman, 1992), pp. 26–7; and the more general treatment in Rosenthal, *Patriarchy and families of privilege*, ch. 3: "Widows". For the exceptionally generous dower entitlements of similarly long-lived London widows, see Caroline M. Barron and Anne F. Sutton (eds), *Medieval London widows 1300–1500* (London, Hambledon Press, 1994), pp. xvii, xxi and *passim*; and see also Henrietta Leyser, *Medieval women. A social history of women in England 450–1500* (London, Weidenfield and Nicolson, 1995), pp. 175–8.

35. McFarlane, *The nobility*, p. 65.

36. Archer, "Rich old ladies", p. 23.

37. Joel T. Rosenthal, "Other victims: peeresses as war widows, 1450–1500", *History* **72**, 1987, pp. 213–30.

38. J. R. Lander, "Marriage and politics in the fifteenth century: the Nevilles and the Wydevilles", *Bulletin of the Institute of Historical Research* **36**, 1963, pp. 129–35.

39. Archer, "Rich old ladies", p. 19 (the quotation is from a late-fourteenth-century source).

40. C. A. J. Armstrong, "The piety of Cicely, duchess of York: a study in late medieval culture", in the same author's *England, France and Burgundy in the fifteenth century* (London, Hambledon Press, 1983), pp. 135–56; and see also Rosenthal, *Patriarchy and families of privilege*, pp. 238–46.

41. Lander, "Marriage and politics", p. 120.

42. Archer, "Rich old ladies", pp. 24–5.

43. Lander, "Marriage and politics", p. 136.

44. Rowena E. Archer, "The estates and finances of Margaret of Brotherton, c.1320–1399", *Historical Research* **60**, 1987, pp. 264–80, and the same author's "Women as landholders and administrators in the later Middle Ages", in *Woman is a worthy wight*, P. J. P. Goldberg (ed.) (Stroud, Alan Sutton, 1992), pp. 149–81; also Ward, *English noblewomen*, ch. 6: "Estates and revenue", and ch. 8: "Religious practice", and Barbara J. Harris, "A new look at the Reformation: aristocratic women and nunneries, 1450–1540", *Journal of British Studies* **32**, 1993, pp. 89–113. For Margaret Beaufort, see Michael K. Jones & Malcolm G. Underwood, *The king's mother. Lady Margaret Beaufort, Countess of Richmond and Derby* (Cambridge, Cambridge University Press, 1992).
45. As quoted by Sherwin B. Nuland, *How we die* (London, Chatto & Windus, 1994), p. 73.

Chapter 5: Knight, esquire and gentleman

1. Christine Carpenter, *Locality and polity. A study of Warwickshire landed society, 1401–1499* (Cambridge, Cambridge University Press, 1992), pp. 44–6. For the earlier emergence of the county gentry as a community, and then for some reservations about what this community comprised before the late fifteenth century, see Peter Coss, *Lordship, knighthood and locality. A study in English society c.1180–c.1280* (Cambridge, Cambridge University Press, 1991), ch. 9: "Conclusion: the origins of the gentry"; also Roger Virgoe, "Aspects of the county community in the fifteenth century", in *Profit, piety and the professions in later medieval England*, Michael Hicks (ed.) (Gloucester, Alan Sutton, 1990), pp. 1–13. The Black Death is given particular prominence in this process, as in everything else he discusses, by Robert C. Palmer, *English law in the age of the Black Death, 1348–1381* (Chapel Hill and London, University of North Carolina Press, 1993), ch. 3: "Creating the gentry"; whereas for Jean Scammell "Henry II was the gentry's midwife, and the petty assizes and the pragmatic concept of the *statuliber*, the greatest single factors in its birth." (The formation of the English social structure: freedom, knights and gentry, 1066–1300, *Speculum* **68**, 1993, p. 618). Deciding "who were the gentry?" has remained just as much a problem for early-modern historians, as in Felicity Heal and Clive Holmes, *The gentry in England and Wales, 1500–1700* (London, Macmillan, 1994), which concludes simply that "the gentry were that body of men and women whose gentility was acknowledged by others" (p. 19).
2. Christine Carpenter, "The fifteenth-century English gentry and their estates", in *Gentry and lesser nobility in late-medieval Europe*, Michael Jones (ed.) (Gloucester, Alan Sutton, 1986), pp. 38–45.
3. Nigel Saul, *Knights and esquires: the Gloucestershire gentry in the fourteenth century* (Oxford, Clarendon Press, 1981), pp. 232–7.
4. Chris Given-Wilson, *The English nobility in the Late Middle Ages: the fourteenth-century political community* (London, Routledge & Kegan Paul, 1987), pp. 71–3; also Michael Bennett, "Careerism in late-medieval England", in *People, politics and community in the later Middle Ages*, Joel Rosenthal & Colin Richmond (eds) (Gloucester, Alan Sutton, 1987), pp. 19–39.
5. Given-Wilson, *The English nobility*, p. 83; for a good recent discussion of the close association of power and landholding in late-medieval England, with particular reference to the upper gentry (the knights), see Simon Payling, *Political society in Lancastrian England. The greater gentry of Nottinghamshire* (Oxford, Clarendon Press, 1991), ch. 1: "The balance of property".

6. Christopher Dyer, "Were there any capitalists in fifteenth-century England?", in *Enterprise and individuals in fifteenth-century England*, Jennifer Kermode (ed.) (Stroud, Alan Sutton, 1991), pp. 10–16.

7. Colin Richmond, *John Hopton. A fifteenth-century Suffolk gentleman* (Cambridge, Cambridge University Press, 1981), p. 30 and *passim*.

8. For this argument, see S. R. Epstein, "Regional fairs, institutional innovation, and economic growth in late-medieval Europe", *Economic History Review* **47**, 1994, pp. 459–82.

9. Robert S. Gottfried, *Epidemic disease in fifteenth-century England. The medical response and the demographic consequences* (Leicester, Leicester University Press, 1978), pp. 49–50. Gottfried describes the national epidemic of 1479–80 as "the most virulent of the fifteenth century".

10. Colin Richmond, "The expenses of Thomas Playter of Sotterley, 1459–60", *Proceedings of the Suffolk Institute of Archaeology and History* **35**, 1981, pp. 43–4; the Playter brass, although damaged, survives at Sotterley Church.

11. Keith Dockray, "Why did fifteenth-century English gentry marry?: the Pastons, Plumptons and Stonors reconsidered", in Jones, *Gentry and lesser nobility*, pp. 70–76.

12. *ibid.*, pp. 74–5.

13. Eric Acheson, *A gentry community. Leicestershire in the fifteenth century, c.1422–c.1485* (Cambridge, Cambridge University Press, 1992), p. 158.

14. *ibid.*, pp. 156–7.

15. *ibid.*, pp. 68–9, 155 (footnote 93). The huge complexity and potency of these links, through all sorts of associations including (but not confined to) the family, has recently been re-emphasized by Christine Carpenter, who entirely rejects the notion of a "county community" and calls for a very different sort of study based on network analysis ("Gentry and community in medieval England", *Journal of British Studies* **33**, 1994, pp. 341–80).

16. For the highly profitable marriage alliances, over several generations, of the Leeks of Cotham, see Payling, *Political society in Lancastrian England*, pp. 44–5; and for the Plumptons' similar but shorter-lived success, see Joan W. Kirby, "A fifteenth-century family, the Plumptons of Plumpton, and their lawyers, 1461–1515", *Northern History* **25**, 1989, p. 109. Although Colin Richmond, briskly refuting the views of his old tutor Bruce McFarlane, has recently denied that the gentry land market was significantly "tight" in the fifteenth century, even he admits that "most property moved by marriage" during this century (*The Paston family in the fifteenth century. The first phase* (Cambridge, Cambridge University Press, 1990), p. 42).

17. Carpenter, *Locality and polity*, pp. 102–3, 116.

18. *ibid.*, pp. 110–12, 115–16.

19. *ibid.*, p. 259.

20. Susan M. Wright, *The Derbyshire gentry in the fifteenth century*, Derbyshire Record Society **8**, 1983, pp. 35–6.

21. *ibid.*, pp. 36–7.

22. *ibid.*, pp. 32, 43–4. For the further development of the use in such a way as to limit widows' rights, see Palmer, *English law in the age of the Black Death*, particularly pp. 119–21, 130–32, in which he again gives the plague the leading role.

23. Carpenter, *Locality and polity*, pp. 112–13.

24. J. N. Hare, "The demesne lessees of fifteenth-century Wiltshire", *Agricultural History Review* **29**, 1981, pp. 4–6; Wright, *The Derbyshire gentry*, p. 16; Christopher Dyer, *Warwickshire farming 1349–c.1520. Preparations for agricultural revolution*, Dugdale Society Occasional Papers **27**, 1981, pp. 4–5.

25. F. R. H. Du Boulay, "Who were farming the English demesnes at the end of the Middle Ages?", *Economic History Review* **17**, 1964–5, pp. 450–51.

26. P. W. Fleming, "The Lovelace dispute: concepts of property and inheritance in fifteenth-century Kent", *Southern History* **12**, 1990, pp. 14–15.

27. Acheson, *A gentry community*, p. 58.

28. Carpenter, *Locality and polity*, pp. 111–12, 168–9; A. Cameron, "Sir Henry Willoughby of Wollaton", *Transactions of the Thoroton Society* **74**, 1970, pp. 11–12; Payling, *Political society in Lancastrian England*, pp. 56–9.

29. Carpenter, *Locality and polity*, pp. 33, 184–6; and see also Dyer, *Warwickshire farming*, p. 17.

30. Carpenter, *Locality and polity*, p. 185. Stock-farming's superior profitability (over arable) in mid-fifteenth-century northern England is emphasized by A. J. Pollard, "The north-eastern economy and the agrarian crisis of 1438–1440", *Northern History* **25**, 1989, pp. 88–105.

31. G. W. Bernard, "The rise of Sir William Compton, early Tudor courtier", *English Historical Review* **96**, 1981, pp. 754–77.

32. *ibid.*, p. 777.

33. Payling, *Political society in Lancastrian England*, p. 49.

34. *ibid.*, pp. 66–7.

35. *ibid.*, p. 73.

36. *ibid.*, pp. 74–7.

37. Acheson, *A gentry community*, pp. 200–201.

Chapter 6: Of monks and nuns

1. William Abel Pantin (ed.), *Documents illustrating the activities of the general and provincial chapters of the English black monks 1215–1540. Vol. III*, Camden Third Series **54**, 1937, pp. 123–4; David Knowles, *The religious orders in England* (Cambridge, Cambridge University Press, 1979), new edn, vol. 3, pp. 159–60.

2. Knowles, *The religious orders*, vol. 2, p. 257.

3. *ibid.*, vol. 3, pp. 161–2.

4. C. H. Williams (ed.), *English historical documents 1485–1558* (London, Eyre & Spottiswoode, 1967), pp. 771–2.

5. Deirdre Le Faye, "Selborne Priory, 1233–1486", *Proceedings of the Hampshire Field Club and Archaeological Society* **30**, 1973, pp. 47–71.

6. A. L. Bedingfeld (ed.), *A cartulary of Creake Abbey*, Norfolk Record Society **35**, 1966, pp. xv–xxiv; *Creake Abbey, Norfolk*, 1970, pp. 3–8. There was an epidemic at Norwich in 1503–4 which seems likely to have been the killer at Creake also (Paul Slack, *The impact of plague in Tudor and Stuart England* (London, Routledge & Kegan Paul, 1985), p. 61.

7. Eileen Power, *Medieval English nunneries c. 1275 to 1535* (Cambridge, Cambridge University Press, 1922), ch. 5: "Financial difficulties". For a more recent comment on this poverty in the later houses, contrasting with the wealth of the greater Anglo-Saxon nunneries, see Sally Thompson, "Why English nunneries had no history: a study of the problems of the English nunneries founded after the Conquest", in *Medieval religious women. Volume One. Distant echoes*, John A. Nichols & Lillian Thomas Shank (eds) (Kalamazoo, Cistercian Publications, 1984), pp. 131–49; and for the same author's general account of these post-Conquest communities, see her *Women religious. The founding of English nunneries after the Norman Conquest* (Oxford, Clarendon Press, 1991).

8. As said by the Dale chronicler (J. C. Dickinson, "Early suppressions of English houses of Austin canons", in *Medieval studies presented to Rose Graham*, Veronica Ruffer & A. J. Taylor (eds) (Oxford, Oxford University Press, 1950), p. 57).

9. David Knowles & R. Neville Hadcock, *Medieval religious houses. England and Wales* (London, Longmans, 1953), pp. 212, 221; also for Wothorpe, see William Dugdale, *Monasticon Anglicanum* (London, 1846), vol. 4, pp. 266–7.

10. Knowles & Hadcock, *Medieval religious houses*, pp. 211–12, 214, 216.

11. *ibid.*, p. 156.

12. *ibid.*, pp. 125–60; Dickinson, "Early suppressions of English houses", pp. 60–69; and see also David M. Robinson, *The geography of Augustinian settlement in medieval England and Wales* (Oxford, British Archaeological Reports, 1980), ch. 4: "Unsuccessful Augustinian foundations".

13. *Calendar of close rolls 1346–1349*, p. 595 (payment is recorded against this debt).

14. *ibid.*, *1349–1354*, pp. 335–6.

15. *Calendar of papal registers: papal letters 1362–1404*, p. 32 (July 1363). The 12 included canons at Cockersand also, Croxton's daughter-house in Lancashire.

16. R. Horrox (trans. and ed.), *The Black Death* (Manchester, Manchester University Press, 1994), pp. 78–9, 85.

17. A. Hamilton Thompson, *The English clergy and their organization in the later Middle Ages* (Oxford, Oxford University Press, 1947), pp. 168–70.

18. Knowles & Hadcock, *Medieval religious houses*, p. 143.

19. A. Hamilton Thompson (ed.), *Visitations of religious houses in the diocese of Lincoln. Volume II. Records of visitations held by William Alnwick, bishop of Lincoln,* AD *1436 to* AD *1449*, Lincoln Record Society **14**, 1918, pp. 206–17.

20. *ibid.*, p. 210; for a recent comment on the work practices of monastic servants, especially those of Westminster, see Barbara Harvey, *Living and dying in England 1100–1540. The monastic experience* (Oxford, Clarendon Press, 1993), pp. 159–63.

21. A. G. Dickens, *Late monasticism and the Reformation* (London, Hambledon Press, 1994), pp. 16–17, 71–3.

22. *ibid.*, pp. 76–7.

23. *ibid.*, p. 15.

24. Barbara Harvey, *Westminster Abbey and its estates in the Middle Ages* (Oxford, Clarendon Press, 1977), p. 331.

25. This is certainly the well-informed concluding judgement of John Hare, "The monks as landlords: the leasing of the monastic demesnes in southern England", in *The Church in pre-Reformation society: essays in honour of F. R. H. Du Boulay*, Caroline M. Barron & Christopher Harper-Bill (eds) (Woodbridge, Boydell Press, 1985), p. 94. For Battle's activity, see the work of the geographer P. F. Brandon, in particular his "Arable farming in a Sussex scarp-foot parish during the Late Middle Ages", *Sussex Archaeological Collections* **100**, 1962, pp. 60–72; "Agriculture and the effects of flooding and weather at Barnhorne, Sussex, during the Late Middle Ages", *Sussex Archaeological Collections* **109**, 1971, pp. 69–93; and "Demesne arable farming in coastal Sussex during the later Middle Ages", *Agricultural History Review* **19**, 1971, pp. 113–34. For Oseney, see David Postles, "The Oseney Abbey flock", *Oxoniensia* **49**, 1984, pp. 141–52.

26. Una Rees, "The leases of Haughmond Abbey, Shropshire", *Midland History* **8**, 1983, pp. 14–28; H. E. Hallam, "The agrarian economy of South Lincolnshire in the mid-fifteenth century", *Nottingham Medieval Studies* **11**, 1967, pp. 86–95.

27. Ian Kershaw, *Bolton Priory rentals and ministers' accounts, 1473–1539*, Yorkshire Archaeological Society Record Series **132**, 1970, p. xv; A. Hamilton Thompson, *History and*

architectural description of the priory of St Mary, Bolton-in-Wharfedale, Thoresby Society **30**, 1928, pp. 111–12, 154–5. For Bolton's earlier prosperity, see Ian Kershaw, *Bolton Priory. The economy of a northern monastery 1286–1325* (Oxford, Oxford University Press, 1973), ch. 6: "The priory's finances".

28. Justin McCann (trans. and ed.), *The Rule of St Benedict* (London, Sheed & Ward, 1972), pp. 84–5.

29. The case for Glastonbury is well-stated by Robert W. Dunning, "Revival at Glastonbury 1530–9", *Studies in Church History* **14**, 1977, pp. 213–22. For two more recent contributions to the debate about quality, see Roger Bowers, "The musicians of the Lady Chapel of Winchester Cathedral Priory, 1402–1539", *Journal of Ecclesiastical History* **45**, 1994, pp. 210–37, and Joan Greatrex, "The English cathedral priories and the pursuit of learning in the later Middle Ages", *ibid.*, pp. 396–411.

30. Harvey, *Westminster Abbey and its estates*, p. 87.

31. As quoted by G. G. Coulton, *Five centuries of religion. Volume III: Getting and spending* (Cambridge, Cambridge University Press, 1936), pp. 375–6.

32. For this, see Horrox, *The Black Death*, pp. 45–54.

33. Ian Keil, "The chamberer of Glastonbury Abbey in the fourteenth century", *Proceedings of the Somersetshire Archaeological and Natural History Society* **107**, 1963, pp. 86, 90 (tables 4 and 6); and see the same author's "Impropriator and benefice in the later Middle Ages", *Wiltshire Archaeological and Natural History Magazine* **58**, 1961–3, pp. 351–63.

34. Power, *Medieval English nunneries*, p. 339. Yvonne Parrey takes issue with Eileen Power's "rather negative assessment" of the condition of the English nunneries in the Late Middle Ages, arguing for the high quality of religious life at Amesbury (Wiltshire) shortly before the Dissolution. Even there, however, in the contemporary homily she quotes, "little is made of any notion of absolute or communal poverty but that vow is understood in terms of obedience to the common will, or indeed the will of Christ, expressed by a religious superior. This seems like a very realistic appraisal of the actual operation of the vow of poverty in many if not most houses, and suggests that the author was not inclined to make unrealistic demands."("'Devoted disciples of Christ': early sixteenth-century religious life in the nunnery at Amesbury", *Historical Research* **67**, 1994, p. 246.)

35. For grumbles of this kind, see Christopher Harper-Bill, "The labourer is worthy of his hire? Complaints about diet in late-medieval English monasteries", in *The Church in pre-Reformation society*, Barron & Harper-Bill (eds), pp. 95–107; and for the remark about medieval road systems which I borrow here for another purpose, see F. M. Stenton, "The road system of medieval England", *Economic History Review* **7**, 1936, p. 21.

36. James P. Carley, *Glastonbury Abbey. The Holy House at the head of the Moors Adventurous* (Woodbridge, Boydell Press, 1988), pp. 76–8.

37. C. H. Williams (ed.), *English historical documents, 1485–1558* (London, Eyre & Spottiswoode, 1967), p. 676.

38. McCann, *The Rule of St Benedict*, pp. 94–7 (my italics).

39. Barbara Harvey, *Living and dying in England, 1100–1540. The monastic experience* (Oxford, Clarendon Press, 1993), p. 71.

40. *ibid.*, ch. 2: "Diet", and pp. 109–11.

41. Owen Ashmore, "The Whalley Abbey bursars' account for 1520", *Transactions of the Historical Society of Lancashire and Cheshire* **114**, 1962, p. 51.

42. *Victoria History of the County of Lancaster. Volume 2* (London, 1908), pp. 132–7.

43. McCann, *The Rule of St Benedict*, pp. 96–7 and note 63.

44. Eleanor Searle & Barbara Ross (eds), *The cellarers' rolls of Battle Abbey 1275–1513*, Sussex Record Society **65**, 1967, pp. 19–20.

45. G. H. Rooke, "Dom William Ingram and his account-book, 1504–1533", *Journal of Ecclesiastical History* **7**, 1956, p. 38.
46. *ibid.*, pp. 31–2; Léon-E. Halkin, *Erasmus. A critical biography* (Oxford, Blackwell, 1993), p. 38.
47. R. A. B. Mynors & Peter G. Bietenholz (eds), *The correspondence of Erasmus. Letters 1122 to 1251. 1520 to 1521* (Toronto, University of Toronto Press, 1988), pp. 237, 239.
48. *ibid.*, p. 227.
49. *ibid.*
50. John P. Dolan (ed.), *The essential Erasmus* (New York, Mentor Books, 1964), p. 92 (from the conclusion of Erasmus's *Enchiridion*).
51. Halkin, *Erasmus*, p. 268.

Chapter 7: Like people, like priest

1. Rosemary Horrox (trans. and ed.), *The Black Death* (Manchester, Manchester University Press, 1994), p. 54.
2. Richard Gyug, "The effects and extent of the Black Death of 1348: new evidence for clerical mortality in Barcelona", *Medieval Studies* **45**, 1983, p. 395.
3. R. A. Davies, "The effect of the Black Death on the parish priests of the medieval diocese of Coventry and Lichfield", *Historical Research* **62**, 1989, pp. 87, 89. For a similar calculation based on court roll evidence, see Norman Groome, "The Black Death in the hundred of Higham Ferrers", *Northamptonshire Past and Present* **6:6**, 1982–3, p. 311 (where "at least half the parishes lost their parsons"). In Herefordshire "over half" of the benefices lost their priests in 1349, the great majority through the death of the incumbent (William J. Dohar, *The Black Death and pastoral leadership. The diocese of Hereford in the fourteenth century* (Philadelphia, University of Pennsylvania Press, 1955), pp. 40–55: "Clerical mortality in the diocese".
4. Davies, "The effect of the Black Death on the parish priests", p. 87.
5. For Henry Knighton on this "glut", see Horrox, *The Black Death*, p. 79. Some pre-plague crowding is also suggested by the Winchester diocese ordination figures, which quite clearly suggest both a growing surplus of clergy before the Black Death and the drying-up by the 1360s of any pool of unemployed clergy which might have filled the vacant benefices in the plague's aftermath (Virginia Davis, "Rivals for ministry? Ordinations of the secular and regular clergy in southern England c.1300–1500", *Studies in Church History* **26**, 1989, pp. 101–3). Both Virginia Davis and Robert Swanson (using the Lichfield ordination lists) agree that clerical recruitment was at its lowest ebb during the first half of the fifteenth century, before staging a recovery from the 1460s (*ibid.*, pp. 103–4, and R. N. Swanson, *Church and society in late-medieval England* (Oxford, Basil Blackwell, 1989), pp. 34–5).
6. Horrox, *The Black Death*, pp. 271–3.
7. *ibid.*, p. 273.
8. *ibid.*, p. 274.
9. A. Hamilton Thompson, "Registers of John Gynewell, bishop of Lincoln, for the years 1347–1350", *Archaeological Journal* **68**, 1911, p. 329; Horrox, *The Black Death*, p. 77; and see also Dohar, *The Black Death and pastoral leadership*, ch. 4: "Clerical recruitment and pastoral provision".
10. Horrox, *The Black Death*, p. 309.

11. *ibid.*, p. 307. For huge post-plague accumulations of such chaplains, some 497 of whom are recorded in London in 1379, see A. K. McHardy (ed.), *The church in London 1375–1392*, London Record Society **13**, 1977, p. xiv; also the same author's "The Lincolnshire clergy in the later fourteenth century", in *England in the fourteenth century. Proceedings of the 1985 Harlaxton Symposium*, W. M. Ormrod (ed.) (Woodbridge, Boydell Press, 1986), where Lincoln is said to have been "swarming with over 150 unbeneficed clerics [in 1377] . . . Boston had 38 unbeneficed men. Grantham, Stamford and Grimsby each had some 14 such chaplains, while Louth had 10" (p. 150). Most of these chaplains were employed as chantry priests. For a comment (not unfavourable) on their quality, see Rosalind Hill, "'*A chaunterie for soules*': London chantries in the reign of Richard II", in *The reign of Richard II*, F. R. H. Du Boulay & Caroline M. Barron (eds) (London, Athlone Press, 1971), pp. 242–55.

12. Horrox, *The Black Death*, pp. 83–4.

13. *ibid.*, p. 36.

14. *ibid.*, pp. 21–3.

15. *ibid.*, p. 34.

16. *ibid.*, p. 69.

17. R. N. Swanson (trans. and ed.), *Catholic England. Faith, religion and observance before the Reformation* (Manchester, Manchester University Press, 1993), p. 127.

18. *ibid.*, p. 126.

19. *ibid.*, p. 139.

20. As said by Boccaccio of country people in the Florentine *contado* (Horrox, *The Black Death*, p. 33).

21. H. F. Westlake, "The parish gilds of the later fourteenth century", *Transactions of the St Paul's Ecclesiological Society* **8**, 1917–20, p. 104; also the same author's *The parish gilds of mediaeval England* (London, Society for Promoting Christian Knowledge, 1919), p. 50.

22. For the doctrine of Purgatory, see in particular Jacques Le Goff, *The birth of Purgatory* (London, Scolar Press, 1984), originally published as *La naissance du Purgatoire* (Paris, Editions Gallimard, 1981). And for chantries in general, see K. L. Wood-Legh, *Perpetual chantries in Britain* (Cambridge, Cambridge University Press, 1965), *passim*. In counting up the Bristol chantries, Clive Burgess notes one such foundation of the late thirteenth century, but nothing again until 1328, with the greatest concentration in the two decades *before* the Black Death. He also observes that the fifteenth-century foundations, of which there continued to be a steady stream, had a much better chance of survival ("Strategies for eternity: perpetual chantry foundation in late medieval Bristol", in *Religious belief and ecclesiastical careers in late medieval England*, Christopher Harper-Bill (ed.) (Woodbridge, Boydell Press, 1991), pp. 1–32. In the York parishes, excluding the Minster, only three chantries are known before 1300; there were "at least 39" foundations in the next 50 years, some 36 of which were concentrated between 1310 and 1340; but the pace slowed down markedly thereafter, 1351–1400 (21), 1401–50 (14), 1451–1500 (7) and then only one other (of 1509) before the suppression (R. B. Dobson, "The foundation of perpetual chantries by the citizens of medieval York", *Studies in Church History* **4**, 1967, pp. 29, 32).

23. Toulmin Smith & Lucy Toulmin Smith (eds), *English gilds*, Early English Text Society, 1870, pp. 74–7.

24. For some recent studies, see Barbara A. Hanawalt, "Keepers of the lights: late medieval English parish gilds", *Journal of Medieval and Renaissance Studies* **14**, 1984, pp. 21–37; Caroline M. Barron, "The parish fraternities of medieval London", in *The Church in pre-Reformation society. Essays in honour of F. R. H. Du Boulay*, Caroline Barron & Christopher

Harper-Bill (eds) (Woodbridge, Boydell Press, 1985), pp. 13–37; Miri Rubin, "Small groups: identity and solidarity in the Late Middle Ages", in *Enterprise and individuals in fifteenth-century England*, Jennifer Kermode (ed.) (Stroud, Alan Sutton, 1991), pp. 132–50; and Gervase Rosser, "Going to the fraternity feast: commensality and social relations in late medieval England", *Journal of British Studies* **33**, 1994, pp. 430–46.

25. Barron, "The parish fraternities of medieval London", pp. 24–5.

26. Alan Kreider, one of the severest critics of the association, deplores "the hoary notion that the chantries were the response of piously petrified Englishmen to the terrors of the Black Death", yet has to concede from his own data that "in many instances this was almost certainly the case" (*English chantries. The road to dissolution* (Cambridge, Mass. and London, Harvard University Press, 1979), p. 86).

27. Swanson, *Catholic England*, pp. 218–20.

28. T. B. Pugh, *Henry V and the Southampton Plot of 1415*, Southampton Records Series **30**, 1988, p. 144. For Henry V's less well-known role as a religious reformer, see Jeremy Catto, "Religious change under Henry V", in *Henry V. The practice of kingship*, G. L. Harriss (ed.) (Oxford, Oxford University Press, 1985), pp. 97–115.

29. Patrick Strong & Felicity Strong, "The last wills and codicils of Henry V", *English Historical Review* **96**, 1981, p. 91.

30. The Inland Revenue uses this formula in relation to capital gains. For Henry's funerary arrangements and bequests, see Christopher Allmand, *Henry V* (London, Methuen, 1992), pp. 174–82; also for his surviving Westminster burial chapel, see Paul Binski, *Westminster Abbey and the Plantagenets. Kingship and the representation of power 1200–1400* (New Haven and London, Yale University Press, 1995), pp. 147–8. For the soaring cost of death in late-medieval Ireland, see Margaret Murphy, "The high cost of dying: an analysis of *pro anima* bequests in medieval Dublin", *Studies in Church History* **24**, 1987, pp. 111–22.

31. P. S. Lewis, *Later medieval France. The polity* (London, Macmillan, 1968), p. 204.

32. G. L. Harriss, *Cardinal Beaufort. A study of Lancastrian ascendancy and decline* (Oxford, Clarendon Press, 1988), pp. 378–9; for the text of Beaufort's will, see J. Nichols, *A collection of all the wills, now known to be extant, of the kings and queens of England etc* (London, Society of Antiquaries, 1780), pp. 321–44.

33. Helen Jewell, "English bishops as educational benefactors in the later fifteenth century", in *The church, politics and patronage in the fifteenth century*, Barrie Dobson (ed.) (Gloucester, Alan Sutton, 1984), pp. 146–67.

34. For some further discussion of these and of the academic colleges, see my *The architecture of medieval Britain: A social history* (New York and London, Yale University Press, 1990), pp. 218–21, 279–84.

35. William Shakespeare, *Henry V*, iv:i:294–6. Although the words are Shakespeare's, the problem and its solution were Henry's own. For the charitable works of Henry V and his successors, see Joel T. Rosenthal, "Kings, continuity and ecclesiastical benefaction in 15th century England", in *People, politics and community in the later Middle Ages*, Joel Rosenthal & Colin Richmond (eds) (Gloucester, Alan Sutton, 1987), pp. 161–75. What was expected of bedesmen and of the sick in offering up prayers for individual founders is discussed by Carole Rawcliffe, "The hospitals of later medieval London", *Medical History* **28**, 1984, pp. 1–21. The mentally ill, Walter Lord Hungerford provided, were to be excluded from his charity on the grounds that they were incapable of praying for his soul (Michael Hicks, "Walter, Lord Hungerford (d.1449) and his chantry in Salisbury Cathedral", *The Hatcher Review* **3:28**, 1989, pp. 394–5).

36. Christine Carpenter, *Locality and polity. A study of Warwickshire landed society, 1401–1499*

(Cambridge, Cambridge University Press, 1992), p. 223.

37. *ibid.*, p. 225.

38. T. F. Reddaway & Lorna E. M. Walker, *The early history of the Goldsmiths' Company 1327–1509* (London, Edward Arnold, 1975), p. 186. For the calculation of days lost, which must include some allowance for obits requiring attendance over two days, see T. F. Reddaway, "The London goldsmiths *circa* 1500", *Transactions of the Royal Historical Society* **12**, 1962, p. 57.

39. Rosser, "Going to the fraternity feast", p. 439. For the role of churchwardens as conscientious administrators of anniversaries, see Clive Burgess, "A service of the dead: the form and function of the anniversary in late medieval Bristol", *Transactions of the Bristol and Gloucestershire Archaeological Society* **105**, 1987, pp. 202–3.

40. As Erasmus wrote in one of his last works (*On mending the peace of the church*, 1533): "The plethora of feast days, which either bishops in deference to popular wish have introduced, or popes have instituted for no real reason, they themselves ought to discreetly reduce in number. I would list among these the feast of the Immaculate Conception, the Nativity of the Blessed Virgin, and the Presentation. I really feel that no feasts should be celebrated that have no basis in Scripture – with the exception, of course, of Sunday." (John P. Dolan (ed.), *The essential Erasmus* (New York, Mentor Books, 1964), p. 385).

41. R. W. Pfaff, *New liturgical feasts in later medieval England* (Oxford, Clarendon Press, 1970), ch. 3: "The Feast of the Visitation".

42. Eamon Duffy, *The stripping of the altars. Traditional religion in England 1400–1580* (New Haven and London, Yale University Press, 1992), pp. 256–65.

43. *ibid.*, p. 263.

44. Dolan, *The essential Erasmus*, p. 383. For the Pastons as "potential and proto-Erasmians", equally unwilling to enter into the spirit of the new cults, see Colin Richmond, "Religion and the fifteenth-century English gentleman", in Dobson, *The church, politics and patronage*, pp. 200, 202.

45. Miri Rubin, *Corpus Christi. The Eucharist in late medieval culture* (Cambridge, Cambridge University Press, 1991), pp. 199–204. The description is Archbishop Melton's of 1322.

46. *Calendar of Patent Rolls 1348–1350*, pp. 97–8. Royal licence was granted at Westminster on 26 May 1348 before the Black Death got to Coventry, although everybody must have known it was on its way.

47. Rubin, *Corpus Christi*, pp. 232–43; and see also the same author's "Corpus Christi fraternities and late-medieval piety", *Studies in Church History* **23**, 1986, pp. 97–109. Margery Kempe, who saw most religious events as the occasion for "boisterous" weeping, nevertheless found the *viaticum* particularly affecting: "And most of all, when she saw the precious sacrament borne about the town with lights and reverence, the people kneeling on their knees, then she had many holy thoughts and meditations, and then she would often cry and roar, as though she would have burst, for the faith and the trust she had in the precious sacrament." (B. A. Windeatt (trans.), *The book of Margery Kempe* (Harmondsworth, Penguin Books, 1985), p. 212).

48. Charles Phythian-Adams, *Desolation of a city. Coventry and the urban crisis of the Late Middle Ages* (Cambridge, Cambridge University Press, 1979), p. 118 (footnote 2).

49. Pfaff, *New liturgical feasts*, p. 63.

50. *ibid.*, p. 85.

51. Duffy, *The stripping of the altars*, p. 293.

52. Swanson, *Catholic England*, pp. 138, 143.

53. Duffy, *The stripping of the altars*, p. 239.

54. Rubin, *Corpus Christi*, p. 310; and see also M. D. Anderson, *History and imagery in British*

churches (London, John Murray, 1971), pp. 97–9 and fig. 8. Bequests for masses of the Name of Jesus start at Norwich in about 1450, and there was "some demand" for Five Wounds masses after 1490 (Norman P. Tanner, *The church in late medieval Norwich 1370–1532* (Toronto, Pontifical Institute of Mediaeval Studies, 1984), pp. 102–3).

55. As in Hugo Legat's eloquent Passion sermon of *c.*1400: " . . . forthurmore he swette, for his passiun was so peinywus, that he swette water & blood in everi membre that he hadde; was he al so reed? ze, for sothe, for he had so mani woundis, what with the bittir scorges, with the scharpe nailis & with the cruel spere, that ther was left no hol place in his bodi, but al so rodi as rose ran on rede blood." (D. M. Grisdale (ed.) *Three Middle English sermons from the Worcester Chapter manuscript F. 10*, Leeds School of English Language Texts and Monographs **5**, 1939, p. 12). For the common occurrence of Passion images at death, see Duffy, *The stripping of the altars*, pp. 242–3; but Peter Heath has found little evidence of *devotio moderna* influences in the 355 Hull wills he has studied, where Christ "rarely appears and then but briefly" and in which "there is only one allusion to the new liturgical devotions, that to the Five Wounds of Christ" ("Urban piety in the later Middle Ages: the evidence of Hull wills", in Dobson, *The church, politics and patronage*, p. 228).

56. Reddaway & Walker, *The early history of the Goldsmiths' Company*, p. 176; Duffy, *The stripping of the altars*, p. 245 (footnote 29). I owe this reference to John Cherry, who illustrates a very similar memorial ring in his *Goldsmiths* (London, British Museum Press, 1992), plate 10.

57. For this fairly obvious point, made nevertheless with great emphasis, see Clive Burgess, "Late medieval wills and pious convention: testamentary evidence reconsidered", in *Profit, piety and the professions in later medieval England*, Michael Hicks (ed.) (Gloucester, Alan Sutton, 1990), pp. 14–33.

58. Reddaway & Walker, *The early history of the Goldsmiths' Company*, pp. 176–7, 306–7; *Calendar of Close Rolls 1485–1500*, pp. 234–6. In what was probably a fairly common precaution, Shaa gave his own soul-care priority over provision for his widow Julian, who was to have in full "that share of his goods to which she was entitled by the custom of London", but only so long as she did not remarry; she would also forfeit those properties if "she disturbed his executors and sought a further share of his goods". Julian Shaa died on 6 July 1494, leaving two daughters (Margaret Riche and Katharine Broun) as her heirs (*Calendar of Inquisitions Post Mortem Henry VII*, i:160–62, 421–3).

59. Clive Burgess, in particular, has made this argument his mission, starting a long series of papers on the subject with his "'For the increase of divine service': chantries in the parish in late medieval Bristol", *Journal of Ecclesiastical History* **36**, 1985, pp. 46–65, and "'By quick and by dead': wills and pious provision in late medieval Bristol", *English Historical Review* **102**, 1987, pp. 837–58.

60. *Calendar of Close Rolls 1485–1500*, p. 235.

61. P. H. Cullum & P. J. P. Goldberg, "Charitable provision in late medieval York: 'To the praise of God and the use of the poor'", *Northern History* **29**, 1993, p. 30.

62. *ibid.*, pp. 24, 38.

63. Roy Martin Haines, *Ecclesia anglicana. Studies in the English church of the later Middle Ages* (Toronto and London, University of Toronto Press, 1989), pp. 208–9, 337–8 (endnote 66). Reciprocity of another kind is evidenced by the readiness of some wealthy Bury burgesses to serve as the godparents of the children of their poorer neighbours, from whom in due course they could anticipate remembrance (Robert Dinn, "Baptism, spiritual kinship and popular religion in late medieval Bury St Edmunds", *Bulletin of the John Rylands University Library of Manchester* **72**, 1990, pp. 93–106).

64. C. H. Williams (ed.), *English Historical Documents 1485–1558* (London, Eyre & Spottiswoode, 1967), p. 654. For a recent defence of the late-medieval Church against Colet's strictures, see Christopher Harper-Bill, "Dean Colet's Convocation Sermon and the pre-Reformation Church in England", *History* **73**, 1988, pp. 191–210. But the "heaping of benefices upon benefices" was certainly not rare, where John Hody, while not holding all of them at once, could nevertheless collect as many as 26 (Robert W. Dunning, "Patronage and promotion in the late-medieval church", in *Patronage. The crown and the provinces in later medieval England*, Ralph A. Griffiths (ed.) (Gloucester, Alan Sutton, 1981), pp. 172–4.

65. Williams, *English Historical Documents 1485–1558*, pp. 654–5. In the King James version the same text (extended) reads: "And there shall be, like people, like priest: and I will punish them for their ways, and reward them their doings." (Hosea iv:9)

66. Erasmus describes Colet's last illness thus: "attacked by it [the sweating sickness] for the third time, he made some sort of recovery, but from the aftermath of that complaint contracted a wasting disease of the intestines which proved fatal. One doctor diagnosed it as a dropsy." (R. A. B. Mynors & Peter G. Bietenholz (eds), *The correspondence of Erasmus. Letters 1122 to 1251. 1520 to 1521* (Toronto, University of Toronto Press, 1988), p. 237).

67. Swanson, *Church and society in late medieval England*, pp. 32–6; and see also Virginia Davis, "Rivals for ministry?", pp. 99–109. Robert Swanson points to the probable link between the economic and recruitment difficulties of the clergy in his recent "Standards of livings: parochial revenues in pre-Reformation England", in Harper Bill, *Religious belief and ecclesiastical careers,* pp. 151–96. Chantry foundations can also be shown to follow much the same curve, with twice as many Yorkshire foundations in 1450–99 as in the previous half-century, and new creations continuing strongly until the 1530s (J. T. Rosenthal, "The Yorkshire chantry certificates of 1546: an analysis", *Northern History* **9**, 1974, p. 30). In York itself, however, growing recession probably contributed to the continuing decline in chantry creations after 1450 (Barrie Dobson, "Citizens and chantries in late medieval York", in *Church and city 1000–1500. Essays in honour of Christopher Brooke*, David Abulafia, Michael Franklin & Miri Rubin (eds) (Cambridge, Cambridge University Press, 1992), p. 327, and note 22 above.

68. G. R. Owst, *The Destructorium Viciorum of Alexander Carpenter* (London, Society for Promoting Christian Knowledge, 1952), p. 21; and see also H. Leith Spencer, *English preaching in the Late Middle Ages* (Oxford, Clarendon Press, 1993), where "a major contention of the present study" is "that preaching in parish churches became more regular in the fifteenth century" (p. 60).

69. See note 59 above. But as Alison McHardy points out, "the excellence and fervour of the chaplains in fifteenth-century Bristol can be contrasted with the laziness and disobedience of those in fourteenth-century Boston"; although she also subscribes to the current more optimistic view of the state of popular religion in late-medieval England, for which "the unbeneficed clergy, the workhorses of the medieval Church, should receive a large share of the credit" (A. K. McHardy, "Careers and disappointments in the late-medieval Church: some English evidence", *Studies in Church History* **26**, 1989, pp. 129–30). Another indicator of quality might be the continuing readiness of Yorkshire's chantry priests, even towards the end of the period, to assign large sums to the purchase of memorial masses for themselves (P. Mackie, "Chaplains in the diocese of York, 1480–1530: the testamentary evidence", *Yorkshire Archaeological Journal* **58**, 1986, p. 132).

70. Spencer, *English preaching in the Late Middle Ages*, p. 92.

71. For this fall-off in recruitment, see Margaret Bowker, *The Henrician Reformation. The dio-*

cese of Lincoln under John Longland 1521–1547 (Cambridge, Cambridge University Press, 1981), pp. 40–44, and the same author's *The secular clergy in the diocese of Lincoln 1495–1520* (Cambridge, Cambridge University Press, 1968), pp. 137–54, where she places great emphasis on royal taxation and on the contemporary erosion of stipends as growing discouragements to clerical recruitment. For the clergy's increasing poverty, see Peter Heath, *The English parish clergy on the eve of the Reformation* (London, Routledge & Kegan Paul, 1969), ch. 8: "The cost of living". But for a more positive view of clerical incomes, see John Pound's "Clerical poverty in early sixteenth-century England: some East Anglian evidence", *Journal of Ecclesiastical History* **37**, 1986, pp. 389–96. And reduced numbers, in R. N. Swanson's opinion, were probably owed as much to better quality-control by the bishops ("Problems of the priesthood in pre-Reformation England", *English Historical Review* **105**, 1990, pp. 861–3).

72. Owst, *The Destructorium Viciorum of Alexander Carpenter*, p. 39. But for a vigorous defence of the view that anticlericalism cannot explain the English Reformation, which originated rather in "the aspirations of particular interest groups [lawyers and politicians]", see Christopher Haigh, "Anticlericalism and the English Reformation", *History* **68**, 1983, pp. 391–407, repeated in the same author's full-length study of *English Reformations. Religion, politics, and society under the Tudors* (Oxford, Clarendon Press, 1993), especially pp. 40–50. The debate continues, as in the entirely contrary conclusions, based on studies of pre-Reformation wills from two somewhat similar eastern towns (Hull and Norwich), of Peter Heath, "Urban piety in the later Middle Ages", pp. 228–9, and Norman P. Tanner, "The Reformation and regionalism: further reflections on the church in late medieval Norwich", in *Towns and townspeople in the fifteenth century*, John A. F. Thomson (ed.) (Gloucester, Alan Sutton, 1988), pp. 140, 144.

Chapter 8: Protest and resolution

1. Christopher Dyer, "Small-town conflict in the later Middle Ages: events at Shipston-on-Stour", *Urban History* **19**, 1992, pp. 183–210. For the Black Death's central importance, if almost certainly over-emphasized, in the contemporary legal and other changes which brought such confrontations about, see Robert C. Palmer, *English law in the age of the Black Death, 1348–1381* (Chapel Hill and London, University of North Carolina Press, 1993), pp. 294–306 and *passim*.

2. *ibid.*, pp. 199–204. Many of the troubles at Shipston related to the chapel-of-ease at Shipston itself, which remained dependent on Tredington. For a similar dispute at Hook (Hampshire), endeavouring to free itself in the 1370s from dependency on Titchfield Church, see D. G. Watts, "Peasant discontent on the manors of Titchfield Abbey, 1245–1405", *Proceedings of the Hampshire Field Club and Archaeological Society* **39**, 1983, pp. 130–32.

3. Dyer, "Small-town conflict in the later Middle Ages", pp. 206, 208–9.

4. *ibid.*, pp. 197, 199. For a recent unqualified statement that "the main cause of these enormous changes [lower rents and rising wages leading to better life styles] in rural society was undoubtedly demographic decline", see Mark Bailey, "Rural society", in *Fifteenth-century attitudes. Perceptions of society in late medieval England*, Rosemary Horrox (ed.) (Cambridge, Cambridge University Press, 1994), p. 152.

5. R. H. Hilton & T. H. Aston (eds), *The English Rising of 1381* (Cambridge, Cambridge University Press, 1984), pp. 8, 17 and *passim*; and see also Rodney Hilton, *Bond men made*

free. Medieval peasant movements and the English Rising of 1381 (London, Temple Smith, 1973), ch. 7: "Social composition". For some Derbyshire gentry families who took full advantage of the 1381 disorders to pursue vendettas of their own, see David Crook, "Derbyshire and the English Rising of 1381", *Historical Research* **60**, 1987, pp. 9–23.

6. Dyer, "Small-town conflict in the later Middle Ages", pp. 201–2.

7. Rosamond Faith, "The 'Great Rumour' of 1377 and peasant ideology", in Hilton & Aston, *The English Rising of 1381*, p. 64.

8. As in the free translation of A. Hamilton Thompson, "The will of Master William Doune, archdeacon of Leicester", *Archaeological Journal* **72**, 1915, pp. 251, 280.

9. Michael J. Haren, "Social ideas in the pastoral literature of fourteenth-century England", in *Religious belief and ecclesiastical careers in late-medieval England*, Christopher Harper-Bill (ed.) (Woodbridge, Boydell Press, 1991), p. 54.

10. Isabel S. T. Aspin (ed.), *Anglo-Norman political songs* (Oxford, Basil Blackwell, 1953), pp. 74–5; also J. R. Maddicott, "Poems of social protest in early fourteenth-century England", in *England in the fourteenth century. Proceedings of the 1985 Harlaxton symposium*, W. M. Ormrod (ed.) (Woodbridge, Boydell Press, 1986), pp. 130–44. Corrupt justices and the strength of the popular hostility towards them which culminated in the Revolt of 1381 are discussed by J. R. Maddicott, *Law and lordship, royal justices as retainers in thirteenth- and fourteenth-century England, Past & Present* supplement **4**, 1978; but for a more positive view of the benefits of the legal system which subsequently emerged from these discontents, see Edward Powell, *Kingship, law, and society. Criminal justice in the reign of Henry V* (Oxford, Clarendon Press, 1989), pp. 19–20 and *passim*.

11. Bartlett Jere Whiting, *Proverbs, sentences, and proverbial phrases from English writings mainly before 1500* (Cambridge, Mass., Harvard University Press, 1968), pp. 489–90. None of Whiting's examples of this very popular saying date before the late fourteenth century.

12. Colin Richmond, "An outlaw and some peasants: the possible significance of Robin Hood", *Nottingham Medieval Studies* 37, 1993, pp. 90–101. For an intelligent summary of the huge Robin Hood literature, with some conclusions of his own, see John Bellamy, *Robin Hood: an historical enquiry* (London, Croom Helm, 1985), *passim*. The Robin Hood plays which continued to be performed at fifteenth-century summer revels, often to inflammatory effect, are discussed by Ronald Hutton, *The rise and fall of Merry England. The ritual year 1400–1700* (Oxford, Oxford University Press, 1994), pp. 31–3.

13. E. B. Fryde, "Peasant rebellion and peasant discontents", in *The agrarian history of England and Wales. Volume III 1348–1500*, Edward Miller (ed.) (Cambridge, Cambridge University Press, 1991), p. 768; A. R. Myers (ed.), *English historical documents 1327–1485* (London, Eyre & Spottiswoode, 1969), pp. 142–3, where the same passage is rendered: "to this [manumission of serfs] they had never assented of their free will, nor would they have done so except to live and die the same day".

14. R. H. Hilton, *The English peasantry in the later Middle Ages* (Oxford, Clarendon Press, 1975), p. 61; Dyer, "Small-town conflict in the later Middle Ages", p. 198.

15. Fryde, "Peasant rebellion and peasant discontents", pp. 764–5. In the parallel case of the Westminster bondmen, Barbara Harvey observes that "gross inequalities characterized the monks' treatment of their tenants in this period; old and new were juxtaposed in a most inflammatory way, in the same street and the same fields" (*Westminster Abbey and its estates in the Middle Ages* (Oxford, Clarendon Press, 1977), p. 246).

16. Christopher Dyer, "The Rising of 1381 in Suffolk: its origins and participants", *Proceedings of the Suffolk Institute of Archaeology* **36**, 1988, p. 279.

17. *ibid.*, pp. 278, 281.

18. Christopher Dyer, "The social and economic background to the rural revolt of 1381", in

Hilton & Aston, *The English Rising of 1381*, p. 12; also Hilton, *Bond men made free*, p. 156. For Walsingham's description in the context of other attacks on muniments, see Steven Justice, *Writing and rebellion. England in 1381* (Berkeley, University of California Press, 1994), p. 18 and *passim*.

19. Robert S. Gottfried, *Bury St Edmunds and the urban crisis: 1290–1539* (Princeton, Princeton University Press, 1982), pp. 222–36; and see also M. D. Lobel, *The borough of Bury St Edmund's. A study in the government and development of a monastic town* (Oxford, Oxford University Press, 1935), pp. 142–55. Walsingham's narrative of the St Albans rising is reprinted in R. B. Dobson's *The Peasants' Revolt of 1381* (London, Macmilllan, 1983), pp. 269–77.

20. Fryde, "Peasant rebellion and peasant discontents", p. 768.

21. Gottfried, *Bury St Edmunds and the urban crisis*, p. 236.

22. Whiting, *Proverbs, sentences, and proverbial phrases*, p. 213; Henry Noble MacCracken (ed.), *The minor poems of John Lydgate. Part II. Secular poems*, Early English Text Society **192**, 1934, p. 472; Derek Pearsall, *John Lydgate* (London, Routledge & Kegan Paul, 1970), pp. 198–200.

23. Geoffrey Brereton (ed.), *Froissart. Chronicles* (Harmondsworth, Penguin Books, 1978), p. 212.

24. *ibid.*, p. 213.

25. Myers, *English historical documents 1327–1485*, p. 1189. For a favourable assessment of the historical value of this literature of complaint, see John Hatcher, "England in the aftermath of the Black Death", *Past & Present* **144**, 1994, pp. 13–19.

26. As quoted by Antonia Gransden, *Historical writing in England II: c. 1307 to the early sixteenth century* (London, Routledge & Kegan Paul, 1982), p. 165.

27. For harvest-workers' agreements, see Christopher Dyer, *Standards of living in the later Middle Ages. Social change in England c. 1200–1520* (Cambridge, Cambridge University Press, 1989), pp. 158–60; and for two sumptuary laws, see Myers, *English historical documents 1327–1485*, pp. 1153–5, 1178; for the last quote, see Dobson, *The Peasants' Revolt of 1381*, p. xl.

28. Margaret Aston, "Corpus Christi and Corpus Regni: heresy and the Peasants' Revolt", *Past & Present* **143**, 1994, pp. 3–47; also Justice, *Writing and rebellion*, pp. 156–68. For some early-sixteenth-century Buckinghamshire evidence of Lollardy concentrating in the richer peasant families, already the leaders of rent-strikes and other forms of economic protest, see Derek Plumb, "The social and economic spread of rural Lollardy: a reappraisal", *Studies in Church History* **23**, 1986, pp. 111–29.

29. Dobson, *The Peasants' Revolt of 1381*, p. 344.

30. Quoted by Hilton, *The English peasantry*, p. 65; J. Kail (ed.), *Twenty-six political and other poems*, Early English Text Society **124**, 1904, pp. xi–xiii, 12.

31. Christopher Dyer, *Lords and peasants in a changing society. The estates of the bishopric of Worcester, 680–1540* (Cambridge, Cambridge University Press, 1980), p. 290.

32. Hilton, *The English peasantry*, pp. 68–9. For a very similar 1450s concession on the abbess's estate at Brede (East Sussex), see Mavis Mate, "The economic and social roots of medieval popular rebellion: Sussex in 1450–1451", *Economic History Review* **45**, 1992, p. 674.

33. Georges Edelen (ed.), *The Description of England by William Harrison* (Ithaca, Cornell University Press, 1968), p. 118.

34. Dobson, *The Peasants' Revolt of 1381*, pp. 306, 308.

35. *ibid.*, pp. xxxii, 316.

36. A. F. Butcher, "English urban society and the Revolt of 1381", in Hilton & Aston, *The

English Rising of 1381, p. 95.

37. *ibid.*, p. 106; unjust taxes were certainly the main cause of the revolt in the view of the usually reliable author of the *Anonimalle Chronicle* (Dobson, *The Peasants' Revolt of 1381*, p. 123). Almost two centuries later, in the rising of 1569, a Lavenham dissident claimed he would have spared "the gentlemen of old contynuance" while hanging the "riche churles", who would probably have included the more successful clothiers of his own small town (Diarmaid MacCulloch, *Suffolk and the Tudors. Politics and religion in an English county 1500–1600* (Oxford, Clarendon Press, 1986), pp. 311–12; I owe this reference to Ian Archer).

38. R. B. Dobson, "The risings in York, Beverley and Scarborough, 1380–1381", in Hilton & Aston, *The English Rising of 1381*, pp. 124–30.

39. *ibid.*, p. 117; Edward Gillett & Kenneth A. MacMahon, *A history of Hull* (Oxford, Oxford University Press for the University of Hull, 1980), p. 28.

40. Stephen Rigby, "Urban 'oligarchy' in late medieval England", in *Towns and townspeople in the fifteenth century*, John A. F. Thomson (ed.) (Gloucester, Alan Sutton, 1988), p. 64.

41. Jennifer I. Kermode, "Obvious observations on the formation of oligarchies in late medieval English towns", in Thomson, *Towns and townspeople*, p. 93; and see also Rigby, "Urban 'oligarchy' in late medieval England", p. 77. In some much smaller towns the proliferation of minor offices through the fifteenth century, far from promoting dissent, was one important reason why urban "rebelliousness" was ceasing to be a problem by the 1430s (Anne Reiber DeWindt, "Local government in a small town: a medieval leet jury and its constituents", *Albion* **23**, 1991, pp. 627–54).

42. For an early statement of this position, see Susan Reynolds, "Medieval urban history and the history of political thought", *Urban History Yearbook*, **1982**, pp. 14–23.

43. Edward Gillett, *A history of Grimsby* (London, Oxford University Press for the University of Hull, 1970), p. 63; also S. H. Rigby, *Medieval Grimsby. Growth and decline* (Hull, University of Hull Press, 1993), pp. 110–11.

44. Mate, "The economic and social roots of medieval popular rebellion", pp. 661–76; Peter Spufford, *Money and its use in medieval Europe* (Cambridge, Cambridge University Press, 1988), ch. 15: "The bullion famines of the later Middle Ages".

45. Mate, "The economic and social roots of medieval popular rebellion", p. 674. In manorial courts, the lords' waning interest in personal pledging (among other things) probably resulted as much from the lack of profitable business which followed population decline (David Postles, "Personal pledging in manorial courts in the later Middle Ages", *Bulletin of the John Rylands University Library of Manchester* **75**, 1993, p. 75).

46. Rigby, *Medieval Grimsby*, pp. 108–12; also the same author's "Urban 'oligarchy' in late medieval England", *passim*. For an earlier urban oligarchy which, while it was much resented in late-fourteenth-century Exeter, nevertheless established itself very firmly both before and after the Revolt, see Maryanne Kowaleski, "The commercial dominance of a medieval provincial oligarchy: Exeter in the late fourteenth century", *Medieval Studies* **46**, 1984, pp. 355–84; and see also the argument for open government even where oligarchies dominated, as in Carl I. Hammer, "Anatomy of an oligarchy: the Oxford town council in the fifteenth and sixteenth centuries", *Journal of British Studies* **18**, 1978, pp. 1–27. It is David Carr's argument that exceptional prosperity at Salisbury in the fifteenth century, far from promoting the rule of a closed elite, kept that elite changing and encouraged a wider than usual participation in city government. ("The problem of urban patriciates: office holders in fifteenth-century Salisbury", *Wiltshire Archaeological and Natural History Magazine* **83**, 1990, pp. 118–35).

47. Ben R. McRee, "Peacemaking and its limits in later medieval Norwich", *English Histori-*

cal Review **109**, 1994, pp. 831–66; Philippa C. Maddern, *Violence and social order. East Anglia 1422–1442* (Oxford, Clarendon Press, 1992), pp. 175–205. For the increasingly important role in city government and law of Norwich's Gild of St George, much promoted by the Wetherby dispute of the 1430s, see Ben McRee, "Religious gilds and civic order: the case of Norwich in the Late Middle Ages", *Speculum* **67**, 1992, pp. 69–97. Dispute and arbitration in mid-fifteenth-century Exeter are usefully discussed by Lorraine Attreed, "Arbitration and the growth of urban liberties in late medieval England", *Journal of British Studies* **31**, 1992, pp. 205–35.

48. Whiting, *Proverbs, sentences, and proverbial phrases*, p. 328. A friend in court, Joan Kirby concludes (after Chaucer) in the case of the Plumptons, was clearly "better . . . than a penny in the purse". ("A fifteenth-century family, the Plumptons of Plumpton, and their lawyers, 1461–1515", *Northern History* **25**, 1989, pp. 106–119).

49. Colin Platt, *Medieval Southampton. The port and trading community, AD 1000–1600* (London, Routledge & Kegan Paul, 1973), pp. 165–8. For a discussion of incorporation and its associated privileges, see also my *The English medieval town* (London, Secker & Warburg, 1976), pp. 142–6.

50. Platt, *Medieval Southampton*, p. 176.

51. Powell, *Kingship, law, and society*, pp. 16–20; J. R. Lander, *English justices of the peace, 1461–1509* (Gloucester, Alan Sutton, 1989), pp. 9–12; Palmer, *English law in the age of the Black Death*, pp. 294–5 and *passim*; Gerald Harriss, "Political society and the growth of government in late medieval England", *Past & Present* **138**, 1993, pp. 47–8.

52. Lander, *English justices of the peace*, p. 160. While in broad agreement with Professor Lander concerning the reasons for the gentry's general conversion to service on the bench, Christine Carpenter is inclined to place it somewhat later, associating it in particular with the final decay of manorial courts, with increasing economic regulation by sixteenth-century Tudor governments, and with the taking on of new responsibilities in religion (*Locality and polity. A study of Warwickshire landed society, 1401–1499* (Cambridge, Cambridge University Press, 1992), p. 341). Before that, any too easy acceptance of the role of the gentry as peace-keepers is contradicted by such repeated resort to violence, aggravated by the county's location on the Welsh Marches, as occurred in fifteenth-century Herefordshire (Ailsa Herbert, "Herefordshire, 1413–61: some aspects of society and public order", in *Patronage, the crown, and the provinces in later medieval England*, Ralph A. Griffiths (ed.) (Gloucester, Alan Sutton, 1981), pp. 102–22).

53. E. Powell, "Arbitration and the law in England in the Late Middle Ages", *Transactions of the Royal Historical Society* **33**, 1983, pp. 49–67; also the same author's "Settlement of disputes by arbitration in fifteenth-century England", *Law and History Review* **2**, 1984, pp. 21–43; and his *Kingship, law, and society*, ch. 4: "Law, politics, and dispute settlement in local society". Most recently, Powell has shown himself to be persuaded still that "there is a case to be made that the reputation of the fifteenth century for lawlessness, corruption and injustice is not wholly deserved" and that "the threat of violence is much more common than its actual occurrence" ("Law and justice", in Horrox, *Fifteenth-century attitudes*, pp. 40–41).

54. Simon Payling, *Political society in Lancastrian England. The greater gentry of Nottinghamshire* (Oxford, Clarendon Press, 1991), p. 189.

55. *ibid.*, pp. 192–5; Alexandra Sinclair, "The great Berkeley law-suit revisited 1417–39", *Southern History* **9**, 1987, pp. 34–50; Simon Payling, "Inheritance and local politics in the later Middle Ages: the case of Ralph, Lord Cromwell, and the Heriz inheritance", *Nottingham Medieval Studies* **30**, 1986, pp. 67–96, and the same author's "The Ampthill dispute: a study in aristocratic lawlessness and the breakdown of Lancastrian govern-

ment", *English Historical Review* **104**, 1989, pp. 881–907; Carpenter, *Locality and polity*, pp. 564–5.

56. Powell, *Kingship, law, and society*, p. 97. For how this worked in practice, see C. E. Moreton, *The Townshends and their world: gentry, law, and land in Norfolk c. 1450–1551* (Oxford, Clarendon Press, 1992), pp. 104–12. Some common late-medieval confrontation rituals which, for all their overt aggression, contributed to the avoidance of violence in fifteenth-century England, are discussed by Charles V. Phythian-Adams, "Rituals of personal confrontation in late medieval England", *Bulletin of the John Rylands University Library of Manchester* **73**, 1991, pp. 65–90.

57. Payling, *Political society in Lancastrian England*, pp. 211–12; and see also for arbitration in general, Ian Rowney, "Arbitration in gentry disputes of the later Middle Ages", *History* **67**, 1982, pp. 367–76. A successful arbitration of 1458 was the subject of Joel T. Rosenthal's early exploration of these procedures in "Feuds and private peace-making: a fifteenth-century example", *Nottingham Medieval Studies* **13**, 1969, pp. 84–90.

58. Powell, *Kingship, law, and society*, pp. 98–100.

59. But neither was it always welcome, for "procedure by love", multiplying in late-medieval England, "seems to have become as embroiled in faction as the ordinary processes of law" (Michael Clanchy, "Law and love in the Middle Ages", in *Disputes and settlements*, J. Bossy (ed.) (Cambridge, Cambridge University Press, 1983), p. 61).

60. Christine Carpenter, "The Beauchamp affinity: a study of bastard feudalism at work", *English Historical Review* **95**, 1980, pp. 524–6; also the same author's *Locality and polity*, pp. 624–5. For good lordship as a restraint on the Percy and Neville affinities, see A. J. Pollard, *North-eastern England during the Wars of the Roses. Lay society, war, and politics 1450–1500* (Oxford, Clarendon Press, 1990), ch. 5: "Service: good lordship and retaining"; and see also Michael Hicks, *Bastard feudalism* (London, Longman, 1995), pp. 153–4, 173–4; and Powell, "Settlement of disputes by arbitration", p. 40. But for magnate-induced disorder and a more sceptical view of magnate peace-keeping generally, see Roger Virgoe, "The murder of James Andrew: Suffolk faction in the 1430s", *Proceedings of the Suffolk Institute of Archaeology and History* **34**, 1980, pp. 263–8, and P. R. Coss, "Bastard feudalism revised", *Past & Present* **125**, 1989, pp. 54–7. Both the good and the bad products of magnate intervention in local peace-keeping are discussed by Susan M. Wright, *The Derbyshire gentry in the fifteenth century*, Derbyshire Record Society **8**, 1983, ch. 9: "Law and order in a gentry society".

61. Stuart A. Moore (ed.), *Letters and papers of John Shillingford, mayor of Exeter 1447–50*, Camden New Series **2**, 1871, p. 16.

62. For the circumstances of the Exeter dispute and its resolution, see Attreed, "Arbitration and the growth of urban liberties", pp. 205–35.

63. Whiting, *Proverbs, sentences, and proverbial phrases*, p. 328.

Chapter 9: Architecture and the arts

1. Nicholas Orme, *Exeter Cathedral as it was 1050–1550* (Exeter, Devon Books, 1986), pp. 17–20. For the cathedral building accounts through this period, see Aubrey M. Erskine (ed.), *The accounts of the fabric of Exeter Cathedral, 1279–1353*, Devon and Cornwall Record Society **24** and **26**, 1981 and 1983.

2. W. M. Ormrod, *The reign of Edward III. Crown and political society in England 1327–1377* (New Haven and London, Yale University Press, 1990), pp. 86–90, and the same author's

"Edward III and the recovery of royal authority in England, 1340–60", *History* **72**, 1987, pp. 4–19.

3. Janet H. Stevenson (ed.), *The Edington cartulary*, Wiltshire Record Society **42**, 1987, pp. xiii-xv, 1–13.

4. *Wiltshire*, 1963, pp. 208–12; also my *The architecture of medieval Britain. A social history* (New Haven and London, Yale University Press, 1990), pp. 217–18.

5. H. M. Colvin (ed.), *The history of the king's works* (London, HMSO, 1963), vol. 2, pp. 872–7.

6. John Maddison, "The architectural development of Patrington Church and its place in the evolution of the Decorated style in Yorkshire", in *Medieval art and architecture in the East Riding of Yorkshire*, Christopher Wilson (ed.) (London, British Archaeological Association, 1989), pp. 133–48; also *Victoria County History. East Yorkshire*, vol. 5, 1984, pp. 106–8.

7. Tideswell's exceptionally grand choir appears to date to c.1360–80 (*Derbyshire*, 1953, pp. 234–5); Tamworth, which burnt down in 1345 just before the plague, was almost immediately rebuilt (*Staffordshire*, 1974, p. 275). But if the work at Tamworth continued, that at neighbouring Lichfield stopped short at 1349, probable as a result of the death by plague of William Ramsey, the former royal mason, who was directing it. Contemporaneously other important building programmes in Lichfield diocese were also halted (J. M. Maddison, "Master masons of the diocese of Lichfield: a study in 14th-century architecture at the time of the Black Death", *Transactions of the Lancashire and Cheshire Antiquarian Society* **85**, 1988, pp. 123–5 and *passim*; I owe this reference to Phillip Lindley).

8. *Derbyshire*, 1953, pp. 40–42.

9. *Bedfordshire, Huntingdon and Peterborough*, 1974, pp. 296–7.

10. *Essex*, 1965, pp. 192–3, 368–9.

11. *Victoria County History. North Yorkshire*, vol. 2, 1923, pp. 68–9.

12. R. D. Bell, M. W. Beresford et al., *Wharram Percy: the church of St Martin*, Society for Medieval Archaeology Monographs **11**, 1987, pp. 204–5 and *passim*.

13. For the use of churches in this way, see L. J. Proudfoot, "The extension of parish churches in medieval Warwickshire", *Journal of Historical Geography* **9**, 1983, pp. 231–46.

14. *Suffolk*, 1974, pp. 314–15; H. Munro Cautley, *Suffolk churches and their treasures* (London, Batsford, 1937), pp. 281–2.

15. H. Munro Cautley, *Norfolk churches* (Ipswich, Norman Adlard & Co., 1949), p. 240; Paul Cattermole & Simon Cotton, "Medieval parish church building in Norfolk", *Norfolk Archaeology* **38**, 1983, p. 263; *Salle Church* guide.

16. *Shropshire*, 1958, p. 303.

17. *Suffolk*, 1981, p. 345. I have modernized Clopton's spelling here.

18. *Cambridgeshire*, 1954, pp. 333–6; *Isleham Church* guide.

19. *Yorkshire: York and the East Riding*, 1978, p. 117; *Dorset,* 1972, pp. 427–8; *South and West Somerset*, 1958, pp. 255–6, and see also the *Cadbury Church* guide for a full listing of the bench-ends of 1538. For St Margaret and her promises, see David Hugh Farmer, *The Oxford dictionary of saints* (Oxford, Clarendon Press, 1978), pp. 260–61; and for church imagery in general, see M. D. Anderson, *The imagery of British churches* (London, John Murray, 1955), ch. 8: "The Passion and Resurrection" and *passim*, subsequently rewritten and extended in the same author's *History and imagery in British churches* (London, John Murray, 1971).

20. *South and West Somerset*, 1958, p. 141 and plate 28a.

21. Cautley, *Norfolk churches*, pp. 22–5, 242; and see also the same author's *Suffolk churches*, pp. 66–70, 76, 81. For a recent full-length study of Seven Sacrament art, placing much

emphasis on these East Anglian fonts, see Ann Eljenholm Nichols, *Seeable signs. The iconography of the Seven Sacraments 1350–1544* (Woodbridge, Boydell Press, 1994), in particular pp. 159–84 (The Sacraments in stone: the theology of the fonts).

22. Hilary Wayment, *The stained glass of the church of St Mary, Fairford, Gloucestershire* (London, Society of Antiquaries, 1984), pp. 10–12, 56; Richard Marks, *Stained glass in England during the Middle Ages* (London, Routledge, 1993), pp. 209–12; for the inscription on John Tame's tomb, see *Fairford Church* guide, p. 8.

23. Malcolm Norris, "Later medieval monumental brasses: an urban funerary industry and its representation of death", in *Death in towns. Urban responses to the dying and the dead, 100–1600*, Steven Bassett (ed.) (Leicester, Leicester University Press, 1992), p. 184 and plate 13.1.

24. *Suffolk*, 1981, pp. 144–5. For cadaver effigies as a class, see Pamela M. King, "The cadaver tomb in England: novel manifestations of an old idea", *Church Monuments* **5**, 1990, pp. 26–38; also Kathleen Cohen, *Metamorphosis of a death symbol. The transi tomb in the Late Middle Ages and the Renaissance* (Berkeley, University of California Press, 1973), p. 91, and Brian Kemp, *English church monuments* (London, Batsford, 1980), pp. 160–61.

25. For John Baret's will, see Samuel Tymms (ed.), *Wills and inventories from the registers of the commissary of Bury St Edmund's and the Archdeacon of Sudbury*, Camden Society **49**, 1850, pp. 15–44; and see also Margaret Aston, "Death", in *Fifteenth-century attitudes. Perceptions of society in late medieval England*, Rosemary Horrox (ed.) (Cambridge, Cambridge University Press, 1994), pp. 224–7 and plate 30.

26. For the Baret family and John Baret II in particular, see Robert S. Gottfried, *Bury St Edmunds and the urban crisis: 1290–1539* (Princeton, Princeton University Press, 1982), pp. 154–9.

27. Tymms, *Wills and inventories from Bury*, p. 17.

28. This was the warning on the transi tomb – believed to be one of the first – of Cardinal Jean de Lagrange (d. 1402) at Avignon (Cohen, *Metamorphosis of a death symbol*, p. 24).

29. *North-West and South Norfolk*, 1962, pp. 196–7 and plate 43; *Northumberland*, 1957, pp. 123–4 and plate 32; *Warwickshire*, 1966, pp. 448–9 and plate 11b.

30. Frederick J. Furnivall (ed.), *The fifty earliest English wills in the court of probate, London*, Early English Text Society **78**, 1882, pp. 116–17; for the origins of Tewkesbury's Despenser connection and the early building works associated with the family's tombs in the abbey church, see Richard Morris, "Tewkesbury Abbey: the Despenser mausoleum", *Transactions of the Bristol and Gloucestershire Archaeological Society* **93**, 1974, pp. 142–55.

31. *Oxfordshire*, 1974, pp. 597–8 and plate 42.

32. Philippa Tristram, *Figures of life and death in medieval English literature* (London, Paul Elek, 1976), p. 160; Cohen, *Metamorphosis of a death symbol*, pp. 29–30 and plate 10.

33. Florence Warren (ed.), *The Dance of Death*, Early English Text Society **181**, 1931, pp. xxi–xxiv, 13; for some of the better known occurrences of the *Dance*, see pp. 97–8.

34. Marks, *Stained glass in England*, p. 84 and fig. 67.

35. *ibid.*, p. 21 and fig. 18; also the same author's "Henry Williams and his 'Ymage of Deth' roundel at Stanford on Avon, Northamptonshire", *Antiquaries Journal* **54**, 1974, pp. 272–4.

36. *Great Chalfield Manor, Wiltshire, 1980*, p. 13 and *passim*.

37. Platt, *The architecture of medieval Britain*, pp. 161, 163; *Holme by Newark Church* guide.

38. Bruce M. S. Campbell, "A fair field once full of folk: agrarian change in an era of population decline, 1348–1500", *Agricultural History Review* **41**, 1993, pp. 60–70.

39. Sarah Pearson, *The medieval houses of Kent: an historical analysis* (London, HMSO for the Royal Commission on the Historical Monuments of England, 1994), pp. 146–7, and the

two same-dated companion volumes from the same publisher: P. S. Barnwell & A. T. Adams, *The house within. Interpreting medieval houses in Kent*, and Sarah Pearson, P. S. Barnwell & A. T. Adams, *A gazetteer of medieval houses in Kent*.

40. Pearson, *The medieval houses of Kent*, pp. 142–3.

41. Michael Zell, *Industry in the countryside. Wealden society in the sixteenth century* (Cambridge, Cambridge University Press, 1994); also Henry Cleere & David Crossley, *The iron industry of the Weald* (Leicester, Leicester University Press, 1985), ch. 5: "Iron in the Weald in the Middle Ages", and ch. 6: "The introduction of the blast furnace"; and Eleanor S. Godfrey, *The development of English glassmaking 1560–1640* (Oxford, Clarendon Press, 1975).

42. Kay Coutin, "The Wealden house", in *Wealden buildings: studies in the timber-framed tradition of building in Kent, Sussex and Surrey, in tribute to R. T. Mason FSA*, John Warren (ed.) (Horsham, Coach Publishing for the Wealden Buildings Study Group, 1990), pp. 72–86. For one of the earlier recognitions of this spread, see S. R. Jones & J. T. Smith, "The Wealden houses of Warwickshire and their significance", *Transactions and Proceedings of the Birmingham Archaeological Society* **79**, 1960–61, pp. 24–35; also J. T. Smith, "The evolution of the English peasant house to the late seventeenth century: the evidence of buildings", *Journal of the British Archaeological Association* **33**, 1970, pp. 122–47.

43. L. R. Poos, *A rural society after the Black Death: Essex 1350–1525* (Cambridge, Cambridge University Press, 1991), ch. 4: "Houses"; Frank Atkinson & R. W. McDowall, "Aisled houses in the Halifax area", *Antiquaries Journal* **47**, 1967, pp. 77–94; also *Rural houses of West Yorkshire, 1400–1830* (London, HMSO for West Yorkshire Metropolitan County Council and the Royal Commission on the Historical Monuments of England, 1986), ch. 2: "The houses of the yeomanry in the Late Middle Ages". For the similar aisled-hall houses in Yorkshire's lowland parishes, see Barbara Hutton, "Timber-framed houses in the Vale of York", *Medieval Archaeology* **17**, 1973, pp. 87–99, and Eric Mercer, *English vernacular houses. A study of traditional farmhouses and cottages* (London, HMSO for the Royal Commission on the Historical Monuments of England, 1975), pp. 14–16. For a fifteenth-century yeoman's farmhouse in Shropshire, which has been particularly well described in its historical context, see M. Morgan, "Padmore, Onibury, Shropshire SO 464794", *Archaeological Journal* **142**, 1985, pp. 340–60. For the farmhouses of late-medieval Hampshire, see the useful (and still continuing) studies of Edward Roberts and his associates (Elizabeth Lewis, Edward Roberts & Kenneth Roberts, *Medieval hall houses of the Winchester area* (Winchester, Winchester City Museum, 1988), *passim*).

44. N. W. Alcock & Michael Laithwaite, "Medieval houses in Devon and their modernization", *Medieval Archaeology* **17**, 1973, pp. 100–125; Matthew Johnson, *Housing culture. Traditional architecture in an English landscape* (London, UCL Press, 1993), ch. 4: "Open houses"; N. W. Alcock, *People at home. Living in a Warwickshire village, 1500–1800* (Chichester, Phillimore, 1993), ch. 4: "Old style: small houses 1532–1600"; also Christopher Dyer, "English peasant buildings in the later Middle Ages (1200–1500)", *Medieval Archaeology* **30**, 1986, pp. 19–45. For the Elizabethan and Restoration rebuildings, see my *The Great Rebuildings of Tudor and Stuart England* (London, UCL Press, 1994), ch. 1: "The first Great Rebuilding".

45. Matthew Johnson, however, puts more emphasis on changes in mentality and "world-view", concluding: "So those building permanent, traditional, middling houses in the 15th century expressed their rise in what they saw as traditional forms: bequests to the Church, and a form of house plan referring to the traditional values of the medieval community." (*Housing culture*, p. 180).

46. Pearson, Barnwell & Adams, *A gazetteer of medieval houses in Kent*, p. 14; *Rufford Old Hall, Lancashire*, 1983, pp. 14–18, 31. Building accounts for two contemporary manor-houses "of the middling sort" were published by John Harvey, "Great Milton, Oxfordshire; and Thorncroft, Surrey. The building accounts for two manor-houses of the late fifteenth century", *Journal of the British Archaeological Association* **18**, 1955, pp. 42–56. And see also the many contracts published by L. F. Salzman, *Building in England down to 1540* (Oxford, Clarendon Press, 1967).

47. Important survivals of late-medieval gentry houses, well described and illustrated in their respective National Trust guides, include Baddesley Clinton (Warwickshire), Bradley and Compton (Devonshire), Cotehele (Cornwall), Ightham Mote (Kent), Lytes Cary (Somerset) and Oxburgh (Norfolk). And see also my *The National Trust guide to late-medieval and Renaissance Britain from the Black Death to the Civil War* (London, George Philip, 1986), ch. 3: "The gentle life". For the same general point, but concerning diet and household sizes, see Christopher Dyer, *Standards of living in the later Middle Ages. Social change in England, c.1200–1520* (Cambridge, Cambridge University Press, 1989), p. 108 and *passim*.

48. For the castles of this period – some effective but mostly not – see my *The architecture of medieval Britain*, pp. 184–93.

49. *ibid.*, pp. 247–52. There is a particularly interesting contemporary compromise between purely domestic building and display-style defence, again of brick, at Sir Thomas Burgh's Gainsborough Hall (Phillip Lindley (ed.), *Gainsborough Old Hall*, Occasional Papers in Lincolnshire History and Archaeology **8**, 1991).

50. For the siege of Caister after Fastolf's death, see Norman Davis (ed.), *Paston letters and papers of the fifteenth century* (Oxford, Clarendon Press, 1971–6), 2 volumes, vol. 1, pp. 340–47, 398–409, 540–48; for one of several threats to Ralph Lord Cromwell, see Roger Virgoe, "William Tailboys and Lord Cromwell: crime and politics in Lancastrian England", *Bulletin of the John Rylands Library* **55**, 1972–3, pp. 459–82.

51. The best account of Haughmond Abbey, which still lacks a good guide, is in the *Victoria History of the County of Shropshire*, Volume 2 (London, 1973), pp. 62–9; but see also David Knowles & J. K. S. St Joseph, *Monastic sites from the air* (Cambridge, Cambridge University Press, 1952), pp. 204–5. A report on the 1907 excavations was published by W. H. St John Hope & H. Brakspear, "Haughmond Abbey, Shropshire", *Archaeological Journal* **66**, 1910, pp. 281–310. For Haughmond's wealth, see Una Rees, "The leases of Haughmond Abbey, Shropshire", *Midland History* **8**, 1983, pp. 14–28; and for further evidence of the canons' successful estate management, see the same author's edition of *The Cartulary of Haughmond Abbey* (Cardiff, Shropshire Archaeological Society and University of Wales Press, 1985), p. 9.

53. For these superiors' lodgings and for other evidence of new comfort-centred building at the religious houses, see my *The abbeys and priories of medieval England* (London, Secker & Warburg, 1984), pp. 152–72; also my *The architecture of medieval Britain*, pp. 200–206.

Chapter 10: What matters

1. This is certainly the conclusion of Edward Miller and John Hatcher in the last sentence of their long-awaited *Medieval England. Towns, commerce and crafts 1086–1348* (London, Longman, 1995), p. 429; and see also S. H. Rigby, *English society in the later Middle Ages. Class, status and gender* (London, Macmillan, 1995), pp. 80–87 ("Population, the manor

and economic change, 1348–1500"). For a general view of these changes both before and after 1348, which includes the archaeological evidence, see my own *Medieval England. A social history and archaeology from the Conquest to 1600* AD (London, Routledge, 1978), ch. 3: "Set-back", and ch. 4: "After the Black Death". For the quotation from Ibn Khaldun, see p. 14 above.

2. Rigby, *English society in the later Middle Ages*, pp. 9–14 and *passim*.

3. For the major work in this field, see Francis Cheetham, *English medieval alabasters, with a catalogue of the collection in the Victoria and Albert Museum* (Oxford, Phaidon, 1984); for the Nottingham collection, see also the same author's *Medieval English alabaster carvings in the Castle Museum, Nottingham* (Nottingham, City of Nottingham Art Galleries and Museums Committee, 1973). The hiding away of books of hours and other devotional works was also probably common enough, while in some parish churches unreformed service books are known to have continued in use for many years (Eamon Duffy, *The stripping of the altars. Traditional religion in England c.1400–c.1580* (New Haven and London, Yale University Press, 1992), pp. 418–19).

4. For the English iconoclasts, see especially Margaret Aston, *England's iconoclasts. Volume I. Laws against images* (Oxford, Clarendon Press, 1988); also the same author's "Iconoclasm in England: official and clandestine", in her *Faith and fire. Popular and unpopular religion 1350–1600* (London, Hambledon Press, 1993), pp. 261–89; and John Phillips, *The reformation of images: destruction of art in England, 1535–1660* (Berkeley, University of California Press, 1973); for the destruction of pictorial glass, see Richard Marks, *Stained glass in England during the Middle Ages* (London, Routledge, 1993), pp. 229–32, 236–8. Eamon Duffy discusses the attack on traditional religion, and the forms it took, in *The stripping of the altars*, part II.

5. Hilary Wayment, *The stained glass of the church of St Mary, Fairford, Gloucestershire* (London, Society of Antiquaries, 1984), p. 7.

6. Florence Warren (ed.), *The Dance of Death*, Early English Text Society **181**, 1931, pp. xxii–xxiii.

7. John Hutchins, *The history and antiquities of the county of Dorset*, 3rd ed., William Shipp and James Whitworth Hodson (eds) (London, J. B. Nichols & Sons, 1861–73), 4 vols, vol. iv, pp. 176–7.

8. M. A. Hicks, "The piety of Margaret, Lady Hungerford (d.1478)", *Journal of Ecclesiastical History* **38**, 1987, p.25 and *passim*.

9. Pamela M. King, "The cadaver tomb in England: novel manifestations of an old idea", *Church Monuments* **5**, 1990, p.26. For some earlier and greater claims, see Millard Meiss, *Painting in Florence and Siena after the Black Death* (Princeton, Princeton University Press, 1951), and also more cautiously Kathleen Cohen, *Metamorphosis of a death symbol. The transi tomb in the Late Middle Ages and the Renaissance* (Berkeley, University of California Press, 1973).

10. Other examples of these subjects are given in my *The architecture of medieval Britain. A social history* (New Haven and London, Yale University Press, 1990), pp. 159–60.

11. For the Fotheringhay statutes, see J. C. Cox, "The college of Fotheringhay", *Archaeological Journal* **61**, 1904, pp. 244–9.

12. Thomas Hearne (ed.), *J. Lelandi antiquarii de rebus Britannicis Collectanea* (London, G. & J. Richardson, 1770), 6 vols, vol. v, pp. 373–81; Leland himself, however, could not have been the recorder of these events. For some discussion of comparable ceremonies, see R. C. Finucane, "Sacred corpes, profane carrion: social ideals and death rituals in the later Middle Ages", and Paul S. Fritz, "From 'public' to 'private': the royal funerals in England, 1500–1830", both in *Mirrors of mortality. Studies in the social history of death*, Joachim

Whaley (ed.) (London, Europa Publications, 1981), pp. 40–79.

13. W. H. St John Hope, *The obituary roll of John Islip, abbot of Westminster, 1500–1532,* Vetusta Monumenta **7**, 1906, plate xxii. Death and burial scenes are included also in the late-fifteenth-century *Pageant of the birth, life, and death of Richard Beauchamp, earl of Warwick KG 1389–1439,* Viscount Dillon and W. H. St John Hope (eds) (London, Longmans Green & Co., 1914).

14. Betty R. Masters & Elizabeth Ralph (eds), *The Church Book of St Ewen's, Bristol 1454–1584,* Bristol and Gloucestershire Archaeological Society Records Section **6**, 1967, p. xxiv.

15. *ibid.,* p. xix.

16. *ibid.,* p.6; the italics are mine.

17. *ibid.,* pp. 182–5.

18. Nigel Llewellyn, for example, in his recent *The art of death. Visual culture in the English death ritual c. 1500–c. 1800* (London, Reaktion Books, 1991), allows plague little or no place in this continuing art, but nevertheless draws a useful distinction between the post-Reformation (i.e. early-modern) rituals of death and those which developed in the nineteenth century. Thus "the final aim of the earlier ritual was to place death in life in order to soften its blow", whereas "the Victorian ritual tended to stress the abnormality and the deep difficulty of death" (p. 136). For the view that this "desocialization of the individual" – i.e. the separation of the living from their dead, taking the form, among other things, of the establishment of out-of-town cemeteries – began much earlier with the Black Death, see Aron Gurevich, *Medieval popular culture: problems of belief and perception* (Cambridge, Cambridge University Press, 1988), p. 152.

19. Christine Carpenter, *Locality and polity. A study of Warwickshire landed society, 1401–1499* (Cambridge, Cambridge University Press, 1992); and see also Simon Payling, *Political society in Lancastrian England. The greater gentry of Nottinghamshire* (Oxford, Clarendon Press, 1991), and Eric Acheson, *A gentry community. Leicestershire in the fifteenth century, c. 1422–c. 1485* (Cambridge, Cambridge University Press, 1992).

20. D. A. Carpenter, "English peasants in politics 1258–1267", *Past & Present* **136**, 1992, pp. 3–42.

21. Martin Ingram, "Ridings, rough music and the 'reform of popular culture' in early modern England", *Past & Present* **105**, 1984, p.96; and see also the same author's *Church courts, sex and marriage in England, 1570–1640* (Cambridge, Cambridge University Press, 1987), ch. 3: "Religion and the people", and his "Ridings, rough music and mocking rhymes in early modern England", in *Popular culture in seventeenth-century England,* Barry Reay (ed.) (London, Routledge, 1988), pp. 166–97. For another general treatment of these themes, see David Underdown, *Revel, riot, and rebellion. Popular politics and culture in England 1603–1660* (Oxford, Clarendon Press, 1985). Rough music and other characteristic elements of the charivari were certainly present in a much earlier incident of 1390, when the granger of Scone woke King Robert III with a trumpet blast and with the banging of basins with sticks. What followed was a settlement of the abbey's grievances, again demonstrating the role of such irreverent displays in reconciling differences even at this early date (I owe this reference to my colleague Dr John McGavin, whose account of the incident has just been published in the *Scottish Historical Review.*).

22. For this point, made with much emphasis, see Alan Macfarlane, *The justice and the mare's ale. Law and disorder in seventeenth-century England* (Oxford, Basil Blackwell, 1981), pp. 173–99 ("Conclusion: English violence in context").

23. For the East Anglian rebellions – also my source for Harington's aphorism – see Diarmaid MacCulloch, *Suffolk and the Tudors. Politics and religion in an English county*

1500–1600 (Oxford, Clarendon Press, 1986), especially ch. 10: "The Age of Rebellions 1525–1570".

24. Zvi Razi, "The myth of the immutable English family", *Past & Present* **140**, 1993, p. 33.

25. S. J. Payling, "Social mobility, demographic change and landed society in late medieval England", *Economic History Review* **45**, 1992, p.70.

26. Geoffrey Brereton (trans. and ed.), *Froissart. Chronicles* (Harmondsworth, Penguin Books, 1978), p. 212.

27. F. A. Greenhill, *Incised effigial slabs. A study of engraved stone memorials in Latin Christendom, c.1100 to c.1700* (London, Faber & Faber, 1976), 2 vols, vol. 2, plate 151a.

28. Warren, *The Dance of Death*, p. 8.

29. As quoted from a contemporary (un-named) source by Mark Bailey, "Rural society", in *Fifteenth-century attitudes*, Rosemary Horrox (ed.) (Cambridge, Cambridge University Press, 1994), p. 162.

Bibliography

Acheson, E., *A gentry community. Leicestershire in the fifteenth century, c.1422–c.1485* (Cambridge, Cambridge University Press, 1992).

Alcock, N. W., *People at home. Living in a Warwickshire village, 1500–1800* (Chichester, Phillimore, 1993).

Alcock, N. W. & M. Laithwaite, "Medieval houses in Devon and their modernization", *Medieval Archaeology* **17**, 1973, pp. 100–125.

Aldred, D. & C. Dyer, "A medieval Cotswold village: Roel, Gloucestershire", *Transactions of the Bristol & Gloucestershire Archaeological Society* **109**, 1991, pp. 139–70.

Allmand, C., *Henry V* (London, Eyre Methuen, 1992).

Anderson, M. D., *The imagery of British churches* (London, John Murray, 1955).

Anderson, M. D., *History and imagery in British churches* (London, John Murray, 1971).

Appleby, A. B., "The disappearance of plague: a continuing puzzle", *Economic History Review* **33**, 1980, pp. 161–73.

Archer, R. E., "Rich old ladies: the problem of late medieval dowagers", in Tony Pollard (ed.), *Property and politics: essays in late medieval English history* (Gloucester, Alan Sutton, 1984), pp. 15–35.

Archer, R. E., "The estates and finances of Margaret of Brotherton, c.1320–1399", *Historical Research* **60**, 1987, pp. 264–80.

Archer, R. E., "Women as landholders and administrators in the later Middle Ages", in Goldberg (ed.), *Woman is a worthy wight*, pp. 149–81.

Armstrong, C. A. J., *England, France and Burgundy in the fifteenth century* (London, Hambledon Press, 1983).

Armstrong, C. A. J., "The piety of Cicely, duchess of York: a study in late medieval culture", in *England, France and Burgundy*, pp. 135–56.

Ashmore, O., "The Whalley Abbey bursars' account for 1520", *Transactions of the Historical Society of Lancashire and Cheshire* **114**, 1962, pp. 49–72.

Aspin, I. S. T. (ed.), *Anglo-Norman political songs* (Oxford, Basil Blackwell, 1953).

Aston, M., *England's iconoclasts. Volume I. Laws against images* (Oxford, Clarendon Press, 1988).

Aston, M., *Faith and fire. Popular and unpopular religion 1350–1600* (London, Hambledon Press, 1993).

Aston, M., "Corpus Christi and Corpus Regni: heresy and the Peasants' Revolt", *Past & Present* **143**, 1994, pp. 3–47.

231

Aston, M., "Death", in Horrox (ed.), *Fifteenth-century attitudes*, pp. 202–27.

Atkinson, F. & R. W. McDowall, "Aisled houses in the Halifax area", *Antiquaries Journal* **47**, 1967, pp. 77–94.

Attreed, L., "Arbitration and the growth of urban liberties in late medieval England", *Journal of British Studies* **31**, 1992, pp. 205–35.

Bailey, M., *A marginal economy? East Anglian Breckland in the later Middle Ages* (Cambridge, Cambridge University Press, 1989).

Bailey, M., "Coastal fishing off south-east Suffolk in the century after the Black Death", *Proceedings of the Suffolk Institute of Archaeology and History* **37**, 1990, pp. 102–14.

Bailey, M., "*Per impetum maris*: natural disaster and economic decline in eastern England, 1275–1350", in Campbell (ed.), *Before the Black Death*, pp. 184–208.

Bailey, M., "A tale of two towns: Buntingford and Standon in the later Middle Ages", *Journal of Medieval History* **19**, 1993, pp. 351–71.

Bailey, M., "Rural society", in Horrox (ed.), *Fifteenth-century attitudes*, pp. 150–68.

Baker, A. R. H., "Evidence in the *Nonarum Inquisitiones* of contracting arable lands in England during the early fourteenth century", *Economic History Review* **19**, 1966, pp. 518–32.

Barnwell, P. S. & A. T. Adams, *The house within. Interpreting medieval houses in Kent* (London, HMSO for the Royal Commission on the Historical Monuments of England, 1994).

Barron, C., "The fourteenth-century poll tax returns for Worcester", *Midland History* **14**, 1989, pp. 1–19.

Barron, C., "The parish fraternities of medieval London", in Barron & Harper-Bill (eds), *The Church in pre-Reformation society*, pp. 13–37.

Barron, C. & C. Harper-Bill (eds), *The Church in pre-Reformation society: essays in honour of F. R. H. Du Boulay* (Woodbridge, Boydell Press, 1985).

Barron, C. M. & A. F. Sutton (eds), *Medieval London widows 1300–1500* (London, Hambledon Press, 1994).

Bassett, S. (ed.), *Death in towns. Urban responses to the dying and the dead, 100–1600* (Leicester, Leicester University Press, 1992).

Bedingfeld, A. L. (ed.), *A cartulary of Creake Abbey*, Norfolk Record Society **35**, 1966.

Bell, R. D., M. W. Beresford et al., *Wharram Percy: the church of St Martin*, Society for Medieval Archaeology monographs **11**, 1987.

Bellamy, J., *Robin Hood: an historical enquiry* (London, Croom Helm, 1985).

Bennett, J. M., "The ties that bind: peasant marriages and families in late-medieval England", *Journal of Interdisciplinary History* **15**, 1984–5, pp. 111–29.

Bennett, J. M., *Women in the medieval English countryside. Gender and household in Brigstock before the plague* (New York and Oxford, Oxford University Press, 1987).

Bennett, M., "Careerism in late-medieval England", in J. Rosenthal & C. Richmond (eds), *People, politics and community in the later Middle Ages* (Gloucester, Alan Sutton, 1987), pp. 19–39.

Bernard, G. W., "The rise of Sir William Compton, early Tudor courtier", *English Historical Review* **96**, 1981, pp. 754–77.

Boccaccio, G., *The Decameron* (trans. G. H. McWilliam) (Harmondsworth, Penguin Books, 1972).

Bowers, R., "The musicians of the Lady Chapel of Winchester Cathedral Priory, 1402–1539", *Journal of Ecclesiastical History* **45**, 1994, pp. 210–37.

Bowker, M., *The secular clergy in the diocese of Lincoln 1495–1520* (Cambridge, Cambridge University Press, 1968).

Bowker, M., *The Henrician Reformation. The diocese of Lincoln under John Longland 1521–1547* (Cambridge, Cambridge University Press, 1981).

Bowsky, W. M. (ed.), *The Black Death. A turning point in history?* (New York, Holt, Rinehart & Winston, 1971).

Bradley, L., "Some medical aspects of plague", in *The plague reconsidered. A new look at its origins and effects in 16th and 17th century England*, Local Population Studies Supplement, 1977, pp. 11–23.

Brandon, P. F., "Arable farming in a Sussex scarp-foot parish during the Late Middle Ages", *Sussex Archaeological Collections* **100**, 1962, pp. 60–72.

Brandon, P. F., "Agriculture and the effects of flooding and weather at Barnhorne, Sussex, during the Late Middle Ages", *Sussex Archaeological Collections* **109**, 1971, pp. 69–93.

Brandon, P. F., "Demesne arable farming in coastal Sussex during the later Middle Ages", *Agricultural History Review* **19**, 1971, pp. 113–34.

Brereton, G. (ed.), *Froissart. Chronicles* (Harmondsworth, Penguin Books, 1978).

Bridbury, A. R., "The Black Death", *Economic History Review* **26**, 1973, pp. 577–92.

Bridbury, A. R., *Economic growth. England in the later Middle Ages* (Hassocks, Harvester Press, 1975), 2nd edn.

Bridbury, A. R., "English provincial towns in the later Middle Ages", *Economic History Review* **34**, 1981, pp. 1–24.

Bridbury, A. R., *Medieval English clothmaking. An economic survey* (London, Heinemann, 1982).

Bridbury, A. R., "Dr Rigby's comment: a reply", *Economic History Review* **39**, 1986, pp. 417–22.

Bridbury, A. R., *The English economy from Bede to the Reformation* (Woodbridge, Boydell Press, 1992).

Britnell, R. H., "The proliferation of markets in England 1200–1349", *Economic History Review* **34**, 1981, pp. 209–21.

Britnell, R. H., *Growth and decline in Colchester, 1300–1525* (Cambridge, Cambridge University Press, 1986).

Britnell, R. H., *The commercialisation of English society 1000–1500* (Cambridge, Cambridge University Press, 1993).

Britnell, R. H., "The Black Death in English towns", *Urban History* **21**, 1994, pp. 195–210.

Brooks, J., "Eaton Hastings: a deserted medieval village", *Berkshire Archaeological Journal* **64**, 1969, pp. 1–8.

Brooks, J., "Tubney, Oxfordshire: medieval and later settlement", *Oxoniensia* **49**, 1984, pp. 121–31.

Burgess, C., "'For the increase of divine service': chantries in the parish in late medieval Bristol", *Journal of Ecclesiastical History* **36**, 1985, pp. 46–65.

Burgess, C., "'By quick and by dead': wills and pious provision in late medieval Bristol", *English Historical Review* **102**, 1987, pp. 837–58.

Burgess, C., "A service of the dead: the form and function of the anniversary in late medieval Bristol", *Transactions of the Bristol and Gloucestershire Archaeological Society* **105**, 1987, pp. 183–211.

Burgess, C., "Late medieval wills and pious convention: testamentary evidence reconsidered", in Hicks (ed.), *Profit, piety and the professions*, pp. 14–33.

Burgess, C., "Strategies for eternity: perpetual chantry foundation in late medieval Bristol", in Harper-Bill (ed.), *Religious belief and ecclesiastical careers*, pp. 1–32.

Butcher, A. F., "Rent, population and economic change in late-medieval Newcastle", *Northern History* **14**, 1978, pp. 67–77.

Butcher, A. F., "Rent and the urban economy: Oxford and Canterbury in the later Middle Ages", *Southern History* **1**, 1979, pp. 11–43.

Butcher, A. F., "English urban society and the Revolt of 1381", in Hilton & Aston (eds), *The English Rising of 1381*, pp. 84–111.

Cameron, A., "Sir Henry Willoughby of Wollaton", *Transactions of the Thoroton Society* **74**, 1970, pp. 10–21.

Cameron, A. & C. O'Brien, "The deserted medieval village of Thorpe-in-the-Glebe, Nottinghamshire", *Transactions of the Thoroton Society* **85**, 1981, pp. 56–67.

Campbell, B. M. S., "Population pressure, inheritance and the land market in a fourteenth-century peasant community", in R. M. Smith (ed.), *Land, kinship and life-cycle*, (Cambridge, Cambridge University Press, 1984), pp. 87–134.

Campbell, B. M. S., "Land, labour, livestock, and productivity trends in English seignorial agriculture, 1208–1450", in B. M. S. Campbell & M. Overton (eds), *Land, labour and livestock: historical studies in European agricultural productivity* (Manchester, Manchester University Press, 1991), pp. 144–82.

Campbell, B. M. S. (ed.), *Before the Black Death. Studies in the "crisis" of the early fourteenth century* (Manchester, Manchester University Press, 1991).

Campbell, B. M. S., "A fair field once full of folk: agrarian change in an era of population decline, 1348–1500", *Agricultural History Review* **41**, 1993, pp. 60–70.

Carley, J. P., *Glastonbury Abbey: The Holy House at the head of the Moors Adventurous* (Woodbridge, Boydell Press, 1988).

Carpenter, C., "The Beauchamp affinity: a study of bastard feudalism at work", *English Historical Review* **95**, 1980, pp. 514–32.

Carpenter, C., "The fifteenth-century English gentry and their estates", in Jones (ed.), *Gentry and lesser nobility*, pp. 36–60.

Carpenter, C., *Locality and polity. A study of Warwickshire landed society, 1401–1499* (Cambridge, Cambridge University Press, 1992).

Carpenter, C., "Who ruled the Midlands in the later Middle Ages?", *Midland History* **19**, 1994, pp. 1–20.

Carpenter, C., "Gentry and community in medieval England", *Journal of British Studies* **33**, 1994, pp. 341–80.

Carpenter, D. A., "English peasants in politics 1258–1267", *Past & Present* **136**, 1992, pp. 3–42.

Carr, D., "The problem of urban patriciates: office holders in fifteenth-century Salisbury", *Wiltshire Archaeological and Natural History Magazine* **83**, 1990, pp. 118–35.

Carus-Wilson, E. M. & O. Coleman, *England's export trade 1275–1547* (Oxford, Clarendon Press, 1963).

Cattermole, P. & S. Cotton, "Medieval parish church building in Norfolk", *Norfolk Archaeology* **38**, 1983, pp. 235–79.

Catto, J., "Religious change under Henry V", in Harriss (ed.), *Henry V*, pp. 97–115.

Cautley, H. M., *Suffolk churches and their treasures* (London, Batsford, 1937).

Cautley, H. M., *Norfolk churches* (Ipswich, Norman Adlard & Co., 1949).

Cheetham, F., *Medieval English alabaster carvings in the Castle Museum, Nottingham* (Nottingham, City of Nottingham Art Galleries and Museums Committee, 1973).

Cheetham, F., *English medieval alabasters, with a catalogue of the collection in the Victoria and Albert Museum* (Oxford, Phaidon, 1984).

Cherry, J., *Goldsmiths* (London, British Museum Press, 1992).

Cherry, M., "The Courtenay earls of Devon: the formation and disintegration of a late-medieval aristocratic affinity", *Southern History* **1**, 1979, pp. 71–97.

Cherry, M., "The struggle for power in mid-fifteenth-century Devonshire", in Griffiths (ed.), *Patronage, the crown, and the provinces*, pp. 123–44.

Clanchy, M., "Law and love in the Middle Ages", in J. Bossy (ed.), *Disputes and settlements* (Cambridge, Cambridge University Press), 1983, pp. 47–67.

Cleere, H. & D. Crossley, *The iron industry of the Weald* (Leicester, Leicester University Press, 1985).

Cohen, K., *Metamorphosis of a death symbol. The transi tomb in the Late Middle Ages and the Renaissance* (Berkeley, University of California Press, 1973).

Cohn, S. K., *The Cult of Remembrance and the Black Death. Six Renaissance cities in central Italy* (Baltimore, Johns Hopkins University Press, 1992).

Colvin, H. M. (ed.), *The history of the king's works. Volume 2* (London, HMSO, 1963).

Colvin, H. M., *Architecture and the after-life* (New Haven and London, Yale University Press, 1991).

Coss, P. R., "Bastard feudalism revised", *Past & Present* **125**, 1989, pp. 27–64.

Coss, P. R., *Lordship, knighthood and locality. A study in English society c.1180–c.1280* (Cambridge, Cambridge University Press, 1991).

Coulton, G. G., *Five centuries of religion. Volume III: Getting and spending* (Cambridge, Cambridge University Press, 1936).

Coutin, K., "The Wealden house", in Warren (ed.), *Wealden buildings*, pp. 72–86.

Cox, J. C., "The college of Fotheringhay", *Archaeological Journal* **61**, 1904, pp. 241–75.

Crawford, A. (ed.), *The household books of John Howard, Duke of Norfolk, 1462–1471, 1481–1483* (Stroud, Alan Sutton, 1992).

Crook, D., "Derbyshire and the English Rising of 1381", *Historical Research* **60**, 1987, pp. 9–23.

Cullum, P. H. & P. J. P. Goldberg, "Charitable provision in late medieval York: 'To the praise of God and the use of the poor'", *Northern History* **29**, 1993, pp. 24–39.

Davies, R. A., "The effect of the Black Death on the parish priests of the medieval diocese of Coventry and Lichfield", *Historical Research* **62**, 1989, pp. 85–90.

Davies, R. R., "Baronial accounts, incomes, and arrears in the later Middle Ages", *Economic History Review* **21**, 1968, pp. 211–29.

Davis, N. (ed.), *Paston letters and papers of the fifteenth century* (Oxford, Clarendon Press, 1971–6), 2 volumes.

Davis, V., "Rivals for ministry? Ordinations of the secular and regular clergy in southern England c.1300–1500", *Studies in Church History* **26**, 1989, pp. 99–109.

Davison, A., *Six deserted villages in Norfolk*, East Anglian Archaeology **44**, 1988.

Day, J., "The great bullion famine of the fifteenth century", *Past & Present* **79**, 1978, pp. 3–54.

DeWindt, A. R., "Local government in a small town: a medieval leet jury and its constituents", *Albion* **23**, 1991, pp. 627–54.

Dickens, A. G., *Late monasticism and the Reformation* (London, Hambledon Press, 1994).

Dickins, B., "Historical graffiti at Ashwell, Hertfordshire", in V. Pritchard, *English medieval graffiti* (Cambridge, Cambridge University Press, 1967), pp. 181–3.

Dickinson, J. C., "Early suppressions of English houses of Austin canons", in V. Ruffer & A. J. Taylor (eds) *Medieval studies presented to Rose Graham* (Oxford, Oxford University Press, 1950), pp. 54–77.

Dillon, Viscount & W. H. St John Hope (eds), *Pageant of the birth, life and death of Richard Beauchamp, earl of Warwick KG 1389–1439* (London, Longmans Green & Co., 1914).

Dinn, R., "Baptism, spiritual kinship, and popular religion in late medieval Bury St Edmunds", *Bulletin of the John Rylands University Library of Manchester* **72**, 1990, pp. 93–106.

Dobson, R. B., "The foundation of perpetual chantries by the citizens of medieval York", *Studies in Church History* **4**, 1967, pp. 22–38.

Dobson, R. B. (ed.), *The Peasants' Revolt of 1381* (London, Macmillan, 1983).

Dobson, R. B., "The risings in York, Beverley and Scarborough, 1380–1381", in Hilton & Aston (eds), *The English Rising of 1381*, pp. 112–42.

Dobson, R. B. (ed.), *The church, politics and patronage in the fifteenth century* (Gloucester, Alan Sutton, 1984).

Dobson, R. B., "Citizens and chantries in late medieval York", in D. Abulafia, M. Franklin & M. Rubin (eds), *Church and city 1000–1500. Essays in honour of Christopher Brooke* (Cambridge, Cambridge University Press, 1992), pp. 311–32.

Dockray, K., "Why did fifteenth-century English gentry marry?: the Pastons, Plumptons and Stonors reconsidered", in Jones (ed.), *Gentry and lesser nobility*, pp. 61–80.

Dohar, W. J., *The Black Death and pastoral leadership. The diocese of Hereford in the fourteenth century* (Philadelphia, University of Pennsylvania Press, 1995).

Dolan, J. P. (ed.), *The essential Erasmus* (New York, Mentor Books, 1964).

Dolls, M. W., *The Black Death in the Middle East* (Princeton, Princeton University Press, 1979).

Du Boulay, F. R. H., "Who were farming the English demesnes at the end of the Middle Ages?", *Economic History Review* **17**, 1964–5, pp. 443–55.

Duffy, E., *The stripping of the altars. Traditional religion in England 1400–1580* (New Haven and London, Yale University Press, 1992).

Dunning, R. W., "Revival at Glastonbury 1530–9", *Studies in Church History* **14**, 1977, pp. 213–22.

Dunning, R. W., "Patronage and promotion in the late-medieval church", in Griffiths (ed.), *Patronage. The crown and the provinces*, pp. 167–80.

Dyer, A., *Decline and growth in English towns 1400–1640* (London, Macmillan, 1991).

Dyer, C., "The deserted medieval village of Woollashill, Worcestershire", *Transactions of the Worcestershire Archaeological Society* **1**, 1965–7, pp. 55–61.

Dyer, C., "A redistribution of incomes in fifteenth-century England?", *Past & Present* **39**, 1968, pp. 11–33.

Dyer, C., *Lords and peasants in a changing society. The estates of the bishopric of Worcester, 680–1540* (Cambridge, Cambridge University Press, 1980).

Dyer, C., *Warwickshire farming 1349–c. 1520. Preparations for agricultural revolution*, Dugdale Society Occasional Papers **27**, 1981.

Dyer, C., "Deserted medieval villages in the West Midlands", *Economic History Review* **35**, 1982, pp. 19–34.

Dyer, C., "The social and economic background to the rural revolt of 1381", in Hilton & Aston (eds), *The English Rising of 1381*, pp. 9–42.

Dyer, C., "Changes in the link between families and land in the west midlands in the fourteenth and fifteenth centuries", in Smith (ed.), *Land, kinship and life-cycle*, pp. 305–11.

Dyer, C., "Changes in the size of peasant holdings in some west midland villages 1400–1540", in Smith (ed.), *Land, kinship and life-cycle*, pp. 277–94.

Dyer, C., "English peasant buildings in the later Middle Ages (1200–1500)", *Medieval Archaeology* **30**, 1986, pp. 19–45.

Dyer, C., "The Rising of 1381 in Suffolk: its origins and participants", *Proceedings of the Suffolk Institute of Archaeology* **36**, 1988, pp. 274–87.

Dyer, C., "Changes in diet in the Late Middle Ages: the case of the harvest workers", *Agricultural History Review* **36**, 1988, pp. 21–37.

Dyer, C., *Standards of living in the later Middle Ages. Social change in England c. 1200–1520* (Cambridge, Cambridge University Press, 1989).

Dyer, C., "The consumer and the market in the later Middle Ages", *Economic History Review*

42, 1989, pp. 305–27.

Dyer, C., "Were there any capitalists in fifteenth-century England?", in Kermode (ed.), *Enterprise and individuals in fifteenth-century England*, pp. 1–24.

Dyer, C., "Small-town conflict in the later Middle Ages: events at Shipston-on-Stour", *Urban History* **19**, 1992, pp. 183–210.

Dyer, C., "The great fire of Shipston-on-Stour", *Warwickshire History* **8**, 1992–3, pp. 179–94.

Dyer, C., "The English medieval village community and its decline", *Journal of British Studies* **33**, 1994, pp. 407–29.

Dymond, D. & R. Virgoe, "The reduced population and wealth of early fifteenth-century Suffolk", *Proceedings of the Suffolk Institute of Archaeology and History* **36**, 1986, pp. 73–100.

Edelen, G. (ed.), *The Description of England by William Harrison* (Ithaca, Cornell University Press, 1968).

Elvey, E. M., "The abbot of Missenden's estates in Chalfont St Peter", *Records of Buckinghamshire* **17**, 1961–5, pp. 20–40.

Epstein, S. R., "Regional fairs, institutional innovation, and economic growth in late-medieval Europe", *Economic History Review* **47**, 1994, pp. 459–82.

Erskine, A. M. (ed.), *The accounts of the fabric of Exeter Cathedral, 1279–1353*, Devon and Cornwall Record Society **24** and **26**, 1981 and 1983.

Everson, P. L., C. C. Taylor, C. J. Dunn, *Change and continuity. Rural settlement in north-east Lincolnshire* (London, HMSO for the Royal Commission on the Historical Monuments of England, 1991).

Faith, R., "The 'Great Rumour' of 1377 and peasant ideology", in Hilton & Aston (eds), *The English Rising of 1381*, pp. 43–73.

Farmer, D. H., *The Oxford dictionary of saints* (Oxford, Clarendon Press, 1978).

Field, R. K., "Migration in the later Middle Ages: the case of the Hampton Lovett villeins", *Midland History* **8**, 1983, pp. 29–48.

Finch, A., "*Repulsa uxore sua*: marital difficulties and separation in the later middle ages", *Continuity and Change* **8**, 1993, pp. 11–38.

Finucane, R. C., "Sacred corpse, profane carrion: social ideals and death rituals in the later Middle Ages", in Whaley (ed.), *Mirrors of mortality*, pp. 40–60.

Fleming, P. W., "The Lovelace dispute: concepts of property and inheritance in fifteenth-century Kent", *Southern History* **12**, 1990, pp. 1–18.

Fritz, P. S., "From 'public' to 'private': the royal funerals in England, 1500–1830", in Whaley (ed.), *Mirrors of mortality*, pp. 61–79.

Fryde, E. B., "Peasant rebellion and peasant discontents", in Miller (ed.), *The agrarian history of England and Wales*, pp. 744–819.

Furnivall, F. J. (ed.), *The fifty earliest English wills in the court of probate, London*, Early English Text Society **78**, 1882.

Gee, E. A., "The painted glass of All Saints' Church, North Street, York", *Archaeologia* **102**, 1969, pp. 151–202.

Gillett, E., *A history of Grimsby* (London, Oxford University Press for the University of Hull, 1970).

Gillett, E. & K. A. MacMahon, *A history of Hull* (Oxford, Oxford University Press for the University of Hull, 1980).

Given-Wilson, C., *The English nobility in the Late Middle Ages. The fourteenth-century political community* (London, Routledge & Kegan Paul, 1987).

Given-Wilson, C., "Wealth and credit, public and private: the earls of Arundel 1306–1397", *English Historical Review* **106**, 1991, pp. 1–26.

Godfrey, E. S., *The development of English glassmaking 1560–1640* (Oxford, Clarendon Press,

1975).

Goldberg, P. J. P, "Female labour, service and marriage in the late-medieval urban North", *Northern History* **22**, 1986, pp. 18–38.

Goldberg, P. J. P., "Women in fifteenth-century town life", in Thomson (ed.), *Towns and townspeople*, pp. 107–28.

Goldberg, P. J. P., "Mortality and economic change in the diocese of York, 1390–1514", *Northern History* **14**, 1988, pp. 38–55.

Goldberg, P. J. P., "Urban identity and the poll taxes of 1377, 1379, and 1381", *Economic History Review* **43**, 1990, pp. 194–216.

Goldberg, P. J. P., *Women, work, and life cycle in a medieval economy. Women in York and Yorkshire c. 1300–1520* (Oxford, Clarendon Press, 1992).

Goldberg, P. J. P. (ed.), *Woman is a worthy wight. Women in English society c. 1200–1500* (Stroud, Alan Sutton, 1992).

Goldberg, P. J. P., "Marriage, migration, and servanthood: the York cause paper evidence", in *Woman is a worthy wight*, pp. 1–15.

Gottfried, R. S., *Epidemic disease in fifteenth-century England. The medical response and the demographic consequences* (Leicester, Leicester University Press, 1978).

Gottfried, R. S., *Bury St Edmunds and the urban crisis: 1290–1539* (Princeton, Princeton University Press, 1982).

Gottlieb, B., *The family in the western world from the Black Death to the Industrial Age* (New York, Oxford University Press, 1993).

Gransden, A., *Historical writing in England II. c. 1307 to the early sixteenth century* (London, Routledge & Kegan Paul, 1982).

Greatrex, J., "The English cathedral priories and the pursuit of learning in the later Middle Ages", *Journal of Ecclesiastical History* **45**, 1994, pp. 396–411.

Greenhill, F. A., *Incised effigial slabs. A study of engraved stone memorials in Latin Christendom, c. 1100 to c. 1700* (London, Faber & Faber, 1976), 2 volumes.

Griffiths, R. A. (ed.), *Patronage, the crown, and the provinces in later medieval England* (Gloucester, Alan Sutton, 1981), pp. 167–80.

Griffiths, R. A., *King and country. England and Wales in the fifteenth century* (London, Hambledon Press, 1991).

Griffiths, R. A., "Duke Richard of York's intentions in 1450 and the origins of the Wars of the Roses", in *King and country*, pp. 277–304.

Grisdale, D. M. (ed.), *Three Middle English sermons from the Worcester Chapter manuscript F. 10* (Leeds School of English Language Texts and Monographs **5**, 1939).

Groome, N., "The Black Death in the hundred of Higham Ferrers", *Northamptonshire Past and Present* **6:6**, 1982–3, pp. 309–11.

Gurevich, A., *Medieval popular culture: problems of belief and perception* (Cambridge, Cambridge University Press, 1988).

Gyug, R., "The effects and extent of the Black Death of 1348: new evidence for clerical mortality in Barcelona", *Medieval Studies* **45**, 1983, pp. 385–98.

Hadwin, J. F., "From dissonance to harmony in the late medieval town?", *Economic History Review* **39**, 1986, pp. 423–6.

Haigh, C., "Anticlericalism and the English Reformation", *History* **68**, 1983, pp. 391–407.

Haigh, C., *English Reformations. Religion, politics, and society under the Tudors* (Oxford, Clarendon Press, 1993).

Haines, R. M., *Ecclesia anglicana. Studies in the English church of the later Middle Ages* (Toronto and London, University of Toronto Press, 1989).

Halkin, L-E., *Erasmus. A critical biography* (Oxford, Blackwell, 1993).

Hallam, H. E., "The agrarian economy of South Lincolnshire in the mid-fifteenth century", *Nottingham Medieval Studies* **11**, 1967, pp. 86–95.

Hallam, H. E., "Age at first marriage and age at death in the Lincolnshire Fenland, 1252–1478", *Population Studies* **39**, 1985, pp. 55–69.

Hammer, C. I., "Anatomy of an oligarchy: the Oxford town council in the fifteenth and sixteenth centuries", *Journal of British Studies* **18**, 1978, pp. 1–27.

Hanawalt, B., "Keepers of the lights: late medieval English parish gilds", *Journal of Medieval and Renaissance Studies* **14**, 1984, pp. 21–37.

Hanawalt, B., *The ties that bound. Peasant families in medieval England* (New York, Oxford University Press, 1986).

Hanawalt, B., *Growing up in medieval London. The experience of childhood in history* (New York, Oxford University Press, 1993).

Hare, J. N., "Durrington: a chalkland village in the Later Middle Ages", *Wiltshire Archaeological Magazine* **74/5**, 1981, pp. 137–47.

Hare, J. N., "The demesne lessees of fifteenth-century Wiltshire", *Agricultural History Review* **29**, 1981, pp. 1–15.

Hare, J. N., "The monks as landlords: the leasing of the monastic demesnes in southern England", in Barron & Harper-Bill (eds), *The Church in pre-Reformation society*, pp. 82–94.

Haren, M. J., "Social ideas in the pastoral literature of fourteenth-century England", in Harper-Bill (ed.), *Religious belief and ecclesiastical careers*, pp. 43–57.

Harper-Bill, C., "The labourer is worthy of his hire? Complaints about diet in late-medieval English monasteries", in Barron & Harper-Bill (eds), *The Church in pre-Reformation society*, pp. 95–107.

Harper-Bill, C., "Dean Colet's Convocation Sermon and the pre-Reformation Church in England", *History* **73**, 1988, pp. 191–210.

Harper-Bill, C. (ed.), *Religious belief and ecclesiastical careers in late medieval England* (Woodbridge, Boydell Press, 1991).

Harris, B. J., "Landlords and tenants in England in the later Middle Ages: the Buckingham estates", *Past & Present* **43**, 1969, pp. 146–50.

Harris, B. J., *Edward Stafford, third duke of Buckingham, 1478–1521* (Stanford, Stanford University Press, 1986).

Harris, B. J., "A new look at the Reformation: aristocratic women and nunneries, 1450–1540", *Journal of British Studies* **32**, 1993, pp. 89–113.

Harris, M. & J. M. Thurgood, "The account of the great household of Humphrey, first duke of Buckingham, for the year 1452–3", *Camden Miscellany* **29**, 1984, pp. 1–57.

Harrison, D. F., "Bridges and economic development 1300–1800", *Economic History Review* **45**, 1992, pp. 240–61.

Harriss, G. L. (ed.), *Henry V. The practice of kingship* (Oxford, Oxford University Press, 1985).

Harriss, G. L., *Cardinal Beaufort. A study of Lancastrian ascendancy and decline* (Oxford, Clarendon Press, 1988).

Harriss, G. L., "Political society and the growth of government in late medieval England", *Past & Present* **138**, 1993, pp. 28–57.

Harvey, B., "The population trend in England between 1300 and 1348", *Transactions of the Royal Historical Society* **16**, 1966, pp. 23–42.

Harvey, B., *Westminster Abbey and its estates in the Middle Ages* (Oxford, Clarendon Press, 1977).

Harvey, B., "Introduction: the 'crisis' of the early fourteenth century", in Campbell (ed.), *Before the Black Death*, pp. 1–24.

Harvey, B., *Living and dying in England 1100–1540. The monastic experience* (Oxford, Clarendon Press, 1993).

Harvey, J., "Great Milton, Oxfordshire; and Thorncroft, Surrey. The building accounts of two manor-houses of the late fifteenth century", *Journal of the British Archaeological Association* **18**, 1955, pp. 42–56.

Harvey, P. D. A., *A medieval Oxfordshire village. Cuxham 1240 to 1400* (Oxford, Oxford University Press, 1965).

Harvey, P. D. A. (ed.), *The peasant land market in medieval England* (Oxford, Clarendon Press, 1984).

Hatcher, J., *Rural economy and society in the duchy of Cornwall 1300–1500* (Cambridge, Cambridge University Press, 1970).

Hatcher, J., "Mortality in the fifteenth century: some new evidence", *Economic History Review* **39**, 1986, pp. 19–38.

Hatcher, J., "England in the aftermath of the Black Death", *Past & Present* **144**, 1994, pp. 3–35.

Hawkins, D., "The Black Death and the new London cemeteries of 1348", *Antiquity* **64**, 1990, pp. 637–42.

Hawthorn, G., *Plausible worlds* (Cambridge, Cambridge University Press, 1991).

Heal, F. & C. Holmes, *The gentry in England and Wales, 1500–1700* (London, Macmillan, 1994).

Hearne, T. (ed.), *J. Lelandi antiquarii de rebus Britannicis Collectanea* (London, G. & J. Richardson, 1770), 6 volumes.

Heath, P., *The English parish clergy on the eve of the Reformation* (London, Routledge & Kegan Paul, 1969).

Heath, P., "Urban piety in the later Middle Ages: the evidence of Hull wills", in Dobson (ed.), *The church, politics and patronage*, pp. 209–34.

Henderson, J., "The Black Death in Florence: medical and communal responses", in Bassett (ed.), *Death in towns*, pp. 136–50.

Herbert, A., "Herefordshire 1413–61: some aspects of society and public order", in Griffiths (ed.), *Patronage, the crown, and the provinces*, pp. 102–22.

Hicks, M., "Walter, Lord Hungerford (d.1449) and his chantry in Salisbury Cathedral", *The Hatcher Review* **3:28**, 1989, pp. 391–99.

Hicks, M. (ed.), *Profit, piety and the professions in later medieval England* (Gloucester, Alan Sutton, 1990).

Hicks, M., *Bastard feudalism* (London, Longman, 1995).

Hill, R., "'A chaunterie for soules': London chantries in the reign of Richard II", in F. R. H. Du Boulay & C. M. Barron (eds), *The Reign of Richard II* (London, Athlone Press, 1971), pp. 242–55.

Hilton, R. H., *Bond men made free. Medieval peasant movements and the English Rising of 1381* (London, Temple Smith, 1973).

Hilton, R. H., *The English peasantry in the later Middle Ages* (Oxford, Clarendon Press, 1975).

Hilton, R. H. & T. H. Aston (eds), *The English Rising of 1381* (Cambridge, Cambridge University Press, 1984).

Holden, B., "The deserted medieval village of Thomley, Oxfordshire", *Oxoniensia* **50**, 1985, pp. 215–38.

Hooke, D. (ed.), *Medieval villages. A review of current work* (Oxford, Oxford University Committee for Archaeology, 1985).

Hooke, D., "Village development in the West Midlands", in *Medieval villages*, pp. 125–54.

Hope, W. H. St John, *The obituary roll of John Islip, abbot of Westminster, 1500–1532*, Vetusta Monumenta 7, 1906.

Hope, W. H. St John & H. Brakspear, "Haughmond Abbey, Shropshire", *Archaeological Journal*

66, 1910, pp. 281–310.

Horrox, R. (ed.), *Selected rentals and accounts of medieval Hull, 1293–1528*, Yorkshire Archaeological Society Records Series **141**, 1981.

Horrox, R. (trans. and ed.), *The Black Death* (Manchester, Manchester University Press, 1994).

Horrox, R. (ed.), *Fifteenth-century attitudes. Perceptions of society in late medieval England* (Cambridge, Cambridge University Press, 1994).

Houlbrooke, R. A., *The English family 1450–1700* (London, Longman, 1984).

Howell, C., *Land, family and inheritance in transition. Kibworth Harcourt 1280–1700* (Cambridge, Cambridge University Press, 1983).

Hurst, J. G. (ed.), *Wharram. A study of settlement on the Yorkshire Wolds*, Society for Medieval Archaeology Monographs **8**, 1979.

Hutchins, J., *The history and antiquities of the county of Dorset*, 3rd edn, W. Shipp & J. W. Hodson (eds) (London, J. B. Nichols, 1861–73), 4 volumes.

Hutton, B., "Timber-framed houses in the Vale of York", *Medieval Archaeology* **17**, 1973, pp. 87–99.

Hutton, R., *The rise and fall of Merry England. The ritual year 1400–1700* (Oxford, Oxford University Press, 1994).

Ingram, M., "Ridings, rough music and the 'reform of popular culture' in early modern England", *Past & Present* **105**, 1984, pp. 79–113.

Ingram, M., *Church courts, sex and marriage in England, 1570–1640* (Cambridge, Cambridge University Press, 1987).

Ingram, M., "Ridings, rough music and mocking rhymes in early modern England", in B. Reay (ed.), *Popular culture in seventeenth-century England* (London, Routledge, 1988), pp. 166–97.

Jack, R. I., *The Grey of Ruthin Valor* (Sydney, Sydney University Press, 1965).

Jewell, H., "English bishops as educational benefactors in the later fifteenth century", in Dobson (ed.), *The church, politics and patronage*, pp. 146–67.

Johnson, M., *Housing culture. Traditional architecture in an English landscape* (London, UCL Press, 1993).

Johnson, P. A., *Duke Richard of York 1411–1460* (Oxford, Clarendon Press, 1988).

Jones, E. D., "Villein mobility in the later Middle Ages: the case of Spalding Priory", *Nottingham Medieval Studies* **36**, 1992, pp. 151–66.

Jones, M. (ed.), *Gentry and lesser nobility in late-medieval Europe* (Gloucester, Alan Sutton, 1986).

Jones, M. K. & M. G. Underwood, *The king's mother. Lady Margaret Beaufort, Countess of Richmond and Derby* (Cambridge, Cambridge University Press, 1992).

Jones, S. R. & J. T. Smith, "The Wealden houses of Warwickshire and their significance", *Transactions and Proceedings of the Birmingham Archaeological Society* **79**, 1960–61, pp. 24–35.

Justice, S., *Writing and rebellion. England in 1381* (Berkeley, University of California Press, 1994).

Kail, J. (ed.), "Twenty-six political and other poems", *Early English Text Society* **124**, 1904.

Keene, D., *Survey of medieval Winchester* (Oxford, Clarendon Press, 1985).

Keil, I., "Impropriator and benefice in the later Middle Ages", *Wiltshire Archaeological and Natural History Magazine* **58**, 1961–3, pp. 351–63.

Keil, I., "The chamberer of Glastonbury Abbey in the fourteenth century", *Proceedings of the Somersetshire Archaeological and Natural History Society* **107**, 1963, pp. 79–92.

Kemp, B., *English church monuments* (London, Batsford, 1980).

Kermode, J. I., "Urban decline? The flight from office in late-medieval York", *Economic His-*

tory Review **35**, 1982, pp. 179–98.

Kermode, J. I., "Merchants, overseas trade, and urban decline: York, Beverley, and Hull *c.*1380–1500", *Northern History* **23**, 1987, pp. 51–73.

Kermode, J. I., "Obvious observations on the formation of oligarchies in late medieval English towns", in Thomson (ed.), *Towns and townspeople*, pp. 87–106.

Kermode, J. I. (ed.), *Enterprise and individuals in fifteenth-century England* (Stroud, Alan Sutton, 1991).

Kershaw, I., *Bolton Priory rentals and ministers' accounts, 1473–1539*, Yorkshire Archaeological Society Records Series **132**, 1970.

Kershaw, I., *Bolton Priory. The economy of a northern monastery 1286–1325* (Oxford, Oxford University Press, 1973).

King, P. M., "The cadaver tomb in England: novel manifestations of an old idea", *Church Monuments* **5**, 1990, pp. 26–38.

Kirby, J. W., "A fifteenth-century family, the Plumptons of Plumpton, and their lawyers, 1461–1515", *Northern History* **25**, 1989, pp. 106–19.

Knowles, D., *The religious orders in England* (Cambridge, Cambridge University Press, 1979), new edn, 3 volumes.

Knowles, D. & R. N. Hadcock, *Medieval religious houses. England and Wales* (London, Longmans, 1953)

Knowles, D. & J. K. S. St Joseph, *Monastic sites from the air* (Cambridge, Cambridge University Press, 1952).

Kowaleski, M., "The commercial dominance of a medieval provincial oligarchy: Exeter in the late fourteenth century", *Medieval Studies* **46**, 1984, pp. 355–84.

Kreider, A., *English chantries. The road to dissolution* (Cambridge, Mass. and London, Harvard University Press, 1979).

Kussmaul, A., *Servants in husbandry in early modern England* (Cambridge, Cambridge University Press, 1981).

Kussmaul, A., *A general view of the rural economy of England 1538–1840* (Cambridge, Cambridge University Press, 1990).

Lander, J. R., "Marriage and politics in the fifteenth century: the Nevilles and the Wydevilles", *Bulletin of the Institute of Historical Research* **36**, 1963, pp. 119–52.

Lander, J. R., *English justices of the peace, 1461–1509* (Gloucester, Alan Sutton, 1989).

Langdon, J., "Water-mills and windmills in the west midlands, 1086–1500", *Economic History Review* **44**, 1991, pp. 424–44.

Le Faye, D., "Selborne Priory, 1233–1486", *Proceedings of the Hampshire Field Club and Archaeological Society* **30**, 1973, pp. 47–71.

Le Goff, J., *The birth of Purgatory* (London, Scolar Press, 1984).

Lewis, E., E. Roberts, K. Roberts, *Medieval hall houses of the Winchester area* (Winchester, Winchester City Museum, 1988).

Lewis, P. S., *Later medieval France. The polity* (London, Macmillan, 1968).

Leyser, H. *Medieval women. A social history of women in England 450–1500* (London, Weidenfeld and Nicolson, 1995).

Lindley, P. (ed.), *Gainsborough Old Hall*, Occasional Papers in Lincolnshire History and Archaeology **8**, 1991.

Llewellyn, N., *The art of death. Visual culture in the English death ritual c. 1500–c. 1800* (London, Reaktion Books, 1991).

Lloyd, T. H., "Some documentary sidelights on the deserted Oxfordshire village of Brookend", *Oxoniensia* **29–30**, 1964–5, pp. 116–28.

Lobel, M. D., *The borough of Bury St Edmund's. A study in the government and development of a monastic town* (Oxford, Oxford University Press, 1935).

Lock, R., "The Black Death in Walsham-le-Willows", *Proceedings of the Suffolk Institute of Archaeology and History* **37**, 1992, pp. 316–37.

Lomas, R., "The Black Death in County Durham", *Journal of Medieval History* **15**, 1989, pp. 127–40.

Lomas, R., *North-East England in the Middle Ages* (Edinburgh, John Donald, 1992).

Loschky, D. & B. D. Childers, "Early English mortality", *Journal of Interdisciplinary History* **24**, 1993, pp. 85–97.

McCann, J. (trans. and ed.), *The Rule of St Benedict* (London, Sheed & Ward, 1972).

MacCracken, H. N. (ed.), *The minor poems of John Lydgate. Part II. Secular poems*, Early English Text Society **192**, 1934.

MacCulloch, D., *Suffolk and the Tudors. Politics and religion in an English county 1500–1600* (Oxford, Clarendon Press, 1986).

McDonnell, J., "Medieval assarting hamlets in Bilsdale, North-East Yorkshire", *Northern History* **22**, 1986, pp. 269–79.

Macfarlane, A., *The origins of English individualism* (Oxford, Basil Blackwell, 1978).

Macfarlane, A., *The justice and the mare's ale. Law and disorder in seventeenth-century England* (Oxford, Basil Blackwell, 1981).

Macfarlane, A., *Marriage and love in England. Modes of reproduction 1300–1840* (Oxford, Basil Blackwell, 1986).

McFarlane, K. B., "The Wars of the Roses", *Proceedings of the British Academy* **50**, 1964, pp. 87–119.

McFarlane, K. B., *The nobility of later medieval England* (Oxford, Oxford University Press, 1973).

McGavin, J., "Robert III's 'rough music': charivari and diplomacy in a medieval Scottish court", *Scottish Historical Review* **74**, 1995, pp. 144–58.

McHardy, A. K. (ed.), *The church in London 1375–1392*, London Record Society **13**, 1977.

McHardy, A. K., "The Lincolnshire clergy in the later fourteenth century", in Ormrod (ed.), *England in the fourteenth century*, pp. 145–51.

McHardy, A. K., "Careers and disappointments in the late-medieval Church: some English evidence", *Studies in Church History* **26**, 1989, pp. 111–30.

McIntosh, M. K., *Autonomy and community. The royal manor of Havering, 1200–1500* (Cambridge, Cambridge University Press, 1986).

Mackie, P., "Chaplains in the diocese of York, 1480–1530: the testamentary evidence", *Yorkshire Archaeological Journal* **58**, 1986, pp. 123–33.

McLaren, D., "Marital fertility and lactation 1570–1720", in M. Prior (ed.), *Women in English society 1500–1800* (London, Methuen, 1985), pp. 22–53.

McRee, B., "Religious gilds and civic order: the case of Norwich in the Late Middle Ages", *Speculum* **67**, 1992, pp. 69–97.

McRee, B. R., "Peacemaking and its limits in later medieval Norwich", *English Historical Review* **109**, 1994, pp. 831–66.

Maddern, P. C., *Violence and social order. East Anglia 1422–1442* (Oxford, Clarendon Press, 1992).

Maddicott, J. R., *Law and lordship: royal justices as retainers in thirteenth- and fourteenth-century England, Past & Present* supplement **4**, 1978.

Maddicott, J. R., "Poems of social protest in early fourteenth-century England", in Ormrod (ed.), *England in the fourteenth century*, pp. 130–44.

Maddison, J. M., "Master masons of the diocese of Lichfield: a study in 14th-century architecture at the time of the Black Death", *Transactions of the Lancashire and Cheshire Antiquarian*

Society **85**, 1988, pp. 107–72.

Maddison, J., "The architectural development of Patrington Church and its place in the evolution of the Decorated style in Yorkshire", in C. Wilson (ed.), *Medieval art and architecture in the East Riding of Yorkshire* (London, British Archaeological Association, 1989), pp. 133–48.

Mamdani, M., *The myth of population control. Family, caste, and class in an Indian village* (New York, Monthly Review Press, 1972).

Manchester, K., "The palaeopathology of urban infections", in Bassett (ed.), *Death in towns*, pp. 8–14.

Manning, R. B., *Village revolts. Social protest and popular disturbances in England, 1509–1640* (Oxford, Clarendon Press, 1988).

Marks, R., "Henry Williams and his 'Ymage of Deth' roundel at Stanford on Avon, Northamptonshire", *Antiquaries Journal* **54**, 1974, pp. 272–4.

Marks, R., *Stained glass in England during the Middle Ages* (London, Routledge, 1993).

Masters, B. R. & E. Ralph (eds), *The Church Book of St Ewen's, Bristol 1454–1584*, Bristol and Gloucestershire Archaeological Society Records Section **6**, 1967.

Mate, M., "Agrarian economy after the Black Death: the manors of Canterbury Cathedral Priory, 1348–91", *Economic History Review* **37**, 1984, pp. 341–54.

Mate, M., "Labour and labour services on the estates of Canterbury Cathedral Priory in the fourteenth century", *Southern History* **7**, 1985, pp. 55–67.

Mate, M., "The economic and social roots of medieval popular rebellion: Sussex in 1450–1451", *Economic History Review* **45**, 1992, pp. 661–76.

Mayhew, N. J., "Population, money supply, and the velocity of circulation in England, 1300–1700", *Economic History Review* **48**, 1995, pp. 238–57.

Meiss, M., *Painting in Florence and Siena after the Black Death* (Princeton, Princeton University Press, 1951).

Mercer, E., *English vernacular houses. A study of traditional farmhouses and cottages* (London, HMSO for the Royal Commission on the Historical Monuments of England, 1975).

Miller, E. (ed.), *The agrarian history of England and Wales. Volume III 1348–1500* (Cambridge, Cambridge University Press, 1991).

Miller, E. & J. Hatcher, *Medieval England. Towns, commerce and crafts 1086–1348* (London, Longman, 1995).

Moore, S. A. (ed.), *Letters and papers of John Shillingford, mayor of Exeter 1447–50*, Camden New Series **2**, 1871.

Moreton, C. E., *The Townshends and their world: gentry, law, and land in Norfolk c. 1450–1551* (Oxford, Clarendon Press, 1992).

Morgan, M., "Padmore, Onibury, Shropshire S0 464794", *Archaeological Journal* **142**, 1985, pp. 340–60.

Morris, R., "Tewkesbury Abbey: the Despenser mausoleum", *Transactions of the Bristol and Gloucestershire Archaeological Society* **93**, 1974, pp. 142–55.

Murphy, M., "The high cost of dying: an analysis of *pro anima* bequests in medieval Dublin", *Studies in Church History* **24**, 1987, pp. 111–22.

Myers, A. R. (ed.), *The household of Edward IV. The Black Book and the Ordinance of 1478* (Manchester, Manchester University Press, 1959).

Myers, A. R. (ed.), *English historical documents 1327–1485* (London, Eyre & Spottiswoode, 1969).

Mynors, R. A. B. & P. G. Bietenholz (eds), *The correspondence of Erasmus. Letters 1122 to 1251. 1520 to 1521* (Toronto, University of Toronto Press, 1988).

Nichols, A. E., *Seeable signs. The iconography of the Seven Sacraments 1350–1544* (Woodbridge, Boydell Press, 1994).

Nichols, J., *A collection of all the wills, now known to be extant, of the kings and queens of England* (London, Society of Antiquaries, 1780).

Nightingale, P., "Monetary contraction and mercantile credit in later medieval England", *Economic History Review* **43**, 1990, pp. 560–75.

Norris, M., "Later medieval monumental brasses: an urban funerary industry and its representation of death", in Bassett (ed.), *Death in towns*, pp. 184–209.

Oestmann, C., *Lordship and community. The Lestrange family and the village of Hunstanton, Norfolk, in the first half of the sixteenth century* (Woodbridge, Boydell Press, 1994).

Orme, N., *Exeter Cathedral as it was 1050–1550* (Exeter, Devon Books, 1986).

Ormrod, W. M. (ed.), "The English government and the Black Death of 1348–49", in *England in the fourteenth century*, pp. 175–88.

Ormrod, W. M., *England in the fourteenth century. Proceedings of the 1985 Harlaxton Symposium* (Woodbridge, Boydell Press, 1986).

Ormrod, W. M., "Edward III and the recovery of royal authority in England, 1340–60", *History* **72**, 1987, pp. 4–19.

Ormrod, W. M., *The reign of Edward III. Crown and political society in England 1327–1377* (New Haven and London, Yale University Press, 1990).

Owst, G. R., *The Destructorium Viciorum of Alexander Carpenter* (London, SPCK, 1952).

Palliser, D. M., "Urban decay revisited", in Thomson (ed.), *Towns and townspeople,* pp. 1–21.

Palmer, R. C., *English law in the age of the Black Death, 1348–1381* (Chapel Hill and London, University of North Carolina Press, 1993).

Pantin, W. A. (ed.), *Documents illustrating the activities of the general and provincial chapters of the English black monks 1215–1540*, vol. III, Camden Third Series **54**, 1937.

Parrey, Y., "'Devoted disciples of Christ': early sixteenth-century religious life in the nunnery at Amesbury", *Historical Research* **67**, 1994, pp. 240–48.

Payling, S. J., "Inheritance and local politics in the later Middle Ages: the case of Ralph, Lord Cromwell, and the Heriz inheritance", *Nottingham Medieval Studies* **30**, 1986, pp. 67–96.

Payling, S. J., "The Ampthill dispute: a study in aristocratic lawlessness and the breakdown of Lancastrian government", *English Historical Review* **104**, 1989, pp. 881–907.

Payling, S. J., *Political society in Lancastrian England. The greater gentry of Nottinghamshire* (Oxford, Clarendon Press, 1991).

Payling, S. J., "Social mobility, demographic change, and landed society in late medieval England", *Economic History Review* **45**, 1992, pp. 51–73.

Pearsall, D., *John Lydgate* (London, Routledge & Kegan Paul, 1970).

Pearson, S., *The medieval houses of Kent: an historical analysis* (London, HMSO for the Royal Commission on the Historical Monuments of England, 1994).

Pearson, S., P. S. Barnwell, A. T. Adams, *A gazetteer of medieval houses in Kent* (London, HMSO for the Royal Commission on the Historical Monuments of England, 1994).

Penn, S. A. C., "Female wage-earners in late fourteenth-century England", *Agricultural History Review* **35**, 1987, pp. 1–14.

Penn, S. A. C. & C. Dyer, "Wages and earnings in late-medieval England: evidence from the enforcement of the labour laws", *Economic History Review* **43**, 1990, pp. 356–76.

Pfaff, R. W., *New liturgical feasts in later medieval England* (Oxford, Clarendon Press, 1970).

Phillips, J., *The reformation of images: destruction of art in England, 1535–1660* (Berkeley, University of California Press, 1973).

Phythian-Adams, C., "Urban decay in late-medieval England", in P. Abrams & E. A Wrigley (eds), *Towns and societies: essays in economic history and historical sociology* (Cambridge, Cambridge University Press, 1978), pp. 159–85.

Phythian-Adams, C., *Desolation of a city. Coventry and the urban crisis of the Late Middle Ages*

(Cambridge, Cambridge University Press, 1979).

Phythian-Adams, C., "Rituals of personal confrontation in late-medieval England", *Bulletin of the John Rylands University Library of Manchester* **73**, 1991, pp. 65–90.

Platt, C., *Medieval Southampton. The port and trading community, AD 1000–1600* (London, Routledge & Kegan Paul, 1973).

Platt, C., *The English medieval town* (London, Secker & Warburg, 1976).

Platt, C., *Medieval England. A social history and archaeology from the Conquest to 1600* AD (London, Routledge, 1978).

Platt, C., *The abbeys and priories of medieval England* (London, Secker & Warburg, 1984).

Platt, C., *The National Trust guide to late-medieval and Renaissance Britain from the Black Death to the Civil War* (London, George Philip, 1986).

Platt, C., *The architecture of medieval Britain. A social history* (New Haven and London, Yale University Press, 1990).

Platt, C., *The Great Rebuildings of Tudor and Stuart England. Revolutions in architectural taste* (London, UCL Press, 1994).

Plumb, D., "The social and economic spread of rural Lollardy: a reappraisal", *Studies in Church History* **23**, 1986, pp. 111–29.

Pollard, A. J., "Estate management in the later Middle Ages: the Talbots and Whitchurch, 1383–1525", *Economic History Review* **25**, 1972, pp. 553–66.

Pollard, A. J., "The north-eastern economy and the agrarian crisis of 1438–1440", *Northern History* **25**, 1989, pp. 88–105.

Pollard, A. J., *North-eastern England during the Wars of the Roses. Lay society, war, and politics 1450–1500* (Oxford, Clarendon Press, 1990).

Poos, L. R., "The rural population of Essex in the later Middle Ages", *Economic History Review* **38**, 1985, pp. 515–30.

Poos, L. R., *A rural society after the Black Death: Essex 1350–1525* (Cambridge, Cambridge University Press, 1991).

Poos, L. R. & R. M. Smith, "'Legal windows onto historical populations'? Recent research on demography and the manor court in medieval England", *Law and History Review* **2**, 1984, pp. 128–52.

Postles, D., "The Oseney Abbey flock", *Oxoniensia* **49**, 1984, pp. 141–52.

Postles, D., "Demographic change in Kibworth Harcourt, Leicestershire, in the later Middle Ages", *Local Population Studies* **48**, 1992, pp. 41–8.

Postles, D., "An English small town in the later Middle Ages: Loughborough", *Urban History* **20**, 1993, pp. 7–29.

Postles, D., "Personal pledging in manorial courts in the later Middle Ages", *Bulletin of the John Rylands University Library of Manchester* **75**, 1993, pp. 65–78.

Pound, J., "Clerical poverty in early sixteenth-century England: some East Anglian evidence", *Journal of Ecclesiastical History* **37**, 1986, pp. 389–96.

Powell, E., "Arbitration and the law in England in the Late Middle Ages", *Transactions of the Royal Historical Society* **33**, 1983, pp. 49–67.

Powell, E., "Settlement of disputes by arbitration in fifteenth-century England", *Law and History Review* **2**, 1984, pp. 21–43.

Powell, E., *Kingship, law, and society. Criminal justice in the reign of Henry V* (Oxford, Clarendon Press, 1989).

Powell, E., "Law and justice", in Horrox (ed.), *Fifteenth-century attitudes*, pp. 29–41.

Power, E., *Medieval English nunneries c.1275 to 1535* (Cambridge, Cambridge University Press, 1922).

Proudfoot, L. J., "The extension of parish churches in medieval Warwickshire", *Journal of*

Historical Geography **9**, 1983, pp. 231–46.

Pugh, T. B. (ed.), *The marcher lordships of South Wales 1415–1536. Select documents* (Cardiff, University of Wales Press, 1963).

Pugh, T. B., "The magnates, knights and gentry", in S. B. Chrimes, C. D. Ross & R. A Griffiths (eds), *Fifteenth-century England, 1399–1509. Studies in politics and society* (Manchester, Manchester University Press, 1972), pp. 86–128.

Pugh, T. B., "The Southampton Plot of 1415", in R. A. Griffiths & J. Sherborne (eds), *Kings and nobles in the later Middle Ages. A tribute to Charles Ross* (Gloucester, Alan Sutton, 1986), pp. 62–89.

Pugh, T. B., "Richard Plantagenet (1411–60), duke of York, as the king's lieutenant in France and Ireland", in J. G. Rowe (ed.), *Aspects of late-medieval government and society: essays presented to J. R. Lander* (Toronto, University of Toronto Press, 1986), pp. 107–41.

Pugh, T. B., *Henry V and the Southampton Plot of 1415*, Southampton Records Series **30**, 1988.

Rawcliffe, C., *The Staffords, earls of Stafford and dukes of Buckingham 1394–1521* (Cambridge, Cambridge University Press, 1978).

Rawcliffe, C., "The hospitals of later medieval London", *Medical History* **28**, 1984, pp. 1–21.

Rawcliffe, C. & S. Flower, "English noblemen and their advisers: consultation and collaboration in the later Middle Ages", *Journal of British Studies* **25**, 1986, pp. 157–77.

Razi, Z., *Life, marriage and death in a medieval parish. Economy, society and demography in Halesowen 1270–1400* (Cambridge, Cambridge University Press, 1980).

Razi, Z., "Family, land and the village community in later medieval England", *Past & Present* **93**, 1981, pp. 3–36.

Razi, Z., "The struggle between the abbots of Halesowen and their tenants in the thirteenth and fourteenth centuries", in T. H. Aston, P. R. Coss, C. Dyer & J. Thirsk (eds), *Social relations and ideas. Essays in honour of R. H. Hilton* (Cambridge, Cambridge University Press, 1983), pp. 151–67.

Razi, Z., "The erosion of the family-land bond in the late fourteenth and fifteenth centuries: a methodological note", in Smith (ed.), *Land, kinship and life-cycle*, pp. 295–304.

Razi, Z., "The myth of the immutable English family", *Past & Present* **140**, 1993, pp. 3–44.

Razzell, P., *Essays in English population history* (London, Caliban Books, 1994).

Reddaway, T. F., "The London goldsmiths *circa* 1500", *Transactions of the Royal Historical Society* **12**, 1962, pp. 49–62.

Reddaway, T. F. & L. E. M. Walker, *The early history of the Goldsmiths' Company 1327–1509* (London, Edward Arnold, 1975).

Rees, U., "The leases of Haughmond Abbey, Shropshire", *Midland History* **8**, 1983, pp. 14–28.

Rees, U. (ed.), *The cartulary of Haughmond Abbey* (Cardiff, Shropshire Archaeological Society and University of Wales Press, 1985).

Reynolds, S., *An introduction to the history of English medieval towns* (Oxford, Oxford University Press, 1977).

Reynolds, S., "Decline and decay in late medieval towns: a look at some of the concepts and arguments", *Urban History Yearbook* **1980**, pp. 76–8.

Reynolds, S., "Medieval urban history and the history of political thought", *Urban History Yearbook* **1982**, pp. 14–23.

Richmond, C., "The nobility and the Wars of the Roses, 1459–61", *Nottingham Medieval Studies* **21**, 1977, pp. 71–86.

Richmond, C., *John Hopton. A fifteenth-century Suffolk gentleman* (Cambridge, Cambridge University Press, 1981).

Richmond, C., "The expenses of Thomas Playter of Sotterley, 1459–60", *Proceedings of the*

Suffolk Institute of Archaeology and History **35**, 1981, pp. 41–52.

Richmond, C., "Religion and the fifteenth-century English gentleman", in Dobson (ed.), *The church, politics and patronage*, pp. 193–208.

Richmond, C., *The Paston family in the fifteenth century. The first phase* (Cambridge, Cambridge University Press, 1990).

Richmond, C., "An outlaw and some peasants: the possible significance of Robin Hood", *Nottingham Medieval Studies* **37**, 1993, pp. 90–101.

Rigby, S. H., "'Sore decay' and 'fair dwellings': Boston and urban decline in the later Middle Ages", *Midland History* **10**, 1985, pp. 47–61.

Rigby, S. H., "Late medieval urban prosperity: the evidence of the lay subsidies", *Economic History Review* **39**, 1986, pp. 411–16.

Rigby, S. H., "Urban 'oligarchy' in late medieval England", in Thomson (ed.), *Towns and townspeople*, pp. 62–86.

Rigby, S. H., "Urban society in early fourteenth-century England: the evidence of the lay subsidies", *Bulletin of the John Rylands University Library of Manchester* **72**, 1990, pp. 169–84.

Rigby, S. H., *Medieval Grimsby: growth and decline* (Hull, University of Hull Press, 1993).

Rigby, S. H., *English society in the later Middle Ages. Class, status and gender* (London, Macmillan, 1995).

Robinson, D. M., *The geography of Augustinian settlement in medieval England and Wales* (Oxford, British Archaeological Reports, 1980).

Rooke, G. H., "Dom William Ingram and his account-book, 1504–1533", *Journal of Ecclesiastical History* **7**, 1956, pp. 30–44.

Rosenthal, J. T., "Feuds and private peace-making: a fifteenth-century example", *Nottingham Medieval Studies* **13**, 1969, pp. 84–90.

Rosenthal, J. T., "The Yorkshire chantry certificates of 1546: an analysis", *Northern History* **9**, 1974, pp. 26–47.

Rosenthal, J. T., "Other victims: peeresses as war widows, 1450–1500", *History* **72**, 1987, pp. 213–30.

Rosenthal, J. T., "Kings, continuity and ecclesiastical benefaction in 15th century England", in Rosenthal and Richmond (eds), *People, politics and community*, pp. 161–75.

Rosenthal, J. T., *Patriarchy and families of privilege in fifteenth-century England* (Philadelphia, University of Pennsylvania Press, 1991).

Rosenthal, J. T., & Richmond, C. (eds), *People, politics and community in the later Middle Ages* (Gloucester, Alan Sutton, 1987).

Rosser, G., "London and Westminster: the suburb in the urban economy in the later Middle Ages", in Thomson (ed.), *Towns and townspeople*, pp. 45–61.

Rosser, G., *Medieval Westminster 1200–1540* (Oxford, Clarendon Press, 1989).

Rosser, G., "Going to the fraternity feast: commensality and social relations in late medieval England", *Journal of British Studies* **33**, 1994, pp. 430–46.

Rowney, I., "Arbitration in gentry disputes of the later Middle Ages", *History* **67**, 1982, pp. 367–76.

Rubin, M., "Corpus Christi fraternities and late-medieval piety", *Studies in Church History* **23**, 1986, pp. 97–109.

Rubin, M., *Corpus Christi. The Eucharist in late medieval culture* (Cambridge, Cambridge University Press, 1991).

Rubin, M., "Small groups: identity and solidarity in the Late Middle Ages", in Kermode (ed.), *Enterprise and individuals*, pp. 132–50.

Rural houses of West Yorkshire, 1400–1830 (London, HMSO for West Yorkshire County Council and the Royal Commission on the Historical Monuments of England, 1986).

Saaler, M., "The manor of Tillingdown: the changing economy of the demesne 1325–71", *Surrey Archaeological Collections* **81**, 1991–2, pp. 19–40.

Salzman, L. F., *Building in England down to 1540* (Oxford, Clarendon Press, 1967).

Saul, A., "Great Yarmouth and the Hundred Years War in the fourteenth century", *Bulletin of the Institute of Historical Research* **52**, 1979, pp. 105–15.

Saul, A., "The herring industry of Great Yarmouth *c.*1280–*c.*1400", *Norfolk Archaeology* **38**, 1981, pp. 34–43.

Saul, A., "English towns in the late middle ages: the case of Great Yarmouth", *Journal of Medieval History* **8**, 1982, pp. 75–88.

Saul, N., *Knights and esquires: the Gloucestershire gentry in the fourteenth century* (Oxford, Clarendon Press, 1981).

Saul, N., *Scenes from provincial life. Knightly families in Sussex 1280–1400* (Oxford, Clarendon Press, 1986).

Scammell, J., "The formation of the English social structure: freedom, knights, and gentry, 1066–1300", *Speculum* **68**, 1993, pp. 591–618.

Schofield, R., "The impact of scarcity and plenty on population change in England, 1541–1871", in R. J. Rotberg & T. K. Rabb (eds), *Hunger and history. The impact of changing food production and consumption patterns on society* (Cambridge, Cambridge University Press, 1985), pp. 67–93.

Searle, E. & B. Ross (eds), *The cellarers' rolls of Battle Abbey 1275–1513*, Sussex Record Society **65**, 1967.

Shaw, D. G., *The creation of a community. The city of Wells in the Middle Ages* (Oxford, Clarendon Press, 1993).

Sinclair, A., "The great Berkeley law-suit revisited 1417–39", *Southern History* **9**, 1987, pp. 34–50.

Slack, P., *The impact of plague in Tudor and Stuart England* (London, Routledge & Kegan Paul, 1985).

Smith, J. T., "The evolution of the English peasant house to the late seventeenth century: the evidence of buildings", *Journal of the British Archaeological Association* **33**, 1970, pp. 122–47.

Smith, L. B., "Seignorial income in the fourteenth century: the Arundels in Chirk", *Bulletin of the Board of Celtic Studies* **28**, 1979, pp. 443–57.

Smith, R. M., "Fertility, economy and household formation in England over three centuries", *Population and Development Review* **7**, 1981, pp. 595–622.

Smith, R. M. (ed.), *Land, kinship and life-cycle* (Cambridge, Cambridge University Press, 1984).

Smith. R. M., "Geographical diversity in the resort to marriage in late medieval Europe: work, reputation, and unmarried females in the household formation systems of northern and southern Europe", in Goldberg (ed.), *Woman is a worthy wight*, pp. 16–59.

Smith, R. M., "Demographic developments in rural England, 1300–48: a survey", in Campbell (ed.), *Before the Black Death*, pp. 25–77.

Smith, T. & L. T. Smith (eds), *English gilds*, Early English Text Society, 1870.

Spencer, H. L., *English preaching in the Late Middle Ages* (Oxford, Clarendon Press, 1993).

Spufford, P., *Money and its use in medieval Europe* (Cambridge, Cambridge University Press, 1988).

Stevenson, J. H. (ed.), *The Edington cartulary*, Wiltshire Record Society **42**, 1987.

Strong, P. & F. Strong, "The last wills and codicils of Henry V", *English Historical Review* **96**, 1981, pp. 79–102.

Swanson, R. N., *Church and society in late-medieval England* (Oxford, Basil Blackwell, 1989).

Swanson, R. N., "Problems of the priesthood in pre-Reformation England", *English Histori-*

cal Review **105**, 1990, pp. 845–69.

Swanson, R. N., "Standards of livings: parochial revenues in pre-Reformation England", in Harper-Bill (ed.), *Religious belief and ecclesiastical careers*, pp. 151–96.

Swanson, R. N. (trans. and ed.), *Catholic England. Faith, religion and observance before the Reformation* (Manchester, Manchester University Press, 1993).

Tanner, N. P., *The church in late medieval Norwich 1370–1532* (Toronto, Pontifical Institute of Mediaeval Studies, 1984).

Tanner, N. P., "The Reformation and regionalism: further reflections on the church in late medieval Norwich", in Thomson (ed.), *Towns and townspeople*, pp. 129–47.

Thompson, A. H., "Registers of John Gynewell, bishop of Lincoln, for the years 1347–1350", *Archaeological Journal* **68**, 1911, pp. 301–60.

Thompson, A. H., "The will of Master William Doune, archdeacon of Leicester", *Archaeological Journal* **72**, 1915, pp. 233–84.

Thompson, A. H. (ed.), *Visitations of religious houses in the diocese of Lincoln. Volume II. Records of visitations held by William Alnwick, bishop of Lincoln, AD 1436 to AD 1449*, Lincoln Record Society **14**, 1918.

Thompson, A. H., *History and architectural description of the priory of St Mary, Bolton-in-Wharfedale*, Thoresby Society **30**, 1928.

Thompson, A. H., *The English clergy and their organization in the later Middle Ages* (Oxford, Oxford University Press, 1947).

Thompson, B., "Monasteries and their patrons at foundation and dissolution", *Transactions of the Royal Historical Society* **4**, 1994, pp. 103–25.

Thompson, S., "Why English nunneries had no history: a study of the problems of the English nunneries founded after the Conquest", in J. A. Nichols & L. T. Shank (eds), *Medieval religious women. Volume one. Distant echoes* (Kalamazoo, Cistercian Publications, 1984), pp. 131–49.

Thompson, S., *Women religious. The founding of English nunneries after the Norman Conquest* (Oxford, Clarendon Press, 1991).

Thomson, J. A. F., "The Courtenay family in the Yorkist period", *Bulletin of the Institute of Historical Research* **45**, 1972, pp. 230–46.

Thomson, J. A. F. (ed.), *Towns and townspeople in the fifteenth century* (Gloucester, Alan Sutton, 1988).

Thrupp, S. L., *The merchant class of medieval London 1300–1500* (Ann Arbor, University of Michigan Press, 1948).

Tittler, R., "For the 'Re-edification of Townes': the rebuilding statutes of Henry VIII", *Albion* **22**, 1990, pp. 591–605.

Tristram, P., *Figures of life and death in medieval English literature* (London, Paul Elek, 1976).

Tymms, S. (ed.), *Wills and inventories from the registers of the commissary of Bury St Edmund's and the archdeacon of Sudbury*, Camden Society **49**, 1850.

Underdown, D., *Revel, riot, and rebellion. Popular politics and culture in England 1603–1660* (Oxford, Clarendon Press, 1985).

Virgoe, R., "William Tailboys and Lord Cromwell: crime and politics in Lancastrian England", *Bulletin of the John Rylands Library* **55**, 1972–3, pp. 459–82.

Virgoe, R., "The murder of James Andrew: Suffolk faction in the 1430s", *Proceedings of the Suffolk Institute of Archaeology and History* **34**, 1980, pp. 263–8.

Virgoe, R., "Aspects of the county community in the fifteenth century", in M. Hicks (ed.), *Profit, piety and the professions in later medieval England* (Gloucester, Alan Sutton, 1990), pp. 1–13.

Wade, J. F., "The overseas trade of Newcastle upon Tyne in the late Middle Ages", *Northern*

History **30**, 1994, pp. 31–48.

Ward, J. C., *English noblewomen in the later Middle Ages* (London, Longman, 1992).

Warren, F. (ed.), *The Dance of Death*, Early English Text Society **181**, 1931.

Warren, J. (ed.), *Wealden buildings: studies in the timber-framed tradition of building in Kent, Sussex and Surrey, in tribute to R. T. Mason FSA* (Horsham, Coach Publishing for the Wealden Buildings Study Group, 1990).

Watts, D. G., "Peasant discontent on the manors of Titchfield Abbey, 1245–1405", *Proceedings of the Hampshire Field Club and Archaeological Society* **39**, 1983, pp. 121–35.

Wayment, H., *The stained glass of the church of St Mary, Fairford, Gloucestershire* (London, Society of Antiquaries, 1984).

Westlake, H. F., *The parish gilds of mediaeval England* (London, Society for Promoting Christian Knowledge, 1919).

Westlake, H. F., "The parish gilds of the later fourteenth century", *Transactions of the St Paul's Ecclesiological Society* **8**, 1917–20, pp. 99–110.

Whaley, J. (ed.), *Mirrors of mortality. Studies in the social history of death* (London, Europa Publications, 1981).

Whiting, B. J., *Proverbs, sentences, and proverbial phrases from English writings mainly before 1500* (Cambridge, Mass., Harvard University Press, 1968).

Williams, C. H. (ed.), *English historical documents 1485–1558* (London, Eyre & Spottiswoode, 1967).

Wilson, C. & R. Woods, "Fertility in England: a long-term perspective", *Population Studies* **45**, 1991, pp. 399–415.

Windeatt, B. A. (trans.), *The Book of Margery Kempe* (Harmondsworth, Penguin Books, 1985).

Wood-Legh, K. L., *Perpetual chantries in Britain* (Cambridge, Cambridge University Press, 1965).

Wright, S. M., *The Derbyshire gentry in the fifteenth century*, Derbyshire Record Society **8**, 1983.

Wrigley, E. A. & R. S. Schofield, *The population history of England 1541–1871. A reconstruction* (Cambridge, Cambridge University Press, 1989), 2nd edn.

Zell, M., *Industry in the countryside. Wealden society in the sixteenth century* (Cambridge, Cambridge University Press, 1994).

Ziegler, P., *The Black Death* (London, Collins, 1969).

Index

1. Major references are indicated by **emboldened** pages.
2. Most references are to England, which is therefore omitted as an entry.
3. Some county entries may not be immediately obvious on a page as the actual word may not be there eg references to *Colchester* are also entered as *Essex*; and *Tamworth* as *Staffordshire*.